**PLACE IN RETURN BOX** to remove this checkout from your record.
**TO AVOID FINES** return on or before date due.
**MAY BE RECALLED** with earlier due date if requested.

GULL LAKE LIBRARY

| DATE DUE | DATE DUE | DATE DUE |
|----------|----------|----------|
|          |          |          |
|          |          |          |
|          |          |          |
|          |          |          |
|          |          |          |
|          |          |          |
|          |          |          |
|          |          |          |
|          |          |          |
|          |          |          |

5/08 K:/Proj/Acc&Pres/CIRC/DateDue.indd

# Managing Wetlands
# on Golf Courses

# Managing Wetlands on Golf Courses

## Gary Libby   Donald F. Harker
## Kay Harker

With contributions from Jean Mackay of
Audubon International

A cooperative publication of the United States Golf Association **USGA** ,
Audubon International AUDUBON INTERNATIONAL,
and the National Fish and Wildlife Foundation.

**WILEY**

JOHN WILEY & SONS, INC.

*Library of Congress Cataloging-in-Publication Data:*

Libby, Gary R.
    Managing wetlands on golf courses / by Gary Libby, Don Harker, Kay
Harker
        p. cm.
    ISBN 0-471-47273-5
    1. wetlands. 2. Wetland management. 3. Golf courses. I. Harker, Donald
F. II. Harker, Kay. III. Title
    QH87.3.L53 2004
    577.68—dc22
                                                        2004012263

Printed in the United States of America

10 9 8 7 6 5 4 3 2 1

# Contents

Foreword ix

Preface xi

Acknowledgments xiii

CHAPTER **1** **Introduction to Wetlands** . . . . . . . . . . . . . . . **1**
  WHAT ARE WETLANDS? 2
  WHY ARE WETLANDS IMPORTANT? 4
  TYPES OF WETLANDS 7
      Estuaries 7
      Rivers, Streams, and Creeks 7
      Lakes and Ponds 9
      Marshes and Wet Meadows 9
      Forested Wetlands 9
      Shrub Wetlands 10
      Bogs 11

CHAPTER **2** **Conservation of Wetlands** . . . . . . . . . . . . . **13**
  IDENTIFYING AND PROTECTING NATURAL WETLANDS 14
      Wetland Protection 15
  INCORPORATING WETLANDS INTO MANAGED AREAS 20
      Natural Landscaping 27
  IMPORTANCE OF VEGETATION ZONES 29
  TRANSITION TO THE TERRESTRIAL ENVIRONMENT 31

CHAPTER **3** **Restoring and Creating Wetlands** . . . . . . . . . **35**

WHAT IS WETLAND RESTORATION? 36

Hydrology 41

Soils 42

Vegetation 42

Additional Suggestions 43

SITE PREPARATION 43

CHOOSING AND OBTAINING APPROPRIATE
WETLAND PLANTS 44

DESIGN CONSIDERATIONS 47

ECOLOGICAL SUCCESSION 47

CONTROLLING EXOTIC SPECIES 53

WILDLIFE CONSIDERATIONS 59

CHAPTER **4** **Structure, Biology, Restoration, and
Management of Wetlands by Type** . . . . . . . . **61**

ESTUARIES 62

Physical Characteristics of Estuaries 62

Plants and Animals of Estuaries 65

Restoration and Management of Estuaries 67

Key Species by Region 69

RIVERS, STREAMS, AND CREEKS 71

Physical Characteristics of Rivers, Streams,
and Creeks 71

Plants and Animals of Rivers, Streams, and
Creeks 77

Restoration and Management of Rivers, Streams,
and Creeks 79

Key Species by Region 80

LAKES AND PONDS 88

Physical Characteristics of Lakes and Ponds 88

Plants and Animals of Lakes and Ponds 97

Restoration and Management of Lakes and
Ponds 104

Key Species by Region 105

MARSHES AND WET MEADOWS  113

Physical Characteristics of Marshes and
Wet Meadows  113

Plants and Animals of Marshes and Wet Meadows  113

Restoration and Management of Marshes
and Wet Meadows  118

Key Species by Region  120

FORESTED WETLANDS  126

Physical Characteristics of Forested Wetlands  126

Plants and Animals of Forested Wetlands  128

Restoration and Management of Forested
Wetlands  129

Key Species by Region  129

SHRUB WETLANDS  134

Physical Characteristics of Shrub Wetlands  134

Plants and Animals of Shrub Wetlands  135

Restoration and Management of Shrub
Wetlands  135

Key Species by Region  135

BOGS  138

Physical Characteristics of Bogs  138

Plants and Animals of Bogs  139

Restoration and Management of Bogs  140

Key Species by Region  140

CHAPTER **5**   **Golf Courses and  Wetlands . . . . . . . . . . . . 145**

PAST AND PRESENT ROLES OF WETLANDS ON
GOLF COURSES  145

Opportunities for Integrating Wetlands
on Golf Courses  146

Wetlands on Existing Golf Courses  147

New Golf Course Developments  149

Golfer and Community Education  151

Environmental Management Planning  151

Self-Assessment Checklist for Managing
Wetlands on Golf Courses  153

APPENDIX **A**   Common and Scientific Names of Organisms  159

APPENDIX **B**   Wetland Resources  169

APPENDIX **C**   Wetland Regulatory Issues  175

Glossary  183

Bibliography and References  187

About the Authors  193

Index  195

# Foreword

*No man is an island*—and no golf course is either. Indeed, every golf course is part of the larger landscape and community in which it is located. Such landscapes are increasingly composed of houses, roads, and commercial and industrial enterprises. Frequently, golf courses are among the few remaining green spaces in a sea of concrete and asphalt.

What this means is that the golf industry not only needs to focus on the game itself, but also needs to be responsive to its role as manager of land, water, wildlife, and natural resources. The concept of superintendent as grass cutter is long gone, replaced by complex demands that require a multitude of skills and extensive technical knowledge.

This book is designed to help with one of the more difficult aspects of golf course environmental management: what to do with wetlands. It offers a basic understanding of different types of wetlands and how they function, as well as information on how to best manage them. It also explores the value of wetlands not only to the environment or community landscape, but also to the game of golf and its role as conservator of open lands.

There is no need to give more examples of wetland loss or degradation. Practical tools like this book can help the golf industry seize the opportunity to showcase its concern for more than the game. It is hoped that this book will be a useful guide for those who are fortunate enough to be managers of wetlands, as well as for those who become interested in creating wetlands on golf courses. Properly sited, designed, and managed golf courses can play a significant role in protecting and improving wetlands and water quality for the benefit of golfers and local communities alike.

RONALD G. DODSON
President and CEO
Audubon International

# Preface

This book can be read from front to back or used as a reference. Chapter 1 is a general introduction to wetlands and wetland types as they are used in this book. Chapter 2 covers basic wetland conservation, and in Chapter 3 the fundamental practices of wetland restoration and creation are presented. Chapter 4 discusses all seven wetland types individually in regard to their ecology, restoration, and management. These sections include common plant species listed by region for all the wetland types. For the purposes of this book, we divided the United States into seven regions. The final chapter (Chapter 5) discusses the concept of wetlands on golf courses. Following the text are three appendices that contain contact and regulatory information about wetland management, creation, and restoration; a Glossary and a Bibliography and References are included as well.

# Acknowledgments

The authors are deeply indebted to many people who helped with this book and wish to thank the following:

The United States Golf Association, especially Mike Kenna, who generously supported this work, and especially the USGA Environmental Research Committee for their support.

The Fish and Wildlife Foundation, especially Peter Stangel, who coordinated the development of this manual for the USGA and offered suggestions and editing.

Ron Dodson, President of Audubon International, for his support, encouragement, and enthusiasm. He generously shared ideas, contacts with golf courses, and the support of his exceptional staff.

Hal Bryan, EcoTech, Inc., for sharing his vast experience in wetland restoration with us and for reading the manuscript critically and offering many helpful suggestions.

Teresa Libby, an artist working in Berea, Kentucky, provided the original artwork for this book.

And last, but not least, our many friends and family members who always had an encouraging word when we needed it.

The authors take responsibility for any errors in this book.

# Introduction to Wetlands

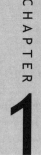

As a game played in a natural setting, golf presents far more than a recreational outlet for golfers. Golf courses are diverse landscapes that can be managed to showcase natural plant communities and wildlife **habitats**—including some of our most valuable: *wetlands*.

Yet golf course superintendents are often unsure of how best to manage wetlands. Questions abound: What is a wetland? When do regulations apply? When is it best to just leave a wetland alone, and when is it best to actively manage it? How can the golf course take advantage of wetlands on-site to enhance their wildlife value and enjoyment by golfers? This book attempts to answer these questions and provides case examples from numerous golf courses that are managing wetlands successfully and with confidence.

## WHAT ARE WETLANDS?

Wetlands are special areas that possess a set of common physical and biological features. These are areas that are covered with water or have saturated soil at least part of the year. Wetlands are "lands where saturation with water is the dominant factor determining the nature of soil development and the types of plant and animal communities living in the soil and on its surface" (Cowardin et al. 1979).

A great diversity of wetlands can be found on golf courses. Some wetlands may appear completely dry during portions of the year. Shrubs and/or relatively large trees, such as cypress and gum, grow in wetlands called swamps, bottomland hardwood forests, and riparian woodlands. A treeless wetland occupied by grasses, rushes, and sedges is referred to as a marsh or wet meadow. An area of predominantly open water may be considered a lake or a pond. Flowing water systems are commonly known as rivers, streams, and creeks. Wetlands are ecological communities with a diversity of living

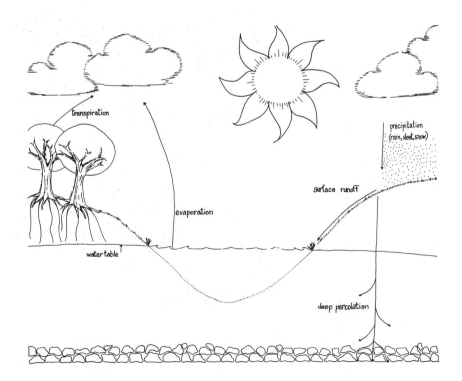

**Figure 1-1** The hydrological cycle showing the major ways in which water moves through the landscape and the atmosphere.

**Figure 1-2** Wetlands on golf courses, such as this wooded wetland at the Country Club of Virginia in Richmond, Virginia, often are located in little used areas of the course. Protecting wetlands ensures that they continue to absorb and filter storm water and provide critical wildlife habitat. (Courtesy of Audubon International.)

organisms such as plants, fish, insects, snails, amphibians, reptiles, birds, and other organisms well adapted to a watery environment.

Wetlands are an integral part of the larger hydrologic cycle. In that cycle, water falls on the land as rain or snow. The water is then taken up by plants, flows back to the ocean or other water bodies, and is taken back into the atmosphere through the energy of the sun (see Figure 1-1).

Rivers, streams, lakes, and other wetlands often receive a significant amount of runoff from the surrounding landscape. The area that drains into a certain river system is called a watershed. The quality of water in the lakes and streams reflects the activity in the watershed. The only way to protect a lake, river, stream, or wetland is proper stewardship of the land in the watershed (see Figure 1-2).

## WHY ARE WETLANDS IMPORTANT?

Wetlands are vital to the planet's water resources. They carry out many functions that are beneficial to plants, animals, and humans. We now realize that wetlands must be protected for the variety of important functions they perform:

- Standing water wetlands (called **lentic** systems) filter water as it moves to streams and influence the rate of flow (especially during storms); they may also act as storage basins during floods. Wetlands improve overall water quality, recharge aquifers (groundwater), and mediate floods by holding storm water runoff.

- Vegetation along flowing waters (called **lotic** systems) helps prevent flooding and erosion by slowing the flow of water and dampening

**Figure 1-3** One hundred twenty acres of wetlands at Old Marsh Golf Club in Palm Beach Gardens, Florida, draw more than 80 species of birds, as well as otters, bobcats, deer, and alligators, to the golf course and residential community. The staff of the golf course has worked closely with the Palm Beach Water Management District on wildlife and plant management and aquatic weed control. Five pairs of sandhill cranes, a threatened species in Florida, live on the property. Golf management proceeds with environmental sensitivity — especially in terms of fertilizer and pesticide use. (Courtesy of Audubon International.)

wave action. Plant roots also hold the soil in place. Both of these qualities reduce the maximum rate of runoff and delay the flood crest in downstream areas.

- Wetlands have a strong influence on water quality because sediments (as much as 80 percent) and heavy metals are deposited, and nitrogen, phosphorus, and other nutrients are extracted and modified by cycling within the marsh system (Kadlec and Kadlec 1979).

- Wetlands provide habitat for many plants and animals. Even upland animals visit wetlands in search of food and water. Some plants and animals that require wetland environments are rare, and wetland conservation and restoration/creation can provide crucial habitat for these species. Thus, wetlands serve as reservoirs of **biodiversity.**

- Wetlands have intrinsic beauty. A pond with water lilies and bald cypress or a salt marsh with swards of waving cordgrass provides a scenic and relaxing setting.

Historically, and unfortunately, wetlands have been considered wastelands in need of draining in order to be useful. In large proportion, wetlands have been drained, dredged, dammed, and otherwise altered drastically from their original state (see Figure 1-3).

## ▶ CASE STUDY

## Old Brockway Golf Course in Kings Beach, California, Serves as a Wetland Mitigation Site

### By David Laurie*

When a Safeway grocery in North Lake Tahoe decided to expand its store and parking area, Old Brockway Golf Course, which borders the store, agreed to mitigate some of the land use change. The project involved creating five water treatment ponds on the adjoining ninth and first holes of the nine-hole public golf course. These created wetlands not only treated storm water runoff, they also enhanced the wildlife habitat and playability of the golf course (see Figure A).

---

*David K. Laurie is the golf course superintendent at Old Brockway Golf Course in Kings Beach, California. The course was designated as a Certified Audubon Cooperative Sanctuary in 1998.

## Implementation and Maintenance

We had an outside contractor provide rough shaping for the wetland areas and enlisted local agencies to help us select appropriate plant material. We chose a specific wildflower mix, as well as indigenous shrubs, trees, and grasses. During plant installation, we irrigated and fertilized these areas to help them get established.

Subsequently, we haven't had to do much to maintain these areas. We no longer water or fertilize them. Occasionally we pull a weed or remove trash that has blown in.

## Success All Around

The success of this project garnered attention from the Tahoe Regional Planning Agency, who named it Best Commercial Project of the Year. The viewing corridor of the golf course, as seen from the nearby roadway, has

**Figure A**  A created wetland at Old Brockway Golf Course improved the beauty and wildlife habitat of the course. (Courtesy of Audubon International.)

been the talk of the town for its beauty. Habitat acreage was increased, and managed acreage, which had been intensely managed in the past, decreased.

Golfers, too, are ecstatic about the project. Though the golf holes are tougher to play, the total beauty of the wetland and wildflower areas more than make up for it. Our pro shop, as well as our local newspaper, kept the public apprised of our progress and success. The project also built pride and confidence in our employees. Because of our initial success, we have repeated this project on hole 2, following the same procedures.

## Project Cost

All costs were covered by the Safeway store.

## TYPES OF WETLANDS

Many wetland classification systems exist and, depending on the scale and the classifier, many types may be recognized. Any classification system involves dividing what is really a continuum. For the purpose of this book, seven general wetland types are presented for incorporation into managed areas: (1) estuaries, (2) rivers, streams, and creeks, (3) lakes and ponds, (4) marshes and wet meadows, (5) forested wetlands, (6) shrub wetlands, and (7) bogs. Detailed information about each of the following types can be found in Chapter 4.

### Estuaries

Waters of most streams and rivers eventually drain into the sea. The interface where fresh water meets salt water is known as an estuary. Estuaries are semienclosed areas in coastal regions (generally influenced by tides) where salt water is diluted and partially mixed with fresh water from the land. Estuaries vary in size from small bays or inlets to extensive open marshes. Estuaries are found along the Atlantic and Gulf coasts of the east and the Pacific coast in the western United States.

### Rivers, Streams, and Creeks

Current, or continuously moving water, is the outstanding feature of streams and rivers. The current in a particular stretch of river or stream is a

**Figure 1-4** Blacklick Creek contributes its name as well as its beauty to Blacklick Woods Golf Course in Reynoldsburg, Ohio. Natural vegetation stabilizes the creek bank, provides wildlife habitat, improves water quality, and reduces the need for intensive maintenance. (Courtesy of Audubon International.)

function of amount of water and topographic relief. Current cuts the channel, molds the character of the stream, and influences the organisms inhabiting the flowing waters. Some streams, however, are intermittent and dry up during part of the year (see Figure 1-4).

Streams may begin as headwaters or outlets of ponds or lakes, or they may arise from springs and seepage areas. In addition, surface runoff, especially after heavy or prolonged rains or rapid snow melt, contributes varying amounts of water to the system. Because precipitation, the source of all runoff and subsurface water, varies seasonally, the rate and volume of stream flow also fluctuate widely from flood conditions to essentially nothing, resulting in a dry stream bed, depending on the size of the stream. In the case of golf courses, irrigation can also be a source of runoff. Rivers, streams, and creeks are found in all regions. The characteristic vegetation, rate of stream flow, and flooding regime vary from region to region.

## Lakes and Ponds

Lakes and ponds are inland depressions or **basins** that contain standing water. They vary in size from less than a hectare to thousands of square kilometers. They may range in depth from less than 1 meter to more than 2000 meters. A lake is a body of water larger than 0.4 hectare and deep enough that it does not freeze from top to bottom in winter. Lakes have deeper waters that do not permit light penetration and plant growth. Ponds are defined as small bodies of standing water (less than 0.4 hectare) so shallow that rooted plants can grow over most of the bottom. Ponds may or may not freeze from top to bottom in winter. Most lakes and ponds have outlet streams; both are changing features on the landscape because filling, no matter how slow, is inevitable. Lakes and ponds are found in all regions. Natural lakes and ponds are abundant in previously glaciated regions. Many human-made lakes and ponds (more appropriately called reservoirs) have been created by damming a river, stream, or depression.

## Marshes and Wet Meadows

Marshes and wet meadows are found in poorly drained, shallow water areas often adjacent to lakes or ponds and along streams or rivers. In some cases, they represent the last filling-in stages of a lake or pond. Marshes and wet meadows are usually saturated or contain water during the growing season. At times, particularly in early fall, the water may dry up and expose the substrate, a condition necessary for the germination of many wetland plants. As plants die, organic matter builds up and may create mounds, called **hummocks,** that are higher than the surrounding wetland. The vegetation may be discontinuous and distributed in small stands or clumps separated from one another. The dominant plants consist of sedges, rushes, reeds, cattails, and a variety of broadleaf aquatic plants. Marshes and wet meadows are found in all regions; however, they vary in species composition, inundation or hydrologic cycles, and basic structure.

## Forested Wetlands

Wooded wetlands may represent a successional stage from a marsh or wet meadow to a moist (mesic) forest. This type of succession, however, occurs

**Figure 1-5** Wetlands can be created in new golf course developments or on established golf courses, like the Carolina National Golf Club in Bolivia, North Carolina. Existing water, soils, and hydrology on-site will determine the most suitable type of wetland to create. (Courtesy of Audubon International.)

over a very long period of time unless the hydrology or substrate is altered. Most forested wetlands are commonly referred to as swamps or bottomland hardwood forests. Forested wetlands may be classified as deep-water or shallow-water swamps. Some trees grow in standing water, and others in periodically flooded areas. Many forested wetlands appear dry during the growing season and may not be saturated. Different types of forested wetlands are found in all regions of the United States (see Figure 1-5).

## Shrub Wetlands

Shrub wetlands are basically intermediate between marshes and wet meadows and forested wetlands. In fact, these wetlands are often transitional in nature. Under certain natural conditions, however, they are maintained over the long term. Although to the casual observer wetlands of this type may have the appearance of a thicket, they contain much biodiversity and serve as habitat for many relatively rare species of plants and animals. Shrub wetlands sometimes occur within marshes and wet meadows and in forested wetlands. Shrub wetlands are found in all regions of the United States.

## Bogs

Bogs develop in areas with very poor drainage. Vegetation consists of sedges, shrubs (usually **heaths**), and sphagnum mosses, typically with peat formation and sometimes with an area of open water. These areas are sometimes called muskegs or mires, and any area that accumulates peat is referred to as a peatland. Cranberries, one of the few native plants cultivated commercially, occur in bogs. Bogs are a typical feature of previously glaciated regions, formed in depressions left by large masses of melting ice. They are also formed in other poorly drained depressions, including mountaintops. Bogs are most common in colder, northern climates with high humidity.

# Conservation of Wetlands

**2**

Managing wetlands on golf courses is done first and foremost to conserve these vital natural resources. This involves identifying existing wetlands and developing a management plan that maintains or enhances water quality, wildlife habitat, and the natural hydrology of the golf course landscape, while protecting the wetlands from negative intrusions by golfers and golf maintenance activities.

## IDENTIFYING AND PROTECTING NATURAL WETLANDS

There are three options for wetlands management on golf courses: wetland preservation, wetland restoration, and wetland creation. *Wetland preservation* means maintaining existing wetlands as a course is built or protecting wetlands present on existing golf courses. *Wetland restoration*, in the broad sense, is the enhancement of degraded or previously existing wetlands. When a wetland is built where none existed before, this is called *wetland creation*. All of these approaches can be used on golf courses to add naturalness to the landscape, create visual appeal, provide habitat for plants and animals, and improve water quality or quantity (i.e., flood control, irrigation). The preferred method is preservation, followed by restoration and creation (see Figure 2-1).

In view of the extensive loss of wetlands in North America and around the world, our emphasis should be to conserve and restore wetlands in a natural state for present and future generations. The best strategy for land managers is the protection of naturally occurring wetlands. Of course, these must first be identified. Streams and ponds are obvious to the land manager, but wet meadows and shrub wetlands are not as easily identified. A pro-

**Figure 2-1** Many golf courses have seasonally wet areas, intermittent streams, or small wetlands, such as this one at Big Canoe Golf Course in Big Canoe, Georgia. Preservation is the preferred method of managing wetlands. (Courtesy of Audubon International.)

fessional with experience in wetland delineation techniques may be needed in some instances (see Appendix C).

Wetland restoration and creation are ways to preserve species that are disappearing as natural wetlands are being drained and developed. Many of our native birds, insects, and larger animals are becoming rare because the plants and natural environments that feed and shelter them are becoming rare. Once wetlands are established, they require less maintenance time and expense than most ornamental landscaping using exotic plants. A wetland must be designed carefully to place each species in soil, moisture, and light conditions that meet its specific needs. The area must be given special attention during the first few seasons after planting. Subsequently, it may require only periodic seasonal maintenance.

Indicative features of wetlands are **hydrophytic** vegetation (e.g., cattails, bulrushes, sedges, etc.), **hydric soils** (e.g., soggy or saturated ground), and/or wetland hydrologic conditions (water drains slowly, holds or remains "perched" in an area, or flows from an area as in a seep or spring). A wetland scientist or botanist can help identify plants in an area to determine how much hydrophytic (water-loving) vegetation is present. Vegetation changes as one goes from upland to lowland, and wetlands are most easily recognized by the plant species that grow there. Hydric soils may be determined by consulting the soil survey for the site (available from the county conservation district), conducting a soil test, or consulting a soil or wetland scientist. Hydrology can be evaluated by a wetland scientist or a hydrologist. The U.S. Army Corps of Engineers administers the permitting of wetland alterations and should be contacted before a wetland is disturbed. In addition, every state has a water quality branch or department that must also give approval for wetland and/or stream disturbances. The Natural Resources Conservation Service (formerly the Soil Conservation Service) and, in certain cases, the Environmental Protection Agency are also involved with wetland regulatory issues.

## Wetland Protection

A wetland can be protected by setting it aside and establishing a buffer area around it. The width of the buffer area depends on the type of wetland. Obviously, bigger is better, insofar as preserving the integrity of the wetland. Buffer areas filter some of the material carried by surface runoff that enters a wetland. As a general rule, stream buffers should be three to five times the average channel width, with a minimum of 20 feet. For other wetlands, a minimum of 25 feet should be used as a buffer width. A critical point in attempting to protect existing wetlands is to maintain the natural hydrology, or levels and flow of water. The wetland should not receive substan-

## HOW ARE WETLANDS DELINEATED?

When a golf course construction or renovation project may impact a wetland, wetland consultants are generally called in to define the wetland's boundaries. Wetland delineation is complicated by the fact that wetland boundaries are often highly variable, inasmuch as water levels fluctuate from year to year. Rather than having distinct beginning and ending points, wetlands often change gradually into uplands as water levels, soil saturation, drainage, and topography change. Experts use a variety of methods to identify and mark a wetland boundary, including site surveys, aerial photography, geographic information system (GIS) maps, soil surveys, and national wetland inventory maps.

On-site observation includes a survey of vegetation, soils, and hydrology.

### VEGETATION

Wetland consultants look at the types of plants growing on-site to delineate the wetland boundary. Plants that are highly adapted to saturated soils and wet conditions are called *hydrophytic*. Consultants identify plants that are almost always found in wetlands (*obligate wetland plants*), as well as those that occur in wetlands most of the time (*facultative wetland plants*). Wetlands generally have some combination of obligate and facultative plant species, depending on the site's hydrology, soils, and topography.

### SOILS

Consultants use a soil probe to take soil samples in various locations in and around a wetland. They look for hydric (wet) soils that developed in conditions where soil oxygen is or was limited by the presence of water for long periods of the growing season. For instance, hydric soils may be gray or black in color, indicating that the iron content has been leached out. Hydric soils usually contain predominantly decomposed plant material (peat or muck) and may have a sulfidic (rotten egg) odor.

### HYDROLOGY

Field observations include the depth of surface water, depth to saturated soils, drainage patterns, watermarks on vegetation, drift lines, and sediment deposits. These wetland indicators help wetland experts determine high and low water flows.

tially more or less water than it did previously. In addition, the water should not carry elevated sediment or contaminant loads into the wetland, or any protection efforts may be in vain.

In some cases it may be beneficial to fence off wetland areas to avoid excessive disturbance by people or other traffic. If the area must be traversed by golfers, a boardwalk can allow people to pass through the area without long-term negative impacts. Informative signs around the borders can help educate people about the importance of protecting wetlands. Successfully protecting existing wetlands also includes monitoring to detect the presence of problems, whether they involve the hydrology, the invasion of an exotic plant species, or problematic animal species (such as white-tailed deer or muskrats). (See Figure 2-2.)

Conservation easements or deed restrictions can be established to ensure protection of a wetland area in perpetuity. This can be an especially important mitigation measure to make certain that natural wetlands will not decline over the long term.

**Figure 2-2** Blackberry Patch Golf Course in Coldwater, Michigan, uses a raised cart path and signs to keep golfers from disturbing wetlands. (Courtesy of Audubon International.)

# WHAT IS A BUFFER?

*By Jean Mackay\**

Maintaining good water quality is a prominent environmental concern for golf courses. The Audubon Cooperative Sanctuary Program and many regional best management practice guidelines routinely recommend that superintendents maintain *vegetated buffers* around water bodies. On sites where fertilizers and pesticides are routinely used, these buffers are an important means of protecting water quality, as well as habitat for aquatic creatures. 'But what, exactly, is a buffer?" people often ask.

A vegetated buffer is an area around the edge of a water body specifically maintained with plants that will reduce storm water flow and potential pollution from runoff. A buffer may be made up primarily of turfgrass or may include a combination of grasses, herbaceous (nonwoody) plants, and shrubs. The plants in a vegetated buffer take in nutrients, trap sediments, reduce erosion, and slow down water as it moves from the land into a pond, lake, or stream.

One type of effective vegetated buffer, often referred to as a *vegetated filter strip,* is turfgrass mown at a height of 3 inches, or as high as possible for the particular turfgrass species. In research trials, such filter strips, maintained at widths between 15 feet and 30 feet, reduced nutrient runoff from adjacent areas by 90 to 99 percent, respectively. Sediment removal rates are generally greater than 70 percent (U.S. Environmental Protection Agency 1993).

### CHOOSING WHAT'S BEST FOR YOUR SITE

In the field, the best height, width, and overall size of a vegetated buffer depend on several factors: slope, type of vegetation, playability, and potential pollution from maintenance practices, including chemical applications (see Figure A).

Many golf courses are able to maintain a full buffer all the way around a pond or stream bank. For sites where this is not feasible, golf courses combine partial vegetated buffers with specialized management zones, such as no-spray zones or limited-spray zones, which may involve spot treatment of disease and weed problems. The use of slow-release or natural organic fertilizers or spoon-feeding also reduces the potential for chemical runoff into water sources.

Vegetated buffers can serve the duel functions of protecting water quality and providing wildlife habitat when emergent and shoreline plants *other*

---

*Jean Mackay is the Director of Educational Services for Audubon International.

*than turfgrass* constitute the buffer around water bodies. Taller emergent vegetation, such as arrowhead, pickerelweed, sedges, and bulrushes, help oxygenate the water and provide food and shelter for a great variety of wildlife.

This type of naturalization alters both the aesthetics and the wildlife value of streams, lakes, and ponds. On golf courses, it may also affect playability, or at least the perception of playability, and therefore must be undertaken with careful consideration. Where taller plants cannot be added, the creation of a turfgrass buffer remains a valuable management strategy.

**Figure A** A combination of turfgrass and taller vegetation provides an effective natural buffer along this stream at Honeybrook Golf Club in Pennsylvania. Such management practices have become increasingly accepted at many golf courses. (Courtesy of Audubon International.)

**References**

Baird, J. H., N. T. Basta, R. L. Huhnke, G. V. Johnson, M. E. Payton, D. E. Storm, C. A. Wilson, M. D. Smolen, D. L. Martin, and J. T. Cole. 2000. "Best Management Practices." In J. M. Clark and M. P. Kenna (eds.), *Fate and Management of Turfgrass Chemicals,* ACS Symposium Series No. 743. Washington, D.C.: American Chemical Society.

Madison, C. E., et al. 1992. "Tillage and Grass Filter Strip Effects upon Sediment and Chemical Losses." *Agronomy Abstracts.* Madison, WI: American Society of Agronomy, 331.

U.S. Environmental Protection Agency. 1993. *Guidance Specifying Management Measures for Sources of Nonpoint Pollution in Coastal Waters,* EPA 840-B-92-002.

## INCORPORATING WETLANDS INTO MANAGED AREAS

The objective of golf course design is to provide players with a challenging and well-maintained, visually appealing course. The lakes and ponds of many golf courses are merely turf-lined water basins that require intense maintenance. A common ground between the typical turf-lined basin and a natural wetland can be reached. Although a totally natural wetland may not be appropriate for some courses, a few fundamental features of natural wetlands can lower maintenance, provide an aesthetically pleasing landscape, and contribute to local biodiversity.

### ► CASE STUDY

## Protecting Wetlands and Water Quality Go Hand in Hand with Development

### By Edward J. P. Hauser, Ph.D. *

Sand Ridge Golf Club (SRGC), an 18-hole golf course complex in Chardon, Ohio, was developed in 1998 on a 359-acre parcel of woodlands and wetlands. The golf course consists of 125 acres, and the remaining 234 acres are open space, including upland mature woods and wetlands.

The club was among the first golf courses in the nation, and the first course in Ohio, to enroll and achieve certification in the Audubon Signature Program. As an Audubon Signature member, SRGC agreed to implement an environmentally sensitive design, which included wetland protection, exotic plant removal, wetland creation, and wetland-upland corridor restoration.

### Significant Wetlands at SRGC

Prior to development, five jurisdictional wetlands, totaling 103.8 acres, were delineated. SRGC received a permit (NWP 26) to fill 0.96 acre and created 10 acres of wetlands and water bodies as part of its mitigation agreement. The wetlands on-site vary from emergent wet meadow to swamp forest to shrub-scrub swamp; the largest wetland on-site (86 acres) contains a small population of a state-listed rare species, *Fraxinus tomentosa* (pumpkin ash), and *Gentiana clausa* (closed gentian), a potentially threatened state species.

---

*Edward J. P. Hauser, Ph.D., is a wetlands consultant in Asheville, North Carolina.

**Figure A**  The headwater stream of the Cuyahoga River flows through Sand Ridge Golf Club. (Courtesy of Audubon International.)

In addition, great blue herons and bald eagles regularly use the wetlands for feeding.

In addition to protecting these significant habitat features, protecting water quality is also of primary importance. The divide for Ohio's Chagrin River and Cuyahoga River watersheds occurs in the large wetland at SRGC. Both rivers of these watersheds are designated as State Scenic Rivers (see Figure A).

## Varied Protection Strategies Yield Excellent Results

SRGC undertook a variety of wetland enhancement and protection measures as part of its stewardship of the property. The five open water zones serve multiple purposes: final "polishing" of tertiary water from the wastewater treatment plant; irrigation; enhancement of wildlife habitats and ecological diversity, including waterfowl and bird habitat; improved aesthetics; and increased variability and challenge in the golf course design, as golfers have to tee over four of the created wetlands (see Figure B).

Ongoing monitoring and enhancement indicate excellent results.

- **Wetland and water quality protection.** Approximately 300 acres of open space, including golf course, wetlands, and uplands, have been placed in a conservation easement in perpetuity with the Chagrin River Land Conservancy.

**Figure B** A bridge crosses a wetland at Sand Ridge Golf Club. All utility lines and irrigation lines were hung under the bridge decking to maintain the wetland's scenic quality and avoid creating any additional fill. (Courtesy of Audubon International.)

- **Water quality protection.** A tertiary wastewater treatment facility was constructed at the time the golf course was built. The third stage of the treatment uses created aquatic bed wetlands to filter wastewater. The tertiary treatment facility processes an estimated 40,000 gallons of water per week, or more than 1 million gallons per year. The wastewater is used for irrigation and no wastewater enters any streams.

- **Exotic plant removal.** A total of 16 acres are included in a permanent exotic species removal program to eliminate *Phragmites australis* (tall reed grass) and *Rhamnus frangula* (buckthorn). Thus far, mechanical removal and seasonal mowing have been used to control about 8 acres of these exotic species, and high-quality native species, including cardinal flower, marshmallow, water shield, and wild raisin, have been planted to take their place.

- **Wetland-upland corridor restoration.** Approximately 22 acres of fairway that received little to no golf play have been transformed into native plant/open field roughs that are now seasonally mowed. In terms of labor, equipment, and chemicals eliminated, this restoration saves an estimated $22,000 per year.

- **Wetland creation.** Approximately 10 acres of wetland have been created, representing Palustrine Aquatic Beds. These wetlands support a number of compatible multiple-use functions: irrigation water, ecofilter wetlands, buffers and ecotones for wildlife between uplands and wetlands and the golf course, waterfowl habitat, and additional ecological diversity. The cost of creating the wetland was approximately $30,000.

---

Wetland restoration or natural landscaping may be appropriate in some areas that are not regulated or considered "jurisdictional" wetlands. Jurisdictional wetlands are those areas that meet the regulatory definition of wetlands. It is important to always to check to see if the area is a regulated wetland. If you walk through an area and end up with wet feet, or if an area is typically too wet to mow without the lawnmower's wheels sinking into the soil, this may be a good place for wet meadow plantings. This treatment will not only beautify the area but will also decrease mowing and maintenance costs as wet meadow plantings need to be cut only once a year rather than once a week (see Figure 2-3). [SB3]

A permit is usually required to alter or fill wetland areas that are considered "jurisdictional waters." The law regarding wetlands allows destruction of a wetland, but only if the loss is mitigated by the creation of a wetland at another location. Adequate mitigation often requires restoration or creation of wetlands at a ratio of 2:1 or greater. Because of the need for a permit, potential mitigation requirements, and the fact that created wetlands may be difficult to maintain, avoidance of disturbance is usually the best alternative.

Once a wetland has been identified, there are two options for protection: (1) Leave the area in an undisturbed condition and allow natural

**Figure 2-3** Robert Trent Jones Golf Club in Gainesville, Virginia, naturalized this slope in front of #11 tee by allowing existing grasses to grow tall and planting hundreds of native perennials. The beautiful result provides an extended buffer along the lake and eliminates the need for intensive maintenance on this slope. (Courtesy of Audubon International.)

## HOW DO WETLAND REGULATIONS APPLY TO GOLF COURSES?

According to the U.S. Army Corps of Engineers, Section 404 of the Clean Water Act (33 U.S.C. 1344) prohibits the discharge of dredged or fill material into waters of the United States without a permit from the Corps of Engineers. The phrase "waters of the United States" refers to navigable waters, but also includes nonnavigable water bodies, perennial and intermittent streams, wetlands, mudflats, and ponds.

Typical activities, although not entirely inclusive, that would require Section 404 permits include depositing fill or dredged material in waters of the United States for such things as

- Utility installations, stream relocations, or culverting

- Site development fills for residential, commercial, or recreational developments

- Construction of revetments, groins, breakwaters, levees, dams, dikes, and weirs

- Placement of riprap and road fills

Because wetland regulations are site and state specific, golf course personnel should contact local authorities when golf course improvement, renovation, or construction projects may impact water bodies.

processes to take their course or (2) actively manage the area. The conservation of natural wetlands may not always be accomplished by leaving them alone, and in many situations restoration or enhancement can greatly increase benefits to wildlife as well as humans. In an undisturbed environment, a wetland is part of a much larger ecosystem. The surrounding natural areas affect the hydrology, as well as the plants and animals. In the human-created environment, some type of active management is usually necessary to maintain the characteristic wetland.

The management of a wetland is sometimes more involved, including such practices as establishing plants, altering the hydrology to meet management goals (may require a permit), and installing structures or creating habitat features to attract particular wildlife species.

## WHEN SHOULD MY GOLF COURSE APPLY FOR A CORPS PERMIT?

According to the U.S. Army Corps of Engineers, the primary governmental agency charged with regulating activities in the nation's waters:

> Permits are required by federal law for almost all projects that involve work in a water of the United States. You should apply for a Corps permit as early as possible during the conceptual stage of a project, while there is still some flexibility in the project design. Since it may take a number of months to process a routine application involving public notice, it is prudent not to wait until permits are obtained from all local and state agencies before going to the Corps.

If you are unsure whether your project requires a permit, contact your nearest Corps office. Performing unauthorized work in waters of the United States or failure to comply with the terms of a valid permit can have serious consequences. Golf courses may face stiff penalties, including fines and requirements to restore the area (see Figure A).

**Figure A**  A 6-acre wetland at Twin Rivers Golf Course in Oviedo, Florida, is surrounded by three golf holes. Carolina willows may eventually grow tall enough to block some golf shots on these holes. "Can these plants be removed? Can they be cut and left to naturally decompose? Can they be chipped and blown back into the area? Should something be planted in their place, and, if so, what are my options?" questioned Superintendent Dan Gillen. Gillen's best option is to contact the local U.S. Army Corps of Engineers to find out what he can and can't do without a permit. (Courtesy of Audubon International.)

**TABLE 2.1.** Wetland Management Techniques

Monitor plants and remove exotic species.

Build trails or walkways to manage pedestrian or golf cart traffic.

Manage the hydrology, or levels and flow of water.

Install structures (nesting boxes/platforms, bat boxes, basking logs).

Create wetland features (pit and mound microtopography).

Mount signs or use ropes or fences where necessary to keep golfers out.

In areas where few, if any, natural wetland areas are present, the conscious design of a wetland will be required. If a wetland is present, the approach may be to enhance it by eliminating exotic plants, determining whether hydrological alterations can be beneficial, planting desirable wetland species (if lacking), installing wildlife structures (e.g., duck boxes, bat boxes, nesting platforms, etc.), constucting protective fencing to keep out unwanted livestock, and establishing buffer areas adjacent to the wetland or corridor connections to the wetland (see Figure 2-4).

## Natural Landscaping

If creation of a full wetland is not possible, managers can practice natural landscaping, which is the arrangement of native plants in a way similar to their arrangement in nature. Natural landscaping can mean planting several species that grow together naturally, combining different native plants from those that grow throughout the region, or just adding a few native shrubs or ferns to an existing area (Harker et al. 1999) On a large site, natural landscaping can mean landscaping large areas with the native species of the region. The first step is to study nearby natural areas carefully, and then recreate the desired landscape, as nearly as possible, the soil, landforms, moisture conditions, and plant arrangements of the natural environment (see Figure 2-5).

Management goals should emphasize the most natural conditions possible by maintaining natural values through the use of natural processes. Natural processes integral to wetland management include

Water flow

Food chains

Nutrient input at rates in natural environment

Balance of plants and animals

Goals should focus on the long-term over short-term benefits.

**Figure 2-4** A buffer of wetland plants at IGM at the Habitat in Malabar, Florida, was created as a result of the course's participation in the Audubon Cooperative Sanctuary Program for Golf Courses. The aquatic plants help to filter runoff from the golf course and provide food and cover for waterbirds and other wildlife. (Courtesy of Audubon International.)

**Figure 2-5** A wetland carry on hole #3 at Black Lake Golf Club in Onaway, Michigan, must be maintained with heightened environmental sensitivity. The mowing height of turfgrass in the rough is raised to create a buffer and delineate the wetland boundary for golfers. (Courtesy of UAW Public Relations and Publications Deptartment.)

Even a 1-meter wide strip of emergent vegetation around a pond or stream can provide food and shelter for birds and amphibians. Birds need insects, leaf litter, and fruiting shrubs, as well as dead wood, both fallen and standing, and herbaceous plants that are allowed to go to seed. With the addition of wetland trees and/or shrubs and some floating-leaved aquatic plants, many more species will be attracted to a wetland. As a general rule, the more diverse the vegetation, the greater the diversity of animals that use the habitat. Improving or creating a wetland with diverse vegetation may take a while. Because the area may appear "derelict," signs explaining that the area is being managed to benefit wildlife may educate people rather than offend them. In these times of continuing significant pressure on the environment, the idea of restoring even one small corner of a damaged landscape is satisfying.

## IMPORTANCE OF VEGETATION ZONES

Aquatic plants are adapted to occupy a particular zone in a given wetland type. Knowing the appropriate zone and wetland type will greatly increase the success of wetland creation and restoration projects. Factors such as light, current speed, water clarity and depth, and soil types determine where particular aquatic plants grow. Various kinds of aquatic plants are described in the following paragraphs (see Figure 2-6).

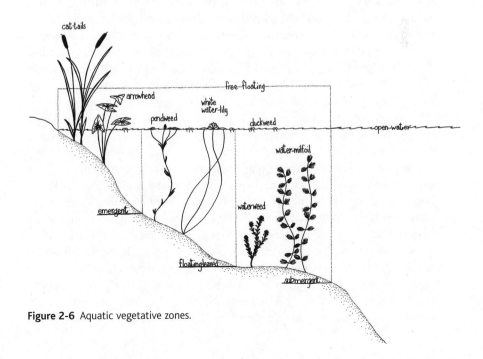

**Figure 2-6** Aquatic vegetative zones.

*Emergents* are plants that grow with their roots, and often their bases, in wet soil or water part or all of their lives. Examples, given in order of shallow to deeper water, are rice cut-grass, whitetop grass, sedges (softstem bulrush, river bulrush, chairmaker's bulrush), cattail, and hardstem bulrush. The more robust species that stand into the next year have been termed persistent emergents, whereas those that deteriorate rapidly are considered nonpersistent (Cowardin et al. 1979). Some trees (bald cypress, swamp tupelo, green ash, red maple) and shrubs (buttonbush, brookside alder) also occur with their bases and root systems in water or wet soil. Emergent plants are generally limited to a water depth of 2 meters or less. They are rooted plants that can tolerate flooded soil but not an extended period of being completely submerged.

*Floating-leaved* plants are those rooted in deeper water that tend to send up broad, floating leaves to the surface, where photosynthesis takes place. They survive well with fluctuating water levels or high turbidity. Examples include American white water lily, yellow pond lily, Carolina fanwort, water shield, and pondweed. Floating-leaved plants have their pores, or stomata (where gas and water exchange occurs), on the upper surface of the leaf, the opposite arrangement to that of most terrestrial plants. A waxy coating repels water from the leaf surface to keep it dry.

*Free-floating* plants are not rooted to the **substrate** but instead have dangling roots that derive nutrients from the water. Examples are lesser duckweed, mosquito fern, water meal, and, in the South, introduced water hyacinth. These plants contain extra spongy or air-filled cavities that make them especially buoyant. Duckweeds are valuable food for water fowl. The tiny roots of duckweed are a microhabitat for algae, water fleas, and microscopic animals. Duckweeds may sometimes cover the entire surface of a pond.

*Submergent* plants are rooted, but their stems and leaves are mostly, if not entirely, underwater. These plants, which flower at the water's surface, include bladderwort, water crowfoot, water milfoil, widgeon grass, waterweed, muskwort, and riverweed. The sago pondweed forms seed heads on the surface, which provides food for ducks, coots, and geese. These animals also feed on its tubers, stems, and leaves.

*Suspended* plants are those that maintain a specific density so as to be suspended in the water column. As portions of submergent plants break off, they may occupy this zone. The most common examples are the tiny phytoplankton, primarily **diatoms.** Other examples include coontail, water naiad or nymph, star-duckweed, waterweed, and horned pondweed.

Vegetation zones can grade into one another gradually, or the transition can be abrupt. Because ponds are not always perfectly circular with evenly sloping contours, a mosaic of vegetation zones is frequently present, with islands of some zones interspersed within others. This is an important consideration, because interspersion creates a greater area of ecotones where

**Figure 2-7** The variety of emergent and floating plants in a "typical" wetland environment at Silver Lake Country Club in Orland Park, Illinois, illustrates how wetland vegetation changes as the wetland gets deeper. Depth of the water level is a key consideration when choosing plants to add to a golf course pond, lake, or wetland shoreline.

diversity is high (Caduto 1990). The combination of life forms and species in a particular wetland constitutes the living, dynamic, interactive plant community (Weller 1994). (See Figure 2-7.)

The plants mentioned here in the various categories of aquatic plants do not occur in every region. It is important to select plants native to the region for a wetland restoration project. Native plants are species that occurred in a certain area prior to European settlement in this country. Most well-written plant identification manuals state whether particular species are native. Native plants are well adapted to regional conditions and will provide valuable habitat and low maintenance while conserving overall biodiversity. For a list of the more characteristic plants for various wetland types in the seven regions discussed in this book, see Chapter 4. For a list of plant suppliers, check with agencies in Appendix B.

## TRANSITION TO THE TERRESTRIAL ENVIRONMENT

The management of a wetland area should not end at the edge of the wetland, but should focus on adjacent areas as well. For example, if a wetland can be situated at the edge of a forest or woodland, wildlife species that are not likely to cross an open turf-dominated area, frequently occupied by humans, will more likely use the area. Management of the surrounding land will also affect the wetland. For example, high levels of fertilizers can cause eutrophication, pesticides can impact wildlife, and so forth.

## PRESERVING WETLAND-UPLAND CONNECTIONS

*By Jean Mackay**

Preserving wetlands sometimes involves more than just protecting the land that is wet. For wetlands to be most beneficial, they have to be connected to other habitats so that a variety of creatures can creep, slither, walk, and fly safely to them from neighboring habitats.

Wetlands are not only relied upon by wildlife species that live in the water, but are also vital to species that use them to meet some of their needs, such as feeding, drinking, or breeding. Thus, for most animals, wetlands and uplands must be connected for both habitats to serve the year-round needs of wildlife.

Yet government regulations rarely stipulate that these connections be preserved when permitting a new development. They merely require that the wetland itself be protected.

"That cuts off the ability of many creatures to get to the wetland," states Larry Woolbright, Director of Research for Audubon International. "For instance, many species of frogs and salamanders move between wooded uplands, where they spend much of the year, and wetlands, where they breed. Protecting only the wetland and developing all around it reduces or eliminates the ability of frogs and salamanders to reproduce—and that can spell the end to once thriving populations."

### GOING BEYOND MINIMUM REQUIREMENTS

Architects and developers can create more environmentally sensitive designs by taking these upland-wetland connections into account in new golf course construction. In some cases this will involve going beyond what the government requires in regard to the "lines" it draws around wetlands. Golf course routing plans should leave upland woods next to wetlands or establish corridors of upland preserves that are linked to the wetlands. In addition, golf course designers can delineate core habitat areas and small habitat patches throughout a property to minimize habitat fragmentation and maximize the wildlife value of protected natural areas (see Figure A).

On-the-ground site surveys and careful analysis of design plans can reveal whether the *primary functions* of a wetland—not just the basin with water in it—will be preserved. Wetland connections, proper drainage, and the final contours of the golf course landscape can enable the wetland to continue absorbing and storing storm water, filtering nutrients, and recharging groundwater.

---

*Jean Mackay is the Director of Educational Services for Audubon International.

"It's critical to protect wetlands right, so that they continue be an essential part of wildlife habitat and watershed integrity," says Woolbright. "When we work with Audubon Signature Program members, we visit the site and designate key wetlands and their upland habitats. Then we work with the architects and developers to make sure these areas are protected."

With thoughtful design considerations and a commitment to conservation, developers can integrate fully functioning wetlands into new golf courses in a way that is good for golf and good for the environment. Preserving wetlands, as well as their functions, benefits developers, golfers, wildlife, and the communities in which they live.

**Figure A** Lost Key Golf Course in Perdido Key, Florida, was designed to take advantage of the natural features of the property. Golf holes are nestled among wetlands, lakes, and upland areas to reduce fragmentation of vegetative communities. The course is a certified Silver Audubon Signature Sanctuary. (Courtesy of Audubon International. Photo by Mike Klemme/golfoto.com)

Buffer zones, whether forested, shrubby, or even with tall herbaceous vegetation, around wetlands help to filter the sediments and chemicals that are carried into wetlands by surface runoff. Moreover, establishing buffer strips and connecting natural habitats can allow a greater variety of wildlife to use the area. Fragmentation is the act of reducing and isolating patches of natural systems. Creating these corridors for animal movement is a way to reverse the impact that fragmentation of natural habitats has had on some species. Rivers and streams are often very important corridors for animal movement. Rivers can be the movement corridors between wetlands that are adjacent to or near the rivers.

# Restoring and Creating Wetlands

New golf course developments and existing golf courses can do much to live up to today's expectations that golf courses be built and managed with sensitivity to the environment. Existing courses with degraded wetland areas, eroded streams, or sterile ponds can take advantage of restoration techniques to greatly improve site conditions. Likewise, new developments can take full advantage of design opportunities that not only minimize or eliminate wetland loss, but actively incorporate functioning wetland systems into the golf course landscape.

## WHAT IS WETLAND RESTORATION?

Wetland restoration is the improvement of any degraded or altered wetland to a more natural state. Wetland creation is the construction of a wetland where one did not previously exist. Wetland restoration is a very active field today. This is primarily due to the new awareness by the public of the importance of wetlands and the federal regulations promulgated as a result of extensive wetland losses suffered in the United States. Overall, the United States has lost more than 50 percent of its wetlands, and in some states the loss is 90 percent (National Research Council 1992). Among the reasons for restoration projects are the creation of wildlife habitat, improvement of water quality, storage of water, and reduction of flooding.

The success of wetland restoration is greater for sites that were previously natural wetlands. If the hydrologic regime has been destroyed on a

**Figure 3-1** Olympia Fields Country Club in Olympia Fields, Illinois, worked with local conservation experts to restore eroded shorelines along Butterfield Creek. Both banks of the creek in this area were stabilized with riprap, and vegetation is allowed to grow in the silt trapped by the riprap. The restoration project improved water quality by reducing sedimentation and erosion and enhanced the visual appeal of the golf course. (Courtesy of Audubon International.)

**Figure 3-2** A variety of consultants, including biologists, ecologists, and wetland regulators from the Army Corps of Engineers, are generally involved in projects where new wetlands are created. Experts help to ensure that wetland hydrology and native plant communities are properly established from the outset. (Courtesy of Audubon International.)

site, it may still be regulated, so it is essential to conduct an investigation for the presence of jurisdictional wetlands. The U.S. Army Corps of Engineers (ACE) has to concur with any wetland delineation to make it official. It is important to remember that some wetlands may not be disturbed without a permit from at least the ACE and, often, local or state agencies. To obtain a permit may require wetland replacement or mitigation, but often the best and cheapest mitigation is avoidance of any jurisdictional wetlands. These natural areas can often be incorporated into your site plan, thereby increasing aesthetic appeal and biodiversity (see Figure 3-1).

Because of the value of wetlands and the significant loss of these plant and animal communities, we recommend restoring such communities whenever appropriate sites are available. If a golf course is going to be developed from an old farm, we encourage close examination to determine the existence of suitable areas that can be restored to wetland. In many cases there are sites, such as along an intermittent stream, where a small wetland may be created that never existed before (see Figure 3-2).

> ► CASE STUDY

## Restoring Wetland Habitat for Migratory Waterfowl

### By Nancy Richardson*

Stevinson Ranch Golf Club—Savannah Course in Stevinson, California, opened in 1995 as the first golf course in California to be certified as an Audubon Signature Sanctuary. The facility includes 18 holes of golf with a clubhouse, practice range, cottages, conference center, and a nature trail set on 996 acres of former rangeland. The site of Stevinson Ranch is unique in that, before construction, it had essentially never been developed; 82 percent consisted of uplands and the rest was marshes, salt pan, and canals.

Stevinson Ranch is located in the Central Valley of California, a region historically known for its wetlands and grasslands that attract thousands of migratory waterfowl and other birds each year. Agriculture within the Central Valley has drastically reduced its once vast wetlands, making those that remain especially vital for birds. Stevinson Ranch sits between two major rivers, the San Joaquin to the south and the Merced to the north. It is in close proximity to three national wildlife refuges, several state wildlife areas, and Yosemite National Park.

A locally and regionally significant seasonal wetland known as Lake Honda lies in the southeastern corner of the property in an area designated as the Grassland Ecological Area. Lake Honda is fed by rainfall, as well as the East Side Canal, an irrigation canal that supplies water for agricultural uses along its length during the growing season from April through mid-November. This area provides prime habitat for migratory waterfowl, including several species of geese, sandhill cranes, cinnamon teal, gadwall, mallards, and black-crowned night herons, among others, as well as numerous species of passerine birds (see Figure A).

### Project Description

During the construction of the Savannah Course, developers not only restored 100 acres of wetlands, but also created 120 acres of new wetlands. The focus of this case study is on the 40 acres of wildlife habitat that were restored within the Lake Honda basin (see Figure A).

Developers and consultants at Stevinson Ranch envisioned a plan to create year-round, rather than seasonal, water in Lake Honda. A proposal

---

*Nancy E. Richardson has served as Director of the Audubon International Signature Program since 1995.

submitted to the U.S. Fish and Wildlife Service, Natural Resources Conservation Service, and Ducks Unlimited secured grant funding for the project, with 50 percent paid by the U.S. Fish and Wildlife Service under the North American Wetlands Conservation Act (NAWCA) Grants Program.

Goals for the project were twofold:

1. Increase the diversity and number of waterfowl species by providing permanent open water to an area already abundant with waterfowl.
2. Provide access for the public to areas previously inaccessible, and offer information about the wildlife inhabiting the Lake Honda basin.

## Construction Process

Construction began on the restoration and expansion of Lake Honda in 2000, with the major portion of the project completed in 2001. Stevinson Ranch staff manages all existing and improved habitat according to a habitat

**Figure A**  Wetland restoration at Stevinson Ranch improved habitat in Lake Honda for migratory waterfowl. (Courtesy of Audubon International.)

management plan developed with assistance from the U.S. Fish and Wildlife Service to improve regional biodiversity.

The construction plan for the restoration project called for excavation of the wetland basin to greater depths and the creation of an island near the northwest end of the lake to provide habitat for nesting birds. Before excavation began, work crews burned off underbrush that prevented ease of access and obscured the view of the lake. Next, they drained the lake by releasing water back into the canal. Silt fences were placed near the perimeter of all disturbed areas to prevent movement of sediment and remained in place until vegetation was eventually established to stabilize the soil. Maintenance staff dredged the lake bed to various depths, providing shallow areas and deeper channels.

Soil removed from the silted-over basin was used to build a 1.3-mile levee around the perimeter of the lake to serve as a nature trail. Because this levee closed a breach in the East Side Canal, two gate valves, one at each end of the levee, were added to allow filling of the lake to desired levels throughout the season and independent control of the lake level. A third valve was subsequently added to provide additional intake control.

Another aspect of the restoration was the removal of undesirable, non-native vegetation, such as tules (*Scirpus* spp), cattails (*Typha* spp.) and giant reed (*Arundo donax*). Native riparian shrubs and trees were added, including valley oak (*Quercus lobata*), Fremont cottonwood (*Populus fremontii*), black willow (*Salix nigra*), and buttonbush (*Cephalanthus occidentalis)*. Crews selectively transplanted these species from existing native vegetation found throughout the property. The bare island was not revegetated manually, but was allowed to naturalize.

## Results

The restoration of Lake Honda has made a positive impact on the number of bird species and other wildlife observed on-site, including wood ducks, hooded mergansers, great egrets, snowy egrets, and great blue heron. Near the end of 2002, the site began to flourish with a greater diversity of plants and wildlife. The island has revegetated naturally and is dense with grasses. Native plant species numbers continue to improve as a result of annual mowing of nonnative and unwanted plant species. The levee and trail area has filled in with grasses and young cottonwoods and willows. Future plans call for laying down a road base along the 1.3-mile nature trail to hold the levee and provide a suitable surface to walk on.

Benches will also be added so that guests may pause to take in the beauty of the site. Several observation turnouts have been cleared along the trail to provide access to the lake. Now that the project is completed and open to the public, interpretive panels have been installed at key viewing points along the perimeter of Lake Honda. At each panel, there is a numbered redwood post that will coincide with a pamphlet featuring 12 key points along the 1.3-mile trail. Guests will be able to pick up a pamphlet in the pro shop and take a self-guided tour into the restored wetland habitat. Observation platforms are to be installed at key points of interest around the lake, along with high power telescopes permanently mounted to allow distance viewing of species. These remaining projects are scheduled to be completed in cooperation with U. S. Fish and Wildlife Service and Ducks Unlimited.

### Project Cost

The total cost of the project was $37,875. The 50/50 funding resulted in $18,937.50 provided through NAWCA and $18,937.50 (including in-kind services) provided by the Kelley family, owners of Stevinson Ranch.

Three main areas must be addressed in considering a wetland creation or restoration plan: hydrology, soils, and vegetation.

### Hydrology

- Its hydrology is the driving force of a wetland. Evaluate the hydrologic conditions for a site, such as water level elevations, velocity, hydroperiod, salinity, nutrient and chemical levels, pH, and sedimentation rates.

- The source of water can be surface flooding from streams, groundwater, or rainwater.

- The watershed/wetland size ratio should be considered. Usually, the larger, the better. Smaller ratios (as low as 1:1) are possible for restoration with isolated, precipitation-driven wetlands in hydric soils.

- The periodicity of inundation or saturation determines the type of community restored or created. For example, a bottomland hardwood forest may require 20–30 days of continuous inundation in the growing season and a period of drydown in the late summer. A shrub swamp may need twice as much inundation with very little drydown.

- The restoration of hydrology may require the removal of berms, the plugging of human-made ditches, the renovation of stream meanders and flood regimes (may not be appropriate in all situations), or the destruction of subsurface drainage tiles.

- The creation of shallow ponds for habitat diversity can increase the numbers of plant and animal species. This is not to be confused with the creation of deeper ponds typically excavated for fish or livestock watering. Moreover, these shallow ponds should not be created in high-quality wetland areas. Clay subsoil from ponds should be used for ditch plugs or berms.

- The use of water control structures, where possible, can provide some ability to manipulate water levels, which is especially important during the early periods of plant establishment.

## Soils

- Select areas of hydric soils for restoration. A list of hydric soils for your region can be obtained from the U.S. Natural Resources Conservation Service (formerly the Soil Conservation Service). Be sure you are not restoring in an existing jurisdictional wetland without a permit.

- Store and replace topsoil during the construction phase.

- Use topsoil or muck from impacted wetlands if possible. Muck is a seed source and also provides many microorganisms characteristic of a wetland but not commercially available.

- Be concerned with erosion possibilities. Slopes should be very gentle and stable even without vegetative cover.

- Use small equipment on-site; large machinery can compact subsoil and restrict root penetration.

## Vegetation

- When possible, select potential restoration locations adjacent to existing wetlands to allow natural regeneration.

- Trees can often be reestablished using bareroot seedlings (usually on 2–3 meter centers) or acorns (2500 per hectare).

- Container-grown stock is often the most successful.

- Adjacent wetlands can be used as a seed source.

- Discourage the collection of native plants from natural areas.

- Herbaceous wetland plants can be installed in small wetlands or in those wetlands where quick establishment is essential.

- In some cases, seeds of wetland plants are used in a temporary matrix of grass like redtop or rye (nonnatives that will die out in standing water) or switch grass. Fescue should be avoided except in the most difficult to establish areas.

- Select species carefully, according to the targeted depth of water.

## Additional Suggestions

- Use nest/roost boxes for wood ducks, bats, or other animals if appropriate. Put in perches (dead snags) for birds to use.

- Managers must be prepared for any adverse impacts wildlife might cause.

- Money should be set aside to monitor and maintain the restored wetland. Be prepared to respond quickly to problems such as erosion or trees dying.

- Plan for buffer areas to protect the wetland from sedimentation, pollution, and other human impacts.

## SITE PREPARATION

Whether to start from scratch (reshape the topography, make hydrologic corrections, and prepare a seed bed) or to begin with revegetation (planting and making minor, gradual improvements in an existing area) can be a difficult decision for some sites. The determination is generally based on elevations and their relation to the present water source(s). If proper hydrologic conditions can be emulated, then the wetland should function well. However, some areas may need earthwork to improve the microtopography, which in turn increases plant and animal diversity. It is always best to get a few opinions from professional wetland scientists, ecologists, or botanists (see Appendix B).

Usually the best approach is to work with what you have, rather than make radical changes. Even simple wetland plantings can change an area into an attractive part of the landscape and set in motion a natural successional path to a natural wetland (see Figure 3.3).

**Figure 3-3** Cattails and yarrow provide an extended and dense buffer for this lake on hole #9 at Haymaker Golf Course in Steamboat Springs, Colorado. Extended buffers are incorporated into the design of new golf courses enrolled in the Audubon Signature Program. (Courtesy of Audubon International.)

## CHOOSING AND OBTAINING APPROPRIATE WETLAND PLANTS

Managers should strive to introduce plants that will attract birds in a natural manner, providing food, shelter, and nesting habitat to increase the carrying capacity of the land. Leave any desirable wetland plants and remove those that are not wanted. Make plant selections and planting designs based on what you want the plants to do for your landscape. This can be a difficult task, given the great diversity of wetland plant communities. Lists of species appropriate for the seven wetland types are arranged by region in Chapter 4. Species were selected on the basis of four criteria:

1. Relative dominance in the wetland type (i.e., it is one of the dominant plants)
2. Wildlife habitat and food value
3. Aesthetic value
4. Availability from commercial growers (i.e., it is commonly cultivated)

Because hundreds or thousands of plant species can be used for most of these wetland types, the lists are only partial. Your state natural heritage program, native plant society, or wildflower preservation society, a local branch of The Nature Conservancy, a fish and wildlife resources agency (Appendix B), and other conservation organizations are excellent sources of information about native plant selections for your landscape (see Harker et al. 1999 for extensive species lists). Many professional consultants who practice wetland creation or restoration can assist in defining and implementing your project (see Appendix B). If there are nature centers or botanical gardens in your area, they may provide valuable sources for information, advice on planting and overall design, or even a cooperative program. Your county extension agent may also be a good source for advice, publications, or information about obtaining native plants. However, some government agencies recommend and provide non-native plants, which should be avoided. Experts in local native plants can review and evaluate plant lists for the inclusion of non-native plants.

Some wetland plants may already exist at your site, or they may "move in" naturally by being blown by the wind or carried by waterfowl. If these species are desirable, they should be encouraged as a complement to those that have been planted (see Figure 3-4).

Just as it is important to be aware of exotic plants, the gardener or restorationist must be familiar with water, light, and soil requirements. As the species considered in this book are listed for large regions, it is important to make sure that a particular plant occurs in your area before using it. Some species that are native outside your area will grow successfully, but it is best to use those native to your region as they are already well adapted and will require the least maintanance.

It may be worthwhile to experiment with various plants in wetland areas, as long as these species are desirable natives and components of the nearby natural systems. You can mix or match plants from various wetland types; for example, many wet meadow species are equally at home along a small stream or adjacent to a lake or pond. For some genera with several common species (such as sedges [*Carex* spp.] or rushes [*Juncus* spp.]) you will need to check on what is available at local nurseries and what is native to your area. Sedges and rushes are found in many different kinds of wet places —marshes, swamps, and bogs, as well as along canals and slow-moving streams. Almost any sunny or lightly shaded place with damp, muddy soil or shallow water is likely to have sedges. Both sedges and rushes are useful for wetland plantings as they provide habitat and food for wildlife and stabilize the banks of ponds and slow-moving streams.

**Figure 3-4** A raised cart path, like this one at Pumpkin Ridge in Cornelias, Oregon, is the preferred method of traversing a wetland when the wetland must be incorporated into the golf course design. (Courtesy of Audubon International.)

Although many wetland plants serve as biological filters there, is a limit to how much of a certain pollutant or chemical a plant can tolerate. Urban runoff contains oil and salts; agricultural and golf course runoff may include nitrogen, phosphorus, sediments, and pesticides. If there are pollutants present, then only the most hardy wetland plants can be used. Several species of bulrushes may be able to act as biological filters, removing contaminants such as mercury, lead, cadmium, and phenol from the aqueous environment. Most studies of plants for use as biological filters have focused on common and widespread species such as bulrushes (*Scirpus* spp.), rushes (*Juncus* spp.), common reeds (*Phragmites australis*), and cattails (*Typha* spp.). Other species may be good choices, but the best species are likely to be the common pioneer wetland grasses and sedges in your area. When using plants to be biological filters, it is important to know the state and local regulations governing disposal of these plants.

## DESIGN CONSIDERATIONS

By its very nature, a wetland setting must have a naturalistic design. The vigorous nature and rapid spread of most aquatic plants make them unsuitable for a formal, intensely structured landscape. As discussed earlier, it is important to plant wetland trees, shrubs, and herbaceous plants that are adapted to site conditions. Blend plants into the landscape in a natural manner, considering the vegetation zones discussed in Chapter 2. Knowledge of a plant's native range and habitat preference gives us a framework in which to place plants in associations. There are differences, both subtle and profound, in the timing, amount, duration, and quality of water required. Knowing which plants require or tolerate what water regimes is essential to success.

## ECOLOGICAL SUCCESSION

The natural orderly change of a plant community over time is known as succession. Succession may even result in the eventual loss of a wetland. Naturally, this would occur over a long period of time (hundreds or thousands of years). These changes are dependent on other variables, such as water regimen and disturbances. Although these changes occur naturally, they are often accelerated by human-made changes in the landscape. We need to consider the dynamics of succession, and how it will affect our wetland areas.

## Specially Designed Wetlands Treat Golf Course Runoff at Raptor Bay Golf Club in Florida

### By Kraig Marquis*

Many golf course superintendents find water quality management one of the most challenging aspects of their jobs. Success in managing water sources for golf, wildlife, aesthetics, irrigation, and overall water quality depends on having a basic understanding of factors influencing water quality and on adopting best management practices (BMPs).

Members of the Audubon Signature Program have a special advantage in working with Audubon International to build in systems that protect water quality from the start. One approach to protecting water quality in lakes uses a unique wetland treatment system known as a *phytozone*. In general terms, a phytozone is similar to a shallow forebay at the edge of a lake. The design is unique, however, because it integrates the treatment benefits of a detention basin and a created wetland.

Raptor Bay is a WCI Communities, Inc., resort-class, championship golf course development with residential time-share units and associated amenities located in Estero, on Florida's Gulf Coast. Raptor Bay Golf Club was designed by Raymond Floyd. In March 2002 it won certification as the third Audubon International Gold Signature Sanctuary golf course in the world, meeting Audubon International's highest standards for development in concert with the environment.

The entire project encompasses approximately 510 acres, of which more than 150 acres will remain undeveloped and preserved in perpetuity under conservation easements. This large preserve area, or Eco-Park, is home to an active nesting pair of bald eagles and several gopher tortoises and is planned to feature a nature trail and interpretive signs detailing the unique ecosystem.

The Raptor Bay property consists primarily of pine flatwoods with pockets of cypress strand and xeric oak scrub vegetation communities. Halfway Creek, classified as a Florida Outstanding Water, runs through the property and drains into the Estero River and then into the Estero Bay.

*Kraig Marguis is Audubon International's Sustainable Communities Coordinator for Florida.

## Phytozones at Raptor Bay

To protect water quality in the created lakes on-site and the water bodies downstream of the project, including Halfway Creek and Estero Bay, approximately 22 acres of phytozones, or small wetland pockets, were constructed to treat runoff from the golf course. The phytozones at Raptor Bay are characterized by a wide earthen berm that separates a shallow pool from the main body of the lake. Each is constructed to receive runoff directly from the storm water drainage system or from swales around the lakes (see Figure A).

Once the runoff is discharged into a phytozone by pipe or swale, it is detained before flowing into the main body of the lake. The phytozone temporarily stores and slows the movement of the runoff and therefore pro-

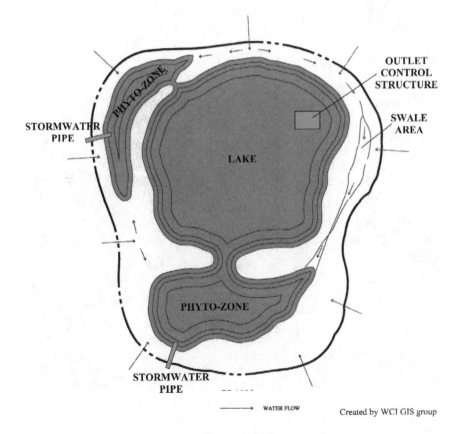

**Figure A** Diagram of Raptor Bay's phytozones. (Courtesy of Audubon International.)

**Figure B** One of Raptor Bay's lakes and two smaller phytozones under construction. (Courtesy of Audubon International.)

**Figure C** When completed, the berm and gradually sloping shallow banks of the phytozones are vegetated with a variety of aquatic plants. The aquatic plants provide added water quality treatment through a combination of trapping solids and taking up dissolved nutrients. (Courtesy of Audubon International.)

**Figure D** Phytozones have dramatically increased the variety of bird species at Raptor Bay.
(Courtesy of Audubon International.)

motes settling of solids and attached pollutants. Vegetation planted in the
phytozone takes up and filters dissolved nutrients (see Figures B and C).

The phytozones at Raptor Bay are sized to treat runoff from smaller,
more frequent storm events, which have the greatest potential to degrade
water quality. Preliminary water monitoring results have indicated that
water quality is good and that the phytozones are functioning effectively.

Phytozones can also have the added benefit of providing habitat and
feeding areas for wading birds and other wildlife. Results from the wildlife
monitoring program at Raptor Bay have indicated a substantial increase in
the variety of bird species on the property. Surveys conducted in December
2001 and December 2002 added 22 new bird species, including 9 new water-
dependent birds, to Raptor Bay's bird list. Rare birds, including listed
species, have been observed feeding along the lake banks and vegetated
berms. These berms are especially popular because they provide additional
forage area and protect the birds from predators and the occasional unknow-
ing golfer searching for a stray golf ball (see Figure D).

**Figure 3-5** Audubon Signature Sanctuary Lost Key Golf Club in Perdido Key, Florida, was designed to take advantage of the natural features of the property. Golf holes are nestled among wetlands, lakes, and upland ecosystems, reducing fragmentation of vegetative communities. A cart path over the wetlands ensures undisturbed water flow and wildlife movement beneath. (Courtesy of Audubon International.)

Generally, as a newly restored wetland ages, the number of plant species present increases (to a certain point). For example, some species, such as oaks and hickories, may not naturally grow in an area until 5–10 years after restoration. This is why we often focus on these species when we are planting. This approach allows us to "jump start" the system, to accelerate succession (see Figure 3-5).

If a wetland is receiving significant loads of sediments, then it is likely to fill in, which will cause a succession in the vegetation. Providing buffer strips and controlling land use practices upstream are the best ways to reduce sedimentation. Although streams can be impacted by excess sedimentation, they can also be limited by a lack of sediment. This is because healthy, natural streams move sediments at a rate that does not allow for buildup (aggradation) or loss (degradation) of sediment. Thus, the amount of sediment transported by the system is in balance, or dynamic equilibrium. Often, well-intended widening or cleaning of stream channels results in channels that aggrade and widen, defeating the purpose of the effort. Understanding natural processes and working with them produces solutions that benefit people and the environment.

## CONTROLLING EXOTIC SPECIES

Exotic plants or animals, or extremely invasive native species, are sometimes a problem in managed areas. To avoid any future problems, exotic plants and animals should be removed when they are discovered. These exotic species compete with native plants and animals and may even dominate a site if they are not controlled. Some exotic species are very difficult to remove and seem to actually thrive on the disturbance caused by attempted removal. To achieve the best results, research exotic species before removal (see Figure 3-6).

**Figure 3-6** Monitoring plants and removing exotic species is an important part of wetland creation and restoration. Crew members at TPC of Michigan in Gaylord, Michigan, conduct a controlled burn to knock back *phragmites* in a wetland area and encourage more desirable wetland plant growth. (Courtesy of Audubon International.)

▶ CASE STUDY

# Removing Exotic Vegetation at The Club at Mediterra, North and South Courses

## By Alicia Oller*

The Mediterra residential and golf course community encompasses approximately 1697 acres in Lee and Collier Counties, Florida, in the Southern Coastal Plain ecological region. A project of the Bonita Bay Group, the Club at Mediterra, North and South Courses, comprises two 18-hole championship golf courses built in 2000–2002. The North and South Courses are certified Audubon International Silver Signature Golf Courses.

The predevelopment project site was composed primarily of pine flatwoods and cypress-pine-cabbage palm, as well as improved and unimproved pasture for cattle grazing. These various habitats had been affected by past land use practices, including agricultural clearing and ditching, cattle grazing, logging, swamp buggy touring, and fire control measures. The sites' hydrology had been altered as a result of the construction of the drainage ditches, elevated roadways, and fire cuts. The spread of exotic vegetation, primarily melaleuca, was accelerated by soil disturbances, wildfires, the use of off-road vehicles, cattle grazing, and reduction of historic groundwater conditions.

The Bonita Bay Group preserved, enhanced, or created approximately 292 acres of wetlands and preserved 60 acres of uplands to satisfy the permitting requirements of federal and state agencies. The two golf courses weave around these preserved and enhanced wetland systems. A coherent wildlife corridor extends throughout the property via connections made between preserved habitat, native landscaped plantings, and surface water management lakes planted with native species.

The four primary goals of the Mediterra wetland restoration project were to

1. Enhance the existing high-quality wetlands by eradicating exotic and nuisance plants
2. Encourage natural recruitment of native plant species by restoring a more historic hydrology and improving soil conditions in wetlands
3. Increase the diversity and wildlife value of the wetland systems by creating deepwater marshes

*Alicia Oller is Project Manager/Senior Scientist with the Audobon International Institute.

4. Provide an aesthetically pleasing and functional environmental amenity for the residents of Mediterra

## Exotic Plant Removal

Prior to golf course development, Mediterra's wetlands had been invaded by a number of exotic and nuisance plants, including Florida's most unwanted—melaleuca and Brazilian pepper. Communities that were once cypress-dominated wetlands had become a monoculture of melaleuca. Other exotics observed included downy rose myrtle, climbing hemp vine, and West Indian marsh grass. When normal conditions of natural communities have been disrupted, even some species of native plants can act as invasives and become undesirable. Some of the nuisance plants that occurred on-site included dog fennel, caesar weed, grapevine, and love vine. Various eradication and maintenance activities were completed both during and after construction to facilitate the removal of these undesirable plants from the property (see Figure A).

**Figure A**  Removing invasive plants enhanced existing wetlands at the club at Mediterra. (Courtesy of Audubon International.)

## Florida's Most Unwanted: Invasive Exotic Plants

Encroachment of nonnative plants in natural communities is a serious problem throughout Florida. Melaleuca and Brazilian pepper are the two most widespread exotic plants. Invasive exotic plants disrupt naturally occurring plant communities. Such non-native plants grow without the elements that keep them in check in their natural environment, such as seasonal weather, disease, insect pests, or other factors. These exotics out-compete native Florida plants and reduce the diversity of the community. This, in turn, can adversely impact wildlife and other natural processes. Natural communities invaded by exotic plants such as melaleuca often become monocultures of the invasive species. The State of Florida spends millions of taxpayers' dollars each year trying to eliminate and control exotic plants (Florida Exotic Pest Plant Council 2003).

Most of the wetland enhancement and restoration activities at Mediterra occurred between May and August 2000 for Phase 1, with a retreatment completed in October 2000. The Phase 2 work was completed in spring 2002.

Prior to any clearing activities, all conservation areas were flagged and staked and silt fence was installed along the boundaries. The exotic vegetation within the wetlands was primarily removed by hand to avoid disturbance of the wetland soil and preserve the desirable native wetland vegetation. Disturbed soils often provide an ideal growing environment for pioneering nuisance vegetation that can out-compete the naturally recruited desirable native species. The Bonita Bay Group believes mechanical removal should be considered only when the wetland grade is to be lowered, such as in wetland creation or restoration areas, or in large areas of exotic vegetation monocultures where hand removal is cost-prohibitive and little to no desirable native vegetation exists.

### Muck Jump-Starts the Created Wetlands

To enhance recruitment of native wetland plant species in the created marshes, muck or wetland topsoil was relocated from both on-site and off-site wetlands previously permitted for impact that did not contain a significant exotic vegetation seed source. However, not enough muck was available for all of the wetland creation areas. In Phase 1, three of five wetlands received a muck blanket. In Phase 2, composted mulch from on-site grinding activities was added to most of the created marshes. The marsh creation areas were excavated approximately 6 inches deeper than the desired final elevation to allow for the addition of a 6-inch deep muck/mulch layer. The final elevations of the marsh creation areas were surveyed to ensure accuracy. In southwest Florida, a few inches of elevation change greatly affects the hydrology and diversity of plant species present in a wetland.

In addition to natural recruitment of wetland plant species, thousands of native species were planted in several enhanced wetland and upland conservation areas. These species included slash pine, dahoon holly, cypress, red maple, wax myrtle, buttonbush, cordgrass, and muhly grass. The marsh creation areas and shallow littoral shelves created along all of the surface water management ponds were planted with native aquatic and wetland species, such as cordgrass, lemon bacopa, bulrush, spike-rush, arrowhead, and pickerelweed.

## Results

The created marshes that received a muck layer from a donor wetland experienced excellent recruitment of wetland species. The wetlands that received the mulch layer also had good recruitment, almost comparable to the recruitment of those that had received muck. The few wetlands that did not receive any organic layer had noticeably poorer recruitment of native plants and less plant diversity. Thus, these areas have taken longer to achieve the aesthetic and functional values of natural wetlands.

Several of the wetland enhancement areas required only removal of exotic vegetation. Once these areas were cleared, the plants within the seed bank germinated and the wetland was soon dominated by native species.

## Maintenance

The Bonita Bay Group has determined that quarterly maintenance is necessary for at least the first 2 years after initial exotic vegetation removal in southwest Florida where melaleuca and Brazilian pepper are prevalent. For several more years, semiannual maintenance is necessary to keep the exotic plants' seedbanks from reestablishing on-site. Gradually, annual maintenance is adequate. Off-site exotic vegetation seed sources will be blown in or carried by other means, such as by birds.

## Project Cost

Exotic removal—$991,000 (The county required exotic vegetation removal over the entire project area. The state and federal agencies required exotic vegetation removal in the conservation areas.)

Plantings (plants and installation)—$325,000

Quarterly maintenance—$150/acre/quarter

## Conclusion

The management activities completed in the wetlands and uplands have resulted in an amazing transformation of natural communities throughout the Club at Mediterra. Several benefits are evident from the work conducted: (1) The seed source for exotic plants in the vicinity has been reduced, (2) a more diverse wildlife habitat has been created and enhanced, (3) the diversity and structure of vegetation within natural communities has increased, and (4) the aesthetic value for the people living and playing in the Mediterra community has been enhanced.

## Summary Points

- Planting costs were reduced in wetland creation areas by use of a muck or mulch layer.

- Disturbed soils often provide an ideal habitat for pioneering nuisance vegetation that often out-competes the naturally recruiting desirable native species.

- Good recruitment of native plants facilitates the enhancement of habitat diversity for wildlife and other wetland functions while also meeting regulatory requirements.

- Monitoring is already showing that communities once dominated by invasive exotic vegetation are now represented by greater diversity and more structural layers of native plant species. The functional value of the enhanced wetlands and uplands in the conservation areas has greatly improved and will continue to improve over time.

## WILDLIFE CONSIDERATIONS

Many animals find their way to newly created wetlands, and others can be easily introduced. Snails, which are useful scavengers that scrape algae off rocks and plant stems and also eat dead organisms, can be introduced into managed wetlands to clean up particulate food left behind by larger organisms. Fish, turtles, and frogs can be readily transplanted, or purchased from commercial sources, and released in newly restored or created wetlands. Be careful not to introduce non-native species into such areas. Newly created wetlands should be allowed to sit for a few weeks after they have been filled so that sediment and any chemicals can settle out before animals are introduced.

Some wildlife can become problematic on managed landscapes. If white-tailed deer are numerous, they may have to be excluded from restoration areas by use of a repellent or an electric fence (at least during the early phases of restoration). Muskrats, nutria, and beavers can cause structural changes in a wetland by digging holes or building dams. They can also eat a large amount of aquatic plants. They should not be excluded from a wetland unless they become too numerous and begin to interfere with other goals. Wetlands should be monitored to assess wildlife activity and determine if any special management techniques are needed. Even the populations of some waterfowl, such as Canada geese, can be overwhelming in some areas. It is important to keep in mind that when we restore or create a wetland for wildlife, we may get more than we expect.

# Structure, Biology, Restoration, and Management of Wetlands by Type

Though often described generically as "water features," golf course streams, ponds, marshes, and forested wetlands require management that is specific to the unique structure and biology of each. This chapter explores the physical characteristics, plants, animals, and management techniques for various types of water bodies. Use it in combination with other local sources of information as a reference for identifying and managing the the specific types of wetlands found on your golf course.

## ESTUARIES

### Physical Characteristics of Estuaries

Where a river meets the sea, a complex interaction of current, tidal action, sedimentation, and salinity occurs. Sediments carried from streams and rivers are deposited in estuaries. As sediments accumulate and form deltas in the upper reaches of the mouth, they shorten the open water part of the estuary. When silt and mud accumulations become high enough to be exposed at low tide, tidal flats develop. These flats divide and braid the original channel of the estuary. Simultaneously, ocean currents and tides erode the coastline and deposit material on the seaward side of the estuary. If material is deposited faster than it is carried away, then barrier beaches, islands, and brackish lagoons appear. Although this process has been constant, the actual formation of estuaries has occurred over a very long period of time, hundreds or thousands of years (see Figure 4-1).

Current and salinity, both complex and variable, shape life in the estuary. Salinity varies vertically and horizontally, often within one tidal cycle. Salt

**Figure 4-1** A display educates public golfers about the tidal marsh present at Eagle's Landing Golf Course, located on Maryland's coast in Berlin. Highlighting the unique natural aspects of the golf course heightens golfer awareness and adds to the enjoyment of the game of golf.

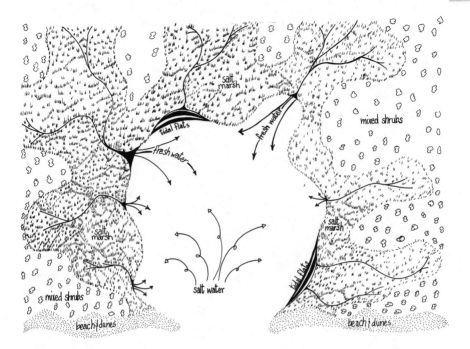

**Figure 4-2**  The estuary is where fresh water meets salt water, creating varying zones of salinity.

water brought in by the tide mixes with fresh water coming down the river. Areas where salt and fresh waters mix are called **brackish** (see Figure 4-2).

Vertical salinity may be constant throughout or stratified, with layers of fresh water near the surface and dense saline water in the lower layers. When winds and currents are strong enough, salinity is constant. Salt water is denser than fresh water, so the fresh water flowing seaward from the river is usually on top of the sea water (see Figure 4-3). However when the tide is coming in, salt water can move in on top of the incoming fresh water.

Because the amount of fresh water entering an estuary varies seasonally, salinity also varies. Salinity is highest during the summer and during periods of drought, when less fresh water flows into the estuary. It is lowest during winter and spring, when rivers and streams are discharging their peak loads. The salinity can change rather rapidly.

Adjacent to the estuary and in the shelter of the spits and offshore bars and islands is the tidal marsh. Although these areas appear as waving acres of grass, they are actually a complex of distinct and clearly demarcated plant associations. The tides play a significant role in plant zonation, for twice a day the salt marsh plants on the outermost tidal flats are submerged in salty water and then exposed to full sun. Their roots extend into poorly drained,

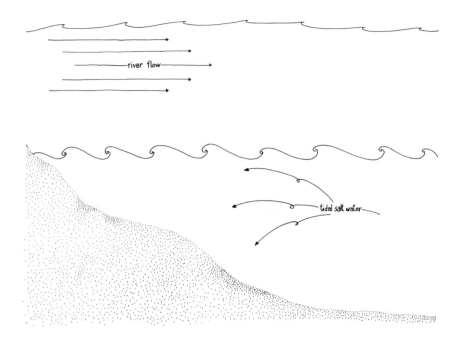

**Figure 4-3** The vertical stratification of an estuary where fresh water enters the marine environment. This is commonly known as the "salt wedge."

poorly aerated soil containing varying concentrations of salt. Only plant species with a wide range of salt tolerance can survive such conditions.

The primary physical features of an estuary are the main channel, the meandering creeks, and the pans (also called pond holes). The creeks are the drainage pathways that carry water back out to the sea. Some channels are formed by water movement around irregularities on the surface. The river itself forms the main channel. After channels or creeks are formed, they may be deepened by scouring and heightened by a steady accumulation of organic matter and silt. In conjunction with these processes, the heads of the creeks erode and small branch creeks develop. Lateral erosion and undercutting causes the banks to cave and fall into the creek in places, cutting off smaller channels. The distribution and pattern of the creek system play an important role in the drainage of the surface water as well as the drainage and movement of the water in the subsoil.

The pond holes, or pans, occurring in tidal marshes are typically round or elliptical depressions. During high tides they are submerged, and at low tide they remain filled with salt water. In shallow pans, the water may evaporate and leave an accumulating concentration of salt on the mud. These depressions occur naturally as the marsh develops. Early plant colonization is irregular, and bare spots on the salt marsh become surrounded by vegetation. The surrounding vegetation causes the adjacent areas to become slightly raised, and a pond hole is formed. If a pond hole, or pan, becomes connected to a creek, it may drain and become vegetated. Other pans, especially in sandy marshes, are derived from creeks. Vigorous growth of marsh plants can partially dam a creek, or lateral erosion may block the channel. Thus, water remains when the tide retreats, inhibiting plant growth. Often a series of pans form on the upper reaches of a single creek. A pan may be caused by the death of small patches of vegetation due to excess salinity or inadequate drainage (referred to as a rotten-spot pan).

Pans may support submerged plants if the depth and the salinity are appropriate. Pools with a firm bottom and sufficient depth to retain tidal water support dense growths of widgeon grass, which has long, threadlike leaves and small black triangular seeds relished by waterfowl. Widgeon grass occurs along the Atlantic, Gulf, and Pacific coasts of the United States. Shallow depressions in which water evaporates are covered with a heavy algal crust and crystallized salt. The edges of these salt flats may be invaded by glasswort, coastal salt grass, sea lavender, or dwarf saltwater cord grass.

## Plants and Animals of Estuaries

The region of transition between fresh water and salt water, where a river enters the ocean, creates a gradient of salinity. That gradient provides a habitat for organisms uniquely adapted to exist in these areas between salt and fresh water. The inhabitants of the region between land and sea are adapted to live in an environment heavily influenced by tides.

Organisms that inhabit an estuary are faced with three challenges: maintenance of position, adjustment to changing salinity, and being underwater and out of water each day. Most estuarine organisms live on the bottom (benthic) and are securely attached, buried in the mud, or occupy crevices around **sessile** organisms. **Motile** inhabitants consist chiefly of crustaceans and fish, largely young of species that spawn offshore in high-salinity water. The position of planktonic organisms is determined by the currents. **Plankton** (algae) blooms can be dramatic in the estuarine river as nutrients precipitate out from chemical reactions where salt and fresh waters meet.

The distribution of life in the estuary is determined by the relative amount of salt in the water. Many estuarine organisms can withstand seawater. Some cannot tolerate lowered salinities, and these species decline along a salinity gradient. Sessile and slightly motile organisms have an optimum salinity range within which they grow best. When salinities vary on either side of this range, populations decline.

In the tidal marsh, saltwater cord grass dominates on the East Coast of North America and Pacific cord grass on the west coast. As a wet grassland species, cord grass is unique. No litter accumulates beneath the stand. Strong tidal currents sweep the floor of the cord grass clean, leaving only thick black mud. Saltwater cord grass is well adapted to grow on the intertidal flats where it dominates. It has a high tolerance for salt water and is able to live in a semisubmerged state.

Along the Atlantic and Gulf coasts, tall saltwater cord grass occupies the portion of the tidal marsh between mean low water and mean high water. At the mean high water line, tall saltwater cord grass declines in abundance as plants of the high marsh dominate. One of the dominant plants of the lower reaches of the high marsh is dwarf saltwater cord grass. This species is short and yellowish, contrasting sharply with the dark green tall saltwater cord grass growing along the banks of the tidal creeks weaving through the marsh. Growing with the dwarf saltwater cord grass are the fleshy, translucent glassworts that turn bright red in fall, sea lavender, spearscale, and sea blite.

At little higher elevation than the dwarf saltwater cord grass is its relative, marsh hay cord grass, and an associate, coastal salt grass. Marsh hay cord grass is a fine, small grass that forms tight mats and often excludes other plants. Dead growth of previous years lies beneath current growth, shielding the ground from the sun and keeping it perpetually moist. When the salinity of the soil is higher or the soil tends to be waterlogged, spike grass occurs. As the microelevation rises several more centimeters above mean high tide and there is some intrusion of fresh water, black needle rush may dominate. Rarely are the rushes covered by ordinary high tides, but they are often submerged by the **neap tides** of spring and fall. Beyond the growth of black needle rush, and often replacing it is a shrubby growth of marsh elder and groundsel. These shrubs tend to invade the high marsh, where there is a slight rise in microelevation, but such invasions may be short-lived as storm tides sweep in and kill the plants. On the upland fringe grow bayberry and rose mallow. Where the water is fresh to brackish, reed, spike-rush, three-square bulrush, and cattails occur.

The oyster bed and oyster reef constitute an interesting feature of the estuary. The oyster is the dominant organism in this formation. Oysters may be attached on every hard object in the intertidal zone, or they may form reefs, areas where clusters of living oysters grow cemented to the almost-buried shells of past generations. Oyster reefs usually lie at right angles to tidal currents, which bring planktonic food, carry away wastes, and sweep the oysters clean of sediment and debris.

Although the animal life of a salt marsh is not particularly diverse, it is certainly interesting. Some animals are permanent residents, mostly living in the sand or mud, and others are seasonal visitors, but most are temporary visitors that come to feed at high or low tide. Along the Atlantic and Gulf coasts, three characteristic animals of the saltwater cord grass stands are the ribbed mussel, the fiddler crab, and the marsh periwinkle. Two conspicuous vertebrates of the intertidal marsh are the diamondback terrapin and the clapper rail. On the high marsh, animal life changes almost as abruptly as the vegetation. A pulmonate snail replaces the marsh periwinkle of the low marsh. Another resident here is the jumping meadow mouse. Replacing the clapper rail on the high marsh are the willet and the seaside and sharp-tailed sparrows. Seaside and sharp-tailed sparrows are common inhabitants of Atlantic and Gulf coast salt marshes. A large fish-eating hawk, the osprey, is common along both the Atlantic and Pacific coasts. Two infamous inhabitants of the salt marsh are salt marsh mosquito and the fierce-biting greenhead fly.

Along the shrubby fringes of the marsh, dense growths of marsh elder and groundsel provide nesting cover for red-winged blackbirds and sites for heron rookeries as well. Remote stands of these shrubs support the nests of smaller herons and egrets, and the pines (as well as man-made structures) support the nests of the fish-eating osprey.

Low tide brings an array of predaceous animals onto the marsh to feed. Herons, egrets, gulls, terns, willets, ibis, and raccoons, among others, inspect the exposed marsh floor and the muddy banks of tidal creeks in search of food. At high tide the food web changes as tidewaters flood the marsh. Killifish (or mummichogs), silversides, four-spined sticklebacks, and flounder, restricted to channel waters at low tide, occupy the marsh at high tide, as does the blue crab. At high tide, too, ribbed mussels and razor clams begin to strain the water for detrital material.

## Restoration and Management of Estuaries

An estuary is not an individual, isolated part of nature and cannot be managed as such. Any estuary is influenced by the adjacent land and how that land is used. Estuaries are relatively stable communities unless a major disturbance occurs. Buffer areas are important, not only to protect the estuary from adverse impacts, but also to protect the mainland during severe weather.

Estuaries are among the most challenging wetland types to restore. The factors that contribute to the difficulty of restoring this type of community are that saturated conditions are usually constant, work must often be done at low tide, and initial stabilization following restoration is difficult because of tides and storms. Estuaries occur in specific areas because a particular set of physical characteristics are present (i.e., fresh water meeting salt water).

For this reason, estuaries cannot be *created*. Preexisting estuaries can be *enhanced* if they are relatively intact, but when more intensive measures are needed (such as fixing the hydrology), then estuaries can be *restored*. Hydrology is the key to success in restoration, and for an estuary, this means that tidal flushing must not be constrained.

The daily inflow and outflow of water must approximate that of a natural estuary. The hydrology of estuaries is dynamic, having both daily and seasonal cycles. If these cycles have been drastically altered, the area will not be able to function as an estuary and the desired vegetation will not become successfully established. Elevations within the estuary must be carefully planned so that it will support the relatively distinct zones of salt marsh vegetation found in natural estuaries. Comparing a natural estuary, with respect to the elevations and zones of vegetation, with one that is being restored can be extremely useful for assessing excavation (if needed) and revegetation plans. The excavation of meandering channels can facilitate restoration of estuarine hydrology.

In estuarine environments where the hydrology is being restored, the hydrology may not become fully functional for a few seasons. This must be taken into account in revegetation efforts. For example, what is used for erosion control in a particular situation—temporary vegetation or human-made structures—may be more important than species composition. Plant species should be selected to perform the erosion control function.

Once the hydrology of the site has been restored, planting may begin. Placement of plants where appropriate growing conditions occur (i.e., tidal flushing) is crucial. Cord grass is generally planted on the flats that occur extensively between the channels and creeks. Cord grass is effective at controlling erosion if conditions are such that it will flourish. In fact, very few other species are as successful in the estuary setting as cord grass. However, an erosion control mix may be amended with other native grasses, rushes, and forbs to improve chances for success. Exact plant placement varies, depending on species. The low marsh species such as saltwater cord grass (Atlantic and Gulf coasts) and Pacific cord grass (Pacific coast) require longer periods of inundation, and high marsh species such as coastal salt grass (Atlantic, Gulf, and Pacific coasts), black needle rush (Atlantic and Gulf coasts), and saltwort (Atlantic, Gulf, and Pacific coasts) require slightly shorter periods. The high marsh species, including groundsel bush (Atlantic and Gulf coasts) and a variety of other shrubs, big cord grass and salt-meadow cord grass (Atlantic and Gulf coasts), do not receive daily tidal flushing. Some species such as widgeon grass (Atlantic, Gulf, and Pacific coasts) may prefer specialized **microhabitats** within an estuary such as pot holes.

## Key Species by Region

### *Atlantic and Gulf Coasts*

| | |
|---|---|
| *Asclepias lanceolata* | Few-flower milkweed |
| *Baccharis halimifolia* | Groundseltree (high tide bush) |
| *Distichlis spicata* | Coastal salt grass |
| *Hibiscus laevis* | Halberd-leaf rose mallow |
| *Hibiscus moscheutos* | Crimson-eyed rose mallow |
| *Ilex opaca* | American holly |
| *Iva frutescens* | Jesuit's-bark |
| *Juncus effusus* | Lamp rush |
| *Juncus gerardii* | Saltmarsh rush (north) |
| *Juncus roemerianus* | Roemer's rush (black needle-rush) (south) |
| *Limonium carolinianum* | Carolina sea lavender |
| *Myrica cerifera* | Southern bayberry (south) |
| *Myrica gale* | Sweetgale (north) |
| *Peltandra virginica* | Green arrow-arum |
| *Salicornia bigelovii* | Dwarf saltwort |
| *Salicornia europea* | Common saltwort |
| *Salicornia virginica* | Woody saltwort |
| *Solidago sempervirens* | Seaside goldenrod |
| *Spartina alterniflora* | Saltwater cord grass |
| *Spartina cynosuroides* | Big cord grass |
| *Spartina patens* | Salt-meadow cord grass |
| *Zizania aquatica* | Indian wild rice |

### *Pacific Coast (Northern Portion)*

Estuarine marshes and tidal flats are found in the estuaries along the Oregon, Washington, and California coasts. Salt marshes occupy sheltered inland margins of bays, lagoons, and estuaries. The soils of these marshes are subject to regular tidal inundation for at least part of the year. Tides directly influence the islands in the lower Columbia basin. The following list should be used as a starting point; a customized list should be developed for your specific site.

| | |
|---|---|
| *Argentina egedii* | Pacific silverweed |
| *Atriplex patula* | Halberd-leaf orache |
| *Carex lyngbyei* | Lyngbye's sedge |
| *Cotula coronopifolia* | Common brassbuttons |
| *Cressa truxillensis* | Spreading alkali-weed |
| *Deschampsia cespitosa* | Tufted hair grass |
| *Distichlis spicata* | Coastal salt grass |
| *Eleocharis parvula* | Little-head spike-rush |
| *Frankenia salina* | Alkali sea-heath |
| *Glaux maritima* | Sea-milkwort |
| *Grindelia integrifolia* | Pudget Sound gumweed |
| *Grindelia paludosa* | Suisun marsh gumweed |
| *Hibiscus moscheutos* | Crimson-eyed rose mallow |
| *Hainardia cylindrica* | Barb grass |
| *Jaumea carnosa* | Marsh jaumea |
| *Juncus balticus* | Baltic rush |
| *Juncus effusus* | Lamp rush |
| *Juncus lesueurii* | Salt rush |
| *Lasthenia minor* | Coastal goldfields |
| *Limonium californicum* | Marsh-rosemary |
| *Puccinellia kurilensis* | Dwarf alkali grass |
| *Salicornia bigelovii* | Dwarf saltwort |
| *Salicornia europea* | Common saltwort |
| *Salicornia maritima* | Sea saltwort |
| *Salicornia virginica* | Woody saltwort |
| *Scirpus americanus* | Chairmaker's bulrush |
| *Scirpus maritimus* | Saltmarsh bulrush |
| *Spartina foliosa* | California cord grass |
| *Spergularia salina* | Sandspurrey |
| *Suaeda californica* | Broom seepweed |
| *Triglochin concinnum* | Slender arrow-grass |
| *Triglochin maritimum* | Seaside arrow-grass |

Prior to initiating full-scale planting it may be useful to plant a transect of a particular species along an environmental gradient (i.e., wetter to dryer) to determine the optimum range for planting. Many excellent sources on restoration of estuaries are available, such as Adam (1990), Broome (1990),

Ranwell (1975), Redfield (1967,1972), Stout (1984), Seliskar and Gallagher (1983), Teal (1986), and Zedler (1982, 1984, 1992).

New plantings may have to be protected from the action of the waves until their root systems become well developed. Coir (coconut) fiber mats or bundles, with plants growing in them, should be installed in areas that need rapid stabilization and establishment of plant cover. The vegetation, whether planted or volunteer, should be monitored periodically to determine the success of revegetation and to see which species are thriving and which are not.

Common reed (*Phragmites australis*) can invade estuarine areas and form continuous stands, or monocultures. Common reed is absent from most natural intact estuaries. Its presence indicates previous disturbance (such as dredging and filling) and disruption of the hydrology. This robust grass is very difficult to control, and a combination of chemical and mechanical methods is often needed for effective control. Once the common reed is under control and the hydrology and vegetation of an estuary are established, it is usually not a serious problem. Enhanced or restored estuaries, however, should be monitored closely to detect common reed infestation before it causes difficulty.

Enhanced and restored estuaries will attract wildlife characteristic of this wetland type. Structures (such as nesting platforms, boxes, and houses) should be used to attract specific species. The structural diversity provided in natural estuarine systems includes open water, mud flats, cordgrass meadows, shrubby areas, tree islands, and adjacent upland woods. These areas all attract a variety of birds and other animals by providing food, water, and cover. Estuarine animals will colonize an enhanced or restored estuary naturally. Some introduction of such wildlife, however, may accelerate wetland functioning and productivity.

Constant change in structure is more characteristic of estuaries than of some other wetland types. Slight variations in elevation have significant impacts on which plants survive. Plant zones should be established (and this may require some trial and error) so that the appropriate species are planted in the various areas. Anchoring the plants with natural fibers or matting or using energy dissipators for the action of the waves can greatly improve the success of plantings.

## RIVERS, STREAMS, AND CREEKS

### Physical Characteristics of Rivers, Streams, and Creeks

Rivers, streams, and creeks are dynamic, flowing aquatic systems greatly influenced by the landscape through which they flow. Wooded lowlands along rivers, streams, and creeks that are only periodically flooded are called riparian forests or bottomland hardwood forests. The major energy or nutrient source of lotic, or flowing water, systems is material carried in from the adjacent areas. This material includes leaf litter and branches dropped from overhanging vegetation or blown in by the wind, and rainwater dripping through leaves and dissolving the nutrient-rich material produced by the leaves. Wind and rain move these nutrients to the stream (see Figure 4-4).

Additional nutrients are washed into the river channel during periods of high water when surrounding swamps, marshes, and meadows are flooded. Other inputs come from subsurface **seepage,** which brings nutrients leached from adjoining forest, agricultural, and residential lands, and from upstream flow carrying both dissolved nutrients and particulate matter. Many streams receive inputs from urban and industrial effluents. A minor source of nutrients is produced in place through primary production (photosynthesis) by algae growing on rocks and by rooted aquatics such as water moss. Even in slow streams where primary production may be substantial, rooted aquatics provide little as immediate sources of energy. They become important only when the plants die and nutrients become available as detrital material. Energy is lost through two pathways, geological (through stream flow feeding downstream systems) and biological (from heat loss through respiration). Dependent on energy input from the outside, stream ecosystems are different from lake and terrestrial ecosystems, whose main source of energy is primary production within the system. Thus, particular concern for management of the entire watershed is more important in flowing-water systems.

Fast or swiftly flowing streams wash small particles downstream and tend to leave behind a stony bottom. A fast stream consists of two essentially different but interrelated habitats, the turbulent **riffle** and the quiet **pool.** The waters of the pool are influenced by processes occurring in the rapids above, and the waters of the rapids are influenced by events in the pool. The riffles are the sites of primary production in the stream. The **periphyton** (algae that are anchored to the substrate) assume dominance and have as much importance as the **phytoplankton** (suspended algae) in lakes and ponds. Diatoms, blue-green and green algae, and water moss constitute the abundant periphyton communities of the riffle areas. As the current slows, a noticeable change takes place in the stream. Silt and decaying organic matter accumulate on the bottom. Animals are able to move about to obtain their food, and a plankton population develops. The structure and composition of the stream community approach those of standing water (see Figure 4-5).

The lay of the land, or **physiognomy,** influences the route of a river stream. The soils and bedrock also influence which path water will take as it cycles through a region. Faster currents at the outside of a bend erode the outer edge of the channel. Slow-moving water on the inside of a bend is

**Figure 4-4** Yellow iris, daylilies, ribbon grass, marsh marigold, and beebalm are among the wildflowers planted along this stream bank at Range End Golf Course in Dillsburg, Pennsylvania. The planting was an attractive way to reduce erosion and create visual interest near the bridge crossing. (Courtesy of Audubon International.)

**Figure 4-5** Aspen Golf Club in Carbondale, Colorado, maintains an extended vegetated buffer and no-spray zone along a stream corridor on the golf course. Higher thresholds for weeds and diseases should be allowed in transition zones near wetlands; weeds may be hand pulled or spot treated to avoid chemical drift or runoff into the water. (Courtesy of Audubon International.)

often a site of sediment deposition. Characteristic features of rivers, streams, and creeks are pools and riffles, meanders, a riparian zone, and a flood zone. Streams and rivers are constantly cutting away at the outside edges of their channels, which often causes the overlying soil to subside into the riverbed and be washed away (Caduto 1990). Mountain streams tend to cut V-shaped channels with steep sides. Rivers at lower elevations exhibit gradually rounded banks, giving way to broad, flat floodplains on level lowland areas adjacent to the rivers, which periodically flood their banks (see Figure 4-6).

Streambanks and riparian zones (vegetation zones along rivers or streams) serve many functions other than keeping the water in the channel. They are home to many plants and animals and protect the stream from detrimental activities on adjacent land. When these areas are covered with trees, shrubs, and herbaceous (nonwoody) plants, they provide shade for the stream, protect the channel from erosion, collect or trap sediments, and absorb nutrients, as well as improve water quality.

Stream order is used as a means of classifying and describing streams. A small headwater stream without any tributaries is a first-order stream. When two first-order streams converge, the stream becomes a second-order stream, and when two second-order streams meet it becomes a third-order stream. The order of a stream can increase only when a stream of the same order joins it. Its order cannot be increased by the entry of a lower-order stream (see Figure 4-7).

In ephemeral and intermittent streams, the stream bed is usually located above the water table. These streams recharge the groundwater and dry up when runoff is insufficient or when water tables drop during dry periods. Perennial streams, being situated at or below the water table, are fed by groundwater throughout the year.

The character of a stream is established by the velocity of the current. The velocity varies from stream to stream, depending on topography, stream size, contour, roughness of the bottom, ambient rainfall, and volume of water. Stream velocity determines the type of materials that constitute the bottom; for example, in a high-gradient stream the current may wash away all but very large rocks and leave a boulder-strewn course. Organisms that live in streams are often washed downstream and replaced by organisms washed in from upstream. Thus, diversity, or the number of different species of organisms, increases as you move downstream. Nutrients are cycled through lotic (flowing) waters in a similar manner.

The temperatures of streams are variable. In general, the temperatures of small, shallow streams parallel but lag air temperatures, warming and cooling with the seasons but never falling below freezing during the winter. Streams that are open and receive direct sunlight are warmer than those

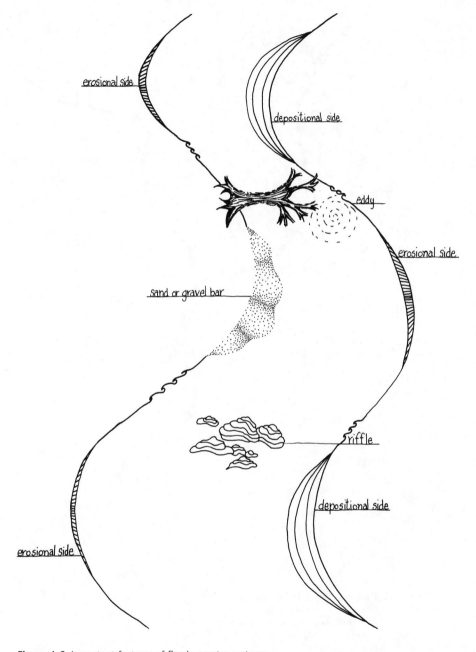

**Figure 4-6** Important features of flowing-water systems.

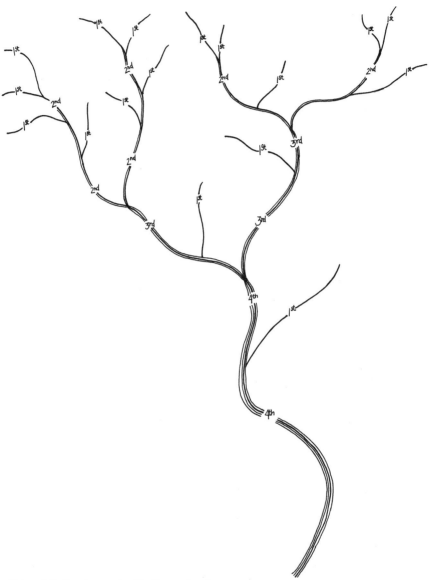

**Figure 4-7** The stream classification system is a useful method to classify creeks, streams, and rivers. The rule is that only when a stream meets another stream of equal order is the order of the resultant stream increased by one.

shaded by trees, shrubs, and steeper banks. This is ecologically important, because temperature affects the composition of the stream community. Stream restoration should mimic these natural conditions.

The continuous swirling and churning of stream water over riffles and falls produces greater contact with the atmosphere. As a result, the oxygen content of the water is high throughout. Only in deep holes or in polluted waters does dissolved oxygen show any significant decline.

Many streams originate as **springs** either in a forest or woodland or in an open field. A spring is a concentrated flow of groundwater rising from an opening in the ground. Springs can range from small seepages, where rising water forms wet areas on the ground, to large fissures in rocks or openings in the ground that are cleared out and enlarged by percolating water. If the rate of flow is great enough, pools of water nearly devoid of suspended matter form around the point of discharge. A stream can also originate where runoff water erodes a channel.

From an ecological perspective, the spring pool is important as a natural constant aquatic environment. As compared with lakes and rivers, its temperature is relatively constant, as are its chemical composition and water velocity. The organisms in a pool do not modify its environment, for almost as rapidly as the water is altered by photosynthesis and aquatic organisms, it is replaced by fresh water from the ground.

Overall production in a stream is influenced, in part, by the nature of the bottom. Pools with sandy bottoms are the least productive, inasmuch as they do not contain substrate for anchored algae or other aquatic organisms. Bedrock, although a solid substrate, is so exposed to currents that only the most tenacious organisms can maintain themselves. Gravel and rubble bottoms support the most abundant life, because they have the greatest surface area for anchored algae. These bottoms also provide other aquatic organisms with sheltered pockets and are more stable.

## Plants and Animals of Rivers, Streams, and Creeks

In-stream habitats include pools, riffles, root mats, plants, undercut banks, and a wide variety of substrate materials. These, along with the depth and flow of the water, usually determine the type of aquatic organisms found in a stream. The major producers in a stream are the periphyton, or attached algae. In many sections of a stream, the benthic invertebrate animals, such as insects, crustaceans, and mollusks constitute the greater volume of living matter or biomass (Caduto 1990). Some stretches of muddy river bottom may be dotted with freshwater mussels and clams (mollusks), especially where there are few or no rooted plants. Pill clams are often abundant in streams and rivers. The varieties of insect larvae differ in abundance on different types of substrate. Mayfly nymphs are most abundant on rubble, caddis fly larvae on bedrock, and dipteran larvae on bedrock and gravel (Pennak and van Gerpen 1947). Benthic organisms are often used to assess water quality. The presence of mayflies, stone flies, and caddis flies in a stream indicates good water quality.

Many aquatic organisms inhabiting streams move back and forth between the riffle and pool habitats. For many fish species, riffles provide food and pools provide shelter. As a general rule, a good trout stream should be half riffles and half pools. Characteristic of the riffle insects are the **nymphs** of mayflies, caddis flies, true flies, stone flies, and alder flies or dobsons. In the pools, the dominant insects are the burrowing mayfly nymphs, dragonflies, damselflies, and water striders.

As the current slows, a noticeable change takes place in streams. Silt and decaying organic matter accumulate on the bottom. Animals are able to move about to obtain their food without being washed downstream, and a plankton community develops. The composition and structure of the stream community become more similar to those of standing water.

As the volume of water increases and the current becomes even slower and the silt deposits heavier, detritus feeders increase. Tube-dwelling annelids and midges are common, as are bottom-feeding catfish, suckers, and the introduced carp. Back swimmers, water boatmen, and diving beetles are insects inhabiting the sluggish stretches and backwaters of rivers; and where water conditions are suitable, muskies, pike, and turtles are common. Rooted aquatic vegetation appears, emergent vegetation grows along the riverbanks, and duckweeds float on the surface. Indeed, the whole aspect approaches that of lakes and ponds, even to zonation along the river margin. The higher water temperatures, weaker currents, and abundant decaying organic matter promote the growth of **protozoan** and other plankton populations.

Common stream salamanders include hellbenders, mud puppies, and waterdogs, as well as mole salamanders, dusky salamanders, and the brook salamanders. Many species of freshwater mussels inhabit our streams. Mussels are filter feeders and indicate good water quality; many species are endangered.

Northern (northern United States) and Louisiana (eastern United States) waterthrushes live along streams, rivers, and forested wetlands and eat mostly insects. The success of the waterthrush is dependent on water quality (because of its insect diet). The Louisiana waterthrush winters in the West Indies, Central America, and South America. The water ouzel, or dipper, lives and nests near clear, fast streams with rapids (western U.S. streams). The dipper actually dives into the water and runs along the bottom with half-open wings. Sandpipers are common throughout the United States around streams, lakes, and wetlands surrounded by vegetation and woods. Wood ducks are common along streams.

Many native plants that grow in streamside areas provide food and cover for wildlife. Box elder and red maple attract the evening grosbeak, pine grosbeak, cardinal, and robin. Yellow birch provides winter food for small birds like the tufted titmouse, northern junco, American goldfinch, and pine siskin. Elderberry is popular with robins, thrushes (including the eastern bluebird), cedar waxwings, cardinals, and purple finches. Cardinal flower, bee balm, jewelweed, and Turk's cap lily attract hummingbirds. Check to see which native plants are important to wildlife in your area.

## Restoration and Management of Rivers, Streams, and Creeks

Rivers, streams, and creeks occur under a specific set of physical conditions (e.g., water draining a region seeking lower elevations). For this reason, these systems cannot be created (although they have been rerouted and channelized in some areas). These systems can be enhanced and restored to more closely resemble natural communities in both structural and functional characteristics. Rivers, streams, and creeks have water flows that can vary greatly during any given year. These flowing-water systems should be allowed the space they need for overbank flooding. We recommend a naturally vegetated buffer strip of at least twice the width of the stream on each side, at a minimum of 25 feet, for smaller streams. For streams wider than 15 feet, a good minimum buffer strip width is 50 feet on each side.

Heavily channelized or engineered streams cycle water through an area faster than normal and do not slow water velocity and reduce downstream flooding as natural systems do. These channelized and engineered watercourses are common in urban areas and other places that require calculated and structured drainage systems. They do, however, lack wildlife habitat and other functional qualities found in natural systems.

Natural streams meander and zigzag through the terrain, carving out their own designs. Over long periods of time, these systems are constantly changing. Sometimes particular bends are abandoned, becoming oxbow wetlands or lakes as the stream carves a new route. Oxbow wetlands are very important to adjacent stream systems; they should be protected and restored.

Before revegetation, the stream banks must be stable. Bank erosion can be a serious problem on some streams, especially in urban or managed areas. Bioengineering is the science of using plants to stabilize slopes and stream banks. The bioengineering techniques in Table 4-1 are useful for stabilizing streams.

**TABLE 4.1** Advantages and Disadvantages of Types of Slope and Stream Bank Methods (Bioengineering)

| Technique | Advantages | Disadvantages |
|---|---|---|
| Live stakes | Low cost<br>Simple | |
| Joint planting | Low cost<br>Simple | |
| Live fascine | Moderate cost<br>Moderately complex | |
| Brush mattress | Moderate cost | Moderate to complex<br>to build |
| Live cribwall | | High cost<br>Complex installation |
| Branch packing | Moderate cost<br>Moderate to complex<br>to build | |
| Conventional vegetation | Low to moderate cost<br>Simple to moderate<br>to build | |
| Conventional bank<br>armoring (riprap) | Low to moderate cost<br>Simple to moderate<br>complexity | |
| Articulated concrete | | High cost<br>Complex installation |

The following list is provided as a starting point for developing a customized list for your specific site.

## Key Species by Region

### Southeastern Region

| | |
|---|---|
| *Acer negundo* | Ash-leaf maple |
| *Acer saccharinum* | Silver maple |
| *Acorus calamus* | Calamus |
| *Betula nigra* | River birch |
| *Carya aquatica* | Water hickory |
| *Cornus* spp. | Dogwoods |
| *Equisetum* spp. | Horsetails |

| | |
|---|---|
| *Eupatorium coelestinum* | Blue mistflower |
| *Fothergilla gardenii* | Dwarf witch-alder |
| *Fothergilla major* | Mountain witch-alder |
| *Fraxinus americana* | White ash |
| *Fraxinus pennsylvanica* | Green ash |
| *Hibiscus laevis* | Halberd-leaf rose mallow |
| *Hibiscus moscheutos* | Crimson-eyed rose mallow |
| *Liquidambar styraciflua* | Sweet gum |
| *Onoclea sensibilis* | Sensitive fern |
| *Osmunda cinnamomea* | Cinnamon fern |
| *Osmunda regalis* | Royal fern |
| *Platanus occidentalis* | American sycamore |
| *Populus deltoides* | Eastern cottonwood |
| *Salix* spp. | Willows |
| *Staphylea trifolia* | Bladdernut |

### Appalachian/Ozark Region

| | |
|---|---|
| *Acer negundo* | Ash-leaf maple |
| *Acer saccharinum* | Silver maple |
| *Acorus calamus* | Calamus |
| *Betula alleghaniensis* | Yellow birch |
| *Betula nigra* | River birch |
| *Equisetum* spp. | Horsetails |
| *Eupatorium coelestinum* | Blue mistflower |
| *Fraxinus americana* | White ash |
| *Fraxinus pennsylvanica* | Green ash |
| *Hibiscus moscheutos* | Crimson-eyed rose mallow |
| *Liquidambar styraciflua* | Sweet gum |
| *Onoclea sensibilis* | Sensitive fern |
| *Osmunda cinnamomea* | Cinnamon fern |
| *Osmunda regalis* | Royal fern |
| *Myosotis laxa* | Bay forget-me-not |
| *Platanus occidentalis* | American sycamore |
| *Populus deltoides* | Eastern cottonwood |

| | |
|---|---|
| *Salix* spp. | Willows |
| *Staphylea trifolia* | Bladdernut |
| *Tsuga canadensis* | Eastern hemlock |

### New England/Great Lakes Region

| | |
|---|---|
| *Acer negundo* | Ash-leaf maple |
| *Acer saccharinum* | Silver maple |
| *Acorus calamus* | Calamus |
| *Betula alleghaniensis* | Yellow birch |
| *Equisetum* spp. | Horsetails |
| *Eupatorium coelestinum* | Blue mistflower |
| *Fraxinus americana* | White ash |
| *Fraxinus nigra* | Black ash |
| *Fraxinus pennsylvanica* | Green ash |
| *Hibiscus moscheutos* | Crimson-eyed rose mallow |
| *Onoclea sensibilis* | Sensitive fern |
| *Osmunda cinnamomea* | Cinnamon fern |
| *Osmunda regalis* | Royal fern |
| *Platanus occidentalis* | American sycamore |
| *Populus balsamifera* | Balsam poplar |
| *Populus grandidentata* | Big-tooth aspen |
| *Salix* spp. | Willows |
| *Staphylea trifolia* | Bladdernut |
| *Tsuga canadensis* | Eastern hemlock |

### Central Plains, Plateaus, and Deserts

| | |
|---|---|
| *Acer negundo* | Ash-leaf maple |
| *Acer saccharinum* | Silver maple |
| *Acorus calamus* | Calamus |
| *Betula nigra* | River birch |
| *Carya aquatica* | Water hickory |
| *Celtis laevigata* | Sugarberry |
| *Equisetum* spp. | Horsetails |
| *Eupatorium coelestinum* | Blue mistflower |
| *Fraxinus americana* | White ash |

| | |
|---|---|
| *Fraxinus pennsylvanica* | Green ash |
| *Hibiscus laevis* | Halberd-leaf rose mallow |
| *Hibiscus moscheutos* | Crimson-eyed rose mallow |
| *Lysichiton americanus* | Yellow skunk cabbage |
| *Onoclea sensibilis* | Sensitive fern |
| *Osmunda cinnamomea* | Cinnamon fern |
| *Osmunda regalis* | Royal fern |
| *Platanus occidentalis* | American sycamore |
| *Populus deltoides* | Eastern cottonwood |
| *Quercus macrocarpa* | Burr oak |
| *Salix* spp. | Willows |

### Rocky Mountains Region

| | |
|---|---|
| *Acer grandidentatum* | Canyon maple |
| *Acer negundo* | Ash-leaf maple |
| *Acorus calamus* | Calamus |
| *Darmera peltata* | Indian rhubarb |
| *Equisetum* spp. | Horsetails |
| *Hibiscus moscheutos* | Crimson-eyed rose mallow |
| *Lysichiton americanus* | Yellow skunk cabbage |
| *Onoclea sensibilis* | Sensitive fern |
| *Picea pungens* | Blue spruce |
| *Populus balsamifera* | Balsam poplar |
| *Populus deltoides* | Eastern cottonwood |
| *Rubus* spp. | Raspberries, blackberries |
| *Salix* spp. | Willows |

### Intermountain Region

| | |
|---|---|
| *Acorus calamus* | Calamus |
| *Amorpha fruticosa* | False indigo bush |
| *Darmera peltata* | Indian rhubarb |
| *Equisetum* spp. | Horsetails |
| *Hibiscus moscheutos* | Crimson-eyed rose mallow |
| *Lysichiton americanus* | Yellow skunk cabbage |

| | |
|---|---|
| *Mimulus* spp. | Monkeyflowers |
| *Onoclea sensibilis* | Sensitive fern |
| *Platanus wrightii* | Arizona sycamore |
| *Populus balsamifera* | Balsam poplar |
| *Salix* spp. | Willows |

### West Coast Region (Northern Portion)

| | |
|---|---|
| *Acer macrophyllum* | Big-leaf maple |
| *Alnus rhombifolia* | White alder |
| *Alnus rubra* | Red alder |
| *Caltha leptosepata* | White marsh marigold |
| *Darmera peltata* | Indian rhubarb |
| *Deschampsia caespitosa* | Tufted hair grass |
| *Equisetum* spp. | Horsetails |
| *Fraxinus latifolia* | Oregon ash |
| *Hibiscus moscheutos* | Crimson-eyed rose mallow |
| *Lysichiton americanus* | Yellow skunk cabbage |
| *Pinus ponderosa* | Ponderosa pine |
| *Populus balsamifera* | Balsam poplar |
| *Quercus garryana* | Oregon white oak |
| *Salix eriocephala* | Missouri willow |
| *Salix lucida* | Shining willow |
| *Salix melanopsis* | Dusky willow |
| *Salix scouleriana* | Scouler's willow |
| *Salix sessilifolia* | Sessile-leaf willow |
| *Tsuga heterophylla* | Western hemlock |
| *Umbellularia californica* | California laurel |

### West Coast Region (Southern Portion)

Riparian forests once formed extensive stands along major streams in areas of the West Coast. Because of flood control, water diversion, agricultural development, and urban expansion, these forests are now reduced and scattered or present as isolated young stands. Such forests develop on soils near streams that provide subsurface water even when the streams or rivers are dry.

| | |
|---|---|
| *Acer negundo* | Ash-leaf maple |
| *Equisetum* spp. | Horsetails |
| *Hibiscus moscheutos* | Crimson-eyed rose mallow |
| *Platanus racemosa* | California sycamore |
| *Populus fremontii* | Fremont's cottonwood |
| *Quercus* | California white oak |
| *Salix goodingii* | Goodding's willow |

In many streamside, or riparian, areas, trees and shrubs will become quickly established on their own from seeds carried in by floodwaters and wind. In some situations, however, planting and/or seeding may accelerate forest establishment, prevent erosion, and keep invasive exotics in check. In areas prone to erosion, plants grown in coir bundles or mats can be used to revegetate and stabilize an area. A variety of biotechnical methods have been used along heavily degraded and eroded streams to control erosion and establish a more natural watercourse.

Some selective cutting or thinning of undesired species or unwanted individuals may be needed during initial revegetation to ensure a desired species composition. Natural flooding of riparian areas should be encouraged as a form of maintenance where possible. Flooding brings in seeds and soil and determines which species will grow along streams. Not all plants can withstand periodic floods; even once-a-year flooding can kill some upland species.

Invasive exotics that are found in streamside areas in the United States include privet, bush honeysuckles, and purple loosestrife (eastern United States) and giant reed and tamarisk (western United States). Control of these riverine invaders is often very difficult and requires persistence over several seasons. Most exotic shrubs can be controlled by cutting the stems and applying chemical herbicide to the cut stumps. These steps may have to be repeated. The herbicide should be applied with a squirt bottle (such as an old dishwashing liquid bottle) or wiped on with a sponge or rag by a person wearing heavy rubber gloves. Adding a few drops of food coloring to the herbicide makes it easy to determine which stumps have already been treated. Be sure that the herbicide covers the entire surface of a cut stump, as conductive tissues are near the edge, just beneath the bark.

In-stream habitats for fish and other aquatic organisms can be established by placing rocks, boulders, or logs in the channel. Large woody debris (e.g., trees, branches, snags) are important to stream ecosystems and should be removed from streams only if they are causing a problem such as a log jam.

## ►CASE STUDY

## Stream Bank Stabilization

## By David Ward, CGCS*

About 1½ miles of Butterfield Creek flows through Olympia Fields Country Club in Olympia Fields, Illinois, and is an important feature on many of the holes. Over the years, however, the stream channel grew wider and deeper as a result of upstream construction, which increased the rate of runoff and flow in the creek. On the 13th hole of the North Course the channel started to cut into an elevated tee bank, causing soil to slump into the creek and threatening the playing surface. Our goal was to control the erosion and stabilize 230 feet of the bank, using vegetation rather than structures (e.g., concrete, pilings, riprap). The use of native prairie and wetland plants would beautify the course as well.

### Implementation and Maintenance

We believed that the project was beyond the scope of what we could do in-house, so we hired Eubanks & Associates, Inc., an environmental engineering firm. Our contract included 1 day's crew training on long-term care of the bank and a 3-year management plan. Eubanks provided most of the labor for the initial project. We moved some soil and worked with Eubanks in other small ways.

Coconut fiber logs were used to stabilize the toe of the slope. After all of the existing foliage was burned off with the use of propane torches, the lower areas were seeded with an emergent shoreline/wet prairie plant mix up to the 100-year flood elevation. The seeded area was then covered with a coconut fiber blanket and anchored with stakes. The upper slope was seeded with a low-profile, dry-to-mesic prairie mix and covered with straw blankets. Shaded areas were planted with an open savannah seed mix and also covered with straw blankets. Oats were used as a nurse crop.

Following seed installation, prairie plugs were planted through the blankets and buttonbush was planted near the coconut logs to aid stabilization.

The plantings would be weeded and "weed wacked" during the first two growing seasons, followed by burning in the spring of the third. More prairie plugs would be added if needed.

---

*Dave Ward, CGCS, was the superintendent of Olympia Fields Country Club from 1991 through 2004. The course achieved certification in the Audubon Cooperative Sanctuary Program in 1994 and was the host of the 2003 U.S. Open Championship.

**Figure A**  Stream bank stabilization controls erosion and enhances the beauty of Butterfield Creek as it flows through Olympia Fields Country Club in Olympia Fields, Illinois.

## Results

After the first year, the bank was stable and there had been acceptable germination of the prairie plants. In the spring of 2002 and the spring of 2003 prairie plugs were planted in the sparse areas. Because of a shift in some underlying boulders, a small portion of the bank slumped into the creek in July 2003 during extremely heavy rains. We had Eubanks come back to restabilize the area and replant it in the same way as in the original project. We planned to install plugs in this area in the spring of 2004 and to have our first controlled burn late in the winter or early in the next spring.

## Golfer Response

Prior to installation, the bank was ugly as a result of past stabilization attempts, and it was collapsing into the creek. In addition, the unsightly bank was visible to those driving into the club. Some members thought we should use steel pilings or concrete to stabilize the bank. We believed it was important to use vegetation both for aesthetic reasons and to accommodate wildlife. After the first year, members were happy with the aesthetics—mostly grass—and we knew that they would be more pleased once the prairie flowers matured and bloomed.

The project required a lot of planning and work, and I'm glad we had professional help. Once it is mature, I think it will be a beautiful improvement.

The project cost almost $60,000. We did not design and price a structural solution, but based on past experience, I'm sure that would have been about double the cost.

Wildlife will use stream corridors that have been enhanced or restored for resting, feeding, and water. Some stream corridors provide the only cover in an area and are important for the movement of animals. Artificial structures such as boxes and houses should be used to attract certain species of birds. In addition, some dead trees (snags) should be left standing to provide shelter for birds and small mammals.

## LAKES AND PONDS

### Physical Characteristics of Lakes and Ponds

Lakes and ponds are bodies of standing water that vary considerably in size, depth, and structure. The environmental conditions of lakes and ponds are very different from those of flowing waters. Light penetrates only to a certain depth, depending on how clear the water is (turbidity). Temperatures vary seasonally and with depth. Decomposition on the bottom and the relatively small portion of water in contact with the air results in a lower oxygen content than that of streams. In some lakes, oxygen decreases with depth. These gradations of oxygen, light, and temperature profoundly influence the distribution and adaptations of life in lakes and ponds.

Every year the waters of lakes and ponds undergo seasonal temperature changes. These changes are less pronounced or nonexistent in the southernmost states. In early spring, the surface water is heated by the sun. When the water reaches 4° Celsius, it sinks. This is the temperature just above freezing, at which water is densest, and which is why the bottoms of lakes are cold. This temporary stratification sets up convection currents. These

**Figure 4-8** Lakes and ponds that do not freeze to the bottom in winter can turn over seasonally. Nutrients are circulated, which causes lakes to vary throughout the year.

currents, along with prevailing winds, uniformly mix the water. This is known as the spring overturn. Early in the growing season, right after the spring overturn, nitrogen, phosphorus, and other nutrients are abundant. As the waters continue to warm, a greater difference in temperature and density develops between the surface and the deeper layers. When this happens, a mixing barrier, or wall, is established (see Figure 4-8).

In the autumn, the air temperature drops and the surface water loses heat to the air. The temperature of the surface water drops and the **thermocline** sinks until the water is once again uniformly mixed. This is the fall overturn. During the fall overturn, nutrients are brought up from the bottom and a brief algal bloom may occur before winter. Nutrient levels are high during the winter. In winter, as the surface water cools to below 4° Celsius, it becomes lighter, remains on the surface, and if the climate is cold enough, freezes. When the surface water is warmed to 4°C, it becomes denser and sinks, creating an inverse temperature stratification (as compared with that of the summer season) with a higher temperature at the bottom. Then spring arrives and the cycle is restarted.

► CASE STUDY

## Pond Enhancements Improve Aesthetics and Water Quality at North Shore Country Club, Glenview, Illinois

### By F. Dan Dinelli, CGCS*

Golf courses can improve their water features by incorporating various components of natural wetlands and ponds. North Shore Country Club in Glenview, Illinois, undertook a major pond improvement project in 2002 to stabilize shorelines and prevent siltation, as well as enhance the beauty and wildlife value of its pond (see Figure A).

Because of the scope of the project, we gathered together an experienced team of architects, aquatic ecosystem experts, and construction and landscape companies to create a detailed plan and carry it out (see Figure B). Our plan included the following:

- Minor dredging

- Shoreline regrading and stabilization

- Employing erosion control fabric to buffer wave action and water level fluctuation

- Removing subsurface drainage to ponds and rerouting surface drainage

- Recreating a safety shelf/spawning bed area for fish

- Adding structure on the bottom for fish habitat (piles of large rock, old clay tile, old Christmas trees)

- Creating a stone outcropping to fish from

- Planting buffers

- Constructing small bays with protected water gardens for beautification, habitat, and function as a nutrient sink

- Reclaiming land in certain areas for walkways and installing paving bricks and degenerated granite stone walks and paths

See Figures C, D, E, and F.

### Pond Project Cost

The cost of the pond improvement project was $140,000.

---

*F. Dan Dinelli, CGCS, is the golf course superintendent at North Shore Country Club.

**Figure A** Our pond project addressed several function-related issues, including shoreline stabilization. The old shoreline is unattractive and eroding. (Courtesy of Audubon International.)

**Figure B** Heavy equipment was brought in to reshape the pond margin. (Courtesy of Audubon International.)

**Figure C**  Pond banks were heavily fortified with yard waste compost as a soil amendment to help stabilize the soil, grow shoreline plants, and absorb nutrients and other potential pollutants. Erosion control fabric was employed to buffer wave action and water level fluctuation. Areas in play were seeded with redtop grass to serve as a shoreline buffer. (Courtesy of Audubon International.)

**Figure D**  We created small bays with rock outcroppings and "safety shelves" to serve as spawning beds for fish. The beds are filled with sand and fine pea gravel, and the bays are landscaped with aquatic plants and wildflowers. These water gardens are dammed off from the main pond so that grass carp can't get in; coarse rock veins through the clay dam allow water exchange. (Courtesy of Audubon International.)

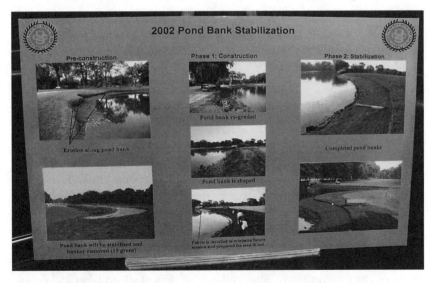

**Figure E**  Educational posters kept members informed about the pond restoration project. (Courtesy of Audubon International.)

**Figure F** The North Shore Country Club created a demonstration wetland in a chroncially wet spot in an out-of-play area along our 12th fairway. It was dug to 6 feet deep and nestled in trees to the southwest so that the afternoon shade could help minimize overheating of the water. A water line was run to the area to freshen the wetland as needed, and a variety of aquatic plants were added. This one little area is the largest wildlife draw we created on the course, with dragonflies, ducks, many songbirds, deer, and some shore birds often seen in the area. (Courtesy of Audubon International.)

During the spring and fall overturns, when water recirculates through the lake, oxygen is replenished in the deep water and nutrients are returned to the top. In winter the reduction of oxygen in unfrozen water is slight, because bacterial decomposition is reduced and water at low temperatures holds a maximum amount of oxygen. Under ice, however, oxygen depletion may be serious and result in a heavy winter fish kill.

There is a very close relationship between land and water and between aquatic and terrestrial ecosystems. Primarily through the water cycle, one influences the other. The water that falls on land runs from the surface or percolates through the soil and deeper layers of the earth to enter springs and streams and eventually reaches lakes, estuaries, and oceans. The water carries with it silt and nutrients in solution, all of which enrich aquatic ecosystems. Humans have added considerably more to the material interchange than occurs under natural conditions. Agriculture, road building, housing construction, and mining have added billions of tons of silt to lakes and estuaries. A heavy load of nutrients, especially nitrogen, phosphorus, sulfur, and organic matter, have been added to aquatic ecosystems. One of the outcomes

## VERNAL POOLS

Many shallow depressions and remnants of old ponds fill with water shortly after the first spring thaw; the water is usually gone by the time summer arrives. These transient pools of water, known as temporary ponds or vernal pools, have sometimes been considered a nuisance or a breeding place for mosquitoes. They contain water only for several months a year, typically in the spring, and are dry the rest of the year. Yet these temporary pools provide valuable habitat for many species of frogs, salamanders, fairy shrimp, and burrowing crayfish. In the eastern United States temporary pools or vernal pools occur in forested or open areas. It is important to be able to recognize these areas during the dry season and to maintain buffers around them for animal migration.

The term **vernal pool** often refers to the pools formed by the accumulation of winter rains on top of a hardpan layer of soil in California. They harbor a large number of endemic and rare species. Such pools have been a feature of the California landscape for thousands of years. Vernal pools were a common feature in the Central Valley of California before agriculture and other development eliminated most of these areas. Three types of vernal pools occur. Valley pools occur most commonly in low places in the San Joaquin Valley, pools in volcanic areas are found throughout California, and terrace pools occur on some of the ancient flood terraces on higher ground.

Because of the extreme environmental conditions, the temporary pond is a difficult place for living organisms to inhabit. For a time the area is submerged; then follows a period of progressively drier conditions; finally, the bottom is dry and covered with woody or herbaceous growth. In winter the depression may hold some ice-covered water collected from melted snow, but most of the area is frozen and snow covered. When the early spring thaw begins, the depression fills with water and the cycle begins again.

of this activity is the excessive nutrient enrichment of our aquatic ecosystems. Because of this the term **eutrophication,** once used only by ecologists, is becoming commonplace. Eutrophication refers to the addition of nutrients to bodies of water—lakes, streams, and estuaries. A body of water with an excessively large supply of nutrients is termed **eutrophic.**

A typical eutrophic lake has a high surface-to-volume ratio; that is, the surface area is large relative to its depth. It has an abundance of nutrients that produce a heavy growth of algae and other aquatic plants. Its bottom is rich in organic sediments, and its deeper waters have continuously or seasonally low concentrations of oxygen. Inflowing waters carry silt, which adds to the bottom sediments and fills in the basins of ponds and lakes. Increased production of phytoplankton and turbidity reduce light penetration and restrict biological productivity to the surface waters. Algae, inflowing organic debris, and the remains of rooted plants settle on the bottom, adding to the highly organic sediments. The activity of **decomposers** depletes the oxygen supply of the bottom sediments and deep water to the point that the deeper parts of the lake are unable to support fish and other forms of life requiring oxygen. Turbidity is also high, causing low visibility. As the basin continues to fill, the volume decreases and the resulting shallowness speeds the cycling of available nutrients and further increases plant production. The ultimate outcome of the successional process is a highly productive swamp or marsh and, eventually, a terrestrial community.

Contrasting with eutrophy is oligotrophy, meaning poor nourishment. **Oligotrophic** lakes are characterized by a low surface-to-volume ratio, water that is clear and appears blue to blue-green in the sunlight, bottom sediments that are largely inorganic, and a high oxygen concentration that extends to the bottom. The nutrient content is low, especially in nitrogen and phosphorus, and nutrients normally added by inflow are quickly taken up by algae. Because the density of algal growth is low, sunlight easily penetrates to considerable depths. Although the number of organisms may be low, the diversity of species is high. Fish life may be dominated by members of the salmon family.

A third type of lake is **dystrophic.** A dystrophic lake has waters that are brownish, resulting from humic materials. It's waters are acidic, it has a reduced rate of bacterial decomposition, and its bottom consists of partially decomposed vegetation or peat. Dystrophication leads to the formation of peat bogs rich in humic materials but low in productivity.

When nutrients in moderate amounts are added in oligotrophic lakes, they are rapidly taken up and circulated. As increasing quantities are added, the condition of the lake or pond begins to change from oligotrophic to mildly eutrophic (mesotrophic) to eutrophic. Increased nutrient input is the result of a heavy influx of wastes, raw sewage, drainage from agricultural lands and other managed lands, river basin development, recreational use of water, industrial processes, runoff from urban areas, and burning of fossil fuels. This accelerated enrichment has been called cultural eutrophication (Hasler 1969). Cultural eutrophication has produced significant biological changes in many lakes. The tremendous increase in nutrients stimulates a dense growth of planktonic algae, dominated by the blue-green forms, and rooted aquatics in shallow water. This growth upsets the normal food chains. The herbivores, mostly grazing **zooplankton,** are unable to consume the bulk of the algae as they normally would. Abnormal quantities of unconsumed algae, as well as the rooted aquatics, die and settle to the bottom.

Lakes that are clear and deep tend to be low in productivity (Reid 1961), become sedimented, less clear, enriched with nutrients, and higher in basic productivity as a part of the succession created by natural filling with rich soils and organic matter. The rate of such eutrophication depends on many factors related to the surrounding uplands, as well as the depth of the lake, the nutrient base stemming from its substrate, the rate of inflow and sedimentation, and the climatic regime (Livingston and Loucks 1979). On the bottom the **aerobic** (requiring oxygen) decomposers are unable to reduce the organic matter to inorganic form and perish from a depletion of oxygen. They are replaced by **anaerobic** (not requiring oxygen) organisms that incompletely decompose the organic matter. Partially decomposed bottom sediments build up the bottom, and sulfate-reducing bacteria release hydrogen sulfide that can poison benthic water. These chemical and environmental changes cause major shifts in the plant and animal life of the affected aquatic ecosystem.

Many lakes that receive treated and untreated wastes are experiencing biological changes affecting the value of water for both recreation and consumption. Murky green water and algal scums make lakes and ponds undesirable for recreational use. Phytoplankton and products of decomposition impart an unsatisfactory flavor to the water and interfere with its proper treatment for drinking water. The rotting mass of vegetation and die-off of fish create objectionable odors.

The shape, size, and surrounding geology and environmental conditions determine the individual character of a lake of pond. No two ponds are exactly alike. Living conditions and water quality varies according to the size, depth, and shape of a pond, its persistence throughout the year, the type of surrounding bedrock and soil, the local climate and topography, and the effects of human activities (Caduto 1990).

Lake and pond conditions also change according to time of day, weather, and season. For example, there is usually a buildup of oxygen during the day, when plants are photosynthesizing, and a decrease at night, when respiring plants and animals use up the oxygen.

## Plants and Animals of Lakes and Ponds

In lakes and ponds the abundance, distribution, and **diversity** of life are influenced by light, temperature, oxygen, and nutrients. The energy source of the lake and pond ecosystem is sunlight. The depth to which light can penetrate is limited by the turbidity of the water and the absorption of light rays. This creates vertical life zones (see Figure 4-9).

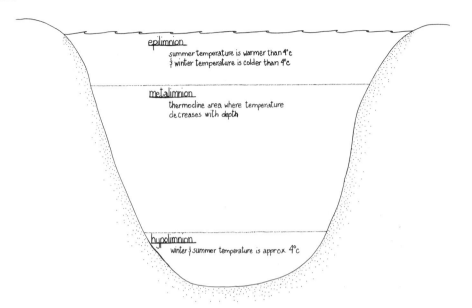

**Figure 4-9** The vertical layers of lakes and ponds.

The region of photosynthetic activity can be subdivided into two subzones. The shallow water, or **littoral** zone, is where light penetrates to the bottom. This area is occupied by rooted plants such as water lilies, rushes, and sedges. Aquatic life is richest and most abundant in this zone. Beyond this is the **limnetic,** or open-water zone, which extends to the depth of effective light penetration. It is inhabited by plant and animal plankton and the **nekton,** free-swimming organisms such as fish, which are capable of moving about voluntarily. The organisms that inhabit the bottom, or **benthic** zone, are known collectively as the **benthos.** While we name and describe these areas separately, they are all dependent on one another in terms of energy flow and nutrient cycles.

Emergent aquatic plants are found in the shallowest water and along the shores of lakes and ponds. These plants have roots and lower stems that are immersed in water and upper stems and leaves that stand above the water. Among these emergents are plants with narrow, tubular, or linear leaves, such as sedges, rushes, bulrushes, reeds, and cattails. Associated emergents include broadleaf plants such as pickerelweed, duck potato, and arrowhead. The distribution and variety of plants vary with water depth and fluctuation of the water level.

Free-floating and floating-leaved aquatic plants, such as duckweed, pondweed, and water lilies, may cover the surface of the shallow water zone. Many floating-leaved plants have poorly developed root systems but highly developed aerating systems. Supporting tissue is greatly reduced, and the spongy tissue in the stems and leaves is filled with large air spaces. The upper surfaces of the floating leaves are heavily waxed to prevent clogging of the **stomata** by water. The underwater leaves of these floating-leaved plants are like those of submerged plants, thin and small, whereas the float-ing leaves are usually large and different in form. The leaves and stems are leathery and tough and able to withstand the action of waves. Floating plants offer food and support for numerous herbivorous animals that feed on both phytoplankton and the floating plants. The undersurfaces and stems of these plants support an interesting assemblage of organisms, such as **desmids** and diatoms, protozoans and minute crustaceans, sponges, hydras, and snails. Mosquitoes and springtails live on the water surface. Floating plants shade the water and provide oxygen.

Submerged plants such as eelgrass, wild celery, riverweed, waterweed, and muskwort are found at water depths beyond that tolerated by emergent vegetation. Submerged plants are highly modified to withstand living com-pletely underwater. They lack cuticle, the waxy outer covering of the leaf that reduces **transpiration** in terrestrial plants. Lacking cuticle, submerged plants can absorb nutrients and gases directly from the water through thin and finely dissected, or ribbonlike, leaves. The buoyancy and support from being submerged in water eliminate the need for supporting tissues in the stems. Air chambers and passages are common in the leaves and stems, where oxygen produced by photosynthesis is stored for use in respiration.

The open water, or limnetic, zone is a world of minute suspended organisms, the plankton. Dominant among them is the phytoplankton, including diatoms, desmids, and the filamentous green algae. Because these tiny plants alone carry on photosynthesis in open water, they form the base on which the rest of limnetic life depends. Suspended with the phytoplank-ton are the animal organisms, or zooplankton, which graze on the minute plants. Phytoplankton constitute the first link in the food chain; zooplank-ton, the second. These animals form an important link in the energy flow in the open water zone (see Figure 4-10).

The movements, abundance, and distribution of phytoplankton and most of the zooplankton are influenced largely by physical and chemical forces such as currents, wind, light, temperature, oxygen, and nutrients. Unable to deter-mine their own positions in the water, these organisms must either float or sink. In the open water zone, fish make up the bulk of the nekton. Their dis-tribution is influenced mostly by food supply, oxygen, and temperature.

Below the depth of effective light, the diversity and abundance of life are influenced by oxygen and temperature; and the organisms depend on the rain of organic material from the layers above as their energy source. In highly productive waters, decomposer organisms so deplete the oxygen that organisms needing oxygen cannot live there.

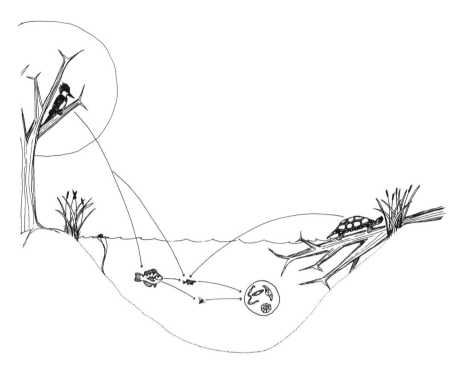

**Figure 4-10** A simplified food web showing the dependence of various organisms on other organisms in the same ecological community.

The bottom ooze of the benthic zone is an area of great biological activity with low oxygen levels. Decomposition by bacteria under these conditions produces smelly hydrogen sulfide and methane-rich byproducts.

Inhabitants of the bottom ooze may include flatworms, rhizopods, protozoans, clams, phantom midges, tardigrades or water bears, and small crustaceans such as isopods and cladocerans. Some organisms, such as the bloodworm or midge **larva** and annelid worms, live buried deep within the ooze.

In shallower water, the bottom-dwelling organisms change. The bottom materials (stones, rubble, gravel, marl, clay) are modified by the action of water, by plant growth, by drift materials, and by recent organic deposits. The increased oxygen, light, and food result in a **richness** of species and an abundance not found in deeper water. Here on the bottom of the littoral zone live, in addition to tube worms, midges, and water bears, numerous other plants and detritus feeders.

Closely associated with the bottom community are the periphyton organisms that are attached to or move on a submerged substrate but do not penetrate it. Small periphyton communities are found on the leaves of submerged aquatics and sticks, rocks, and other debris. The types of organisms found here depend on movement of water, temperature, kind of substrate, and depth.

The periphyton found on living plants are lightly attached. They are fast-growing organisms consisting primarily of algae and diatoms. These rarely live more than one season. Periphyton on stones, wood, and debris form a more crustlike growth of blue-green algae, diatoms, water mosses, and sponges. Burrowing into and living in this crust are a host of associated animals—rotifers, hydras, copepods, insect larvae—and a wide variety of protozoans.

Life is abundant around the sheltering beds of emergent plants. Damselflies and dragonflies lay their eggs on submerged stems just below the waterline. The water scorpion, nearly 2 inches long and resembling a walking stick, has a long air tube on its abdomen. Through this tube it draws air from the atmosphere while it hangs its head and feeding forelegs below the surface and waits to seize any prey that ventures near. Conspicuous diving insects are back swimmers, diving beetles, and water boatmen.

Fish, such as pickerel, bass, and sunfish, find shelter, food, and protection among the emergent and floating plants. Catfish and bullheads, often tolerant of extreme conditions of turbidity, feed close to the bottom. The fish of lakes and ponds lack the strong lateral muscles characteristic of fish living in swift water; some, such as the sunfish, have compressed bodies that permit them to move with ease through masses of aquatic plants.

Many species of turtles inhabit lakes and ponds. Common turtles include the eastern painted, spotted, and mud turtles, as well as the snapping turtle, stinkpot, and musk turtle. Frogs are common inhabitants of lakes and ponds; snakes are occasionally seen here too. A common predator on amphibian eggs is the red-spotted newt. This is the aquatic adult stage of the immature land-dwelling red eft, which is commonly seen in leaf litter and among rotting logs on the forest floor.

Food, cover, and nesting sites attract many birds to lakes and ponds. Wading birds search for food along the shorelines. Many birds, fish, and animals raise their young along the productive shoreline. Green-backed and great blue herons stalk the shallows, and belted kingfishers perch on nearby branches. Red-winged blackbirds, purple gallinules, Virginia rails, American bitterns, and marsh wrens frequent the cattails (Caduto 1990). Where the land meets the water sandpipers, killdeer, snowy egrets, and the lesser yellowlegs, among others, are commonly seen. Shallow, weedy areas provide food for dabbling ducks such as black ducks and mallards, wood ducks, and teal. Geese and, occasionally, swans may also be seen here. Lakes and ponds provide habitat for many diving birds, such as ruddy ducks, common mergansers, ring-necked ducks, American coots, and grebes. Kingbirds and cedar waxwings hunt insects along the shore. Bald eagles may be seen around a lake during the winter, feeding on fish.

## AMPHIBIAN CONSERVATION ON GOLF COURSES

Golf courses with wetlands and shallow ponds have excellent opportunities to attract and sustain populations of amphibians, including frogs and salamanders. These creatures have survived for more than 250 million years, yet currently are in decline throughout much of the world as a result of habitat loss, disease, and other environmental factors. The following checklist suggests a variety of ways golf courses can improve wetland, pond, and woodland habitats for amphibians.

### IDENTIFY AND MONITOR FROGS AND SALAMANDERS

☐ Learn the life history and vocalizations of local frogs so that you can identify the amphibian species on your golf course.

☐ Survey amphibian species in nearby natural areas and compare species variety with that of your golf course.

☐ Monitor amphibians on your property and submit data to the U.S. Geological Survey (USGS) North American Amphibian Monitoring Program (NAAMP) or Frogwatch USA.

### ENHANCE BREEDING HABITAT

☐ Improve water quality in ponds, wetlands, and streams.

☐ Create no-mow, no-spray buffer zones to provide habitat and filter pollutants.

☐ Add shallow water areas by creating *littoral shelves* along the edges of deeper ponds or lakes.

☐ Enhance shallow water areas with emergent plants.

☐ Protect seasonal wetlands and shallow ponds without fish—these habitats are extremely important for amphibian breeding.

☐ Create a natural corridor between upland woods and ponds or wetland sites so that amphibians can travel safely between the two.

## ENHANCE COVER

☐ Add shelters, such as rock piles, brush piles, logs, or a small wall, to terrestrial habitats and damp places where amphibians are most likely to be.

☐ Add logs or downed limbs in shallow areas of streams and ponds to serve as shelter and places to lay eggs.

☐ Create buffers of taller grasses or native plants along the shoreline of a stream, pond, or wetland.

☐ Leave woodland understory intact, including a shrub layer, leaf litter, and downed limbs.

☐ Refrain from draining ponds in winter.

## REDUCE HAZARDS

☐ Do not stock fish in a shallow pond; fish are major predators of amphibian adults, larvae, and eggs.

☐ Naturalize wet or seasonally wet areas with native plant material and keep lawn mowers away.

☐ Practice integrated pest management to reduce chemical use and choose the least toxic products when needed.

☐ Always apply chemicals according to label instructions and under proper weather conditions to prevent drift and runoff.

☐ Prevent the loss of wetlands — especially small wetlands and seasonal ponds or pools.

## CONNECT AQUATIC AND TERRESTRIAL HABITATS

☐ Retain or create habitat corridors connecting wetlands and woodlands.

☐ Link together as many natural and restored areas as possible.

☐ Limit traffic and maintenance activities and maintain good ground cover in corridors.

☐ Naturalize property borders to serve as natural travel corridors and sheltered areas that connect habitats on and off your property.

Muskrats are common pond dwellers. They use cattails as food and as material to build their lodges. Muskrats eat other plants besides cattails, such as water lilies, pondweeds, and arrowheads, and they are especially fond of mussels (Caduto 1990). The nutria, a rodent that was introduced into the southern marshes of the United States in 1899, is now common throughout the South. These large rodents can become so numerous that massive "eat outs" result, whereby vegetation is stripped from sections of a marsh, sometimes harming populations of fish, amphibians, and other life that rely on these plants for cover (Caduto 1990). In addition, mink and raccoons forage along the shorelines of ponds and lakes.

## *Vernal Ponds*

Animal life in a temporary pond is at low ebb during the late winter and early spring. Flatworms and copepods may be present, but the most typical inhabitant is the fairy shrimp. Fairy shrimp are confined to temporary ponds or ponds that undergo considerable drawdown of water during the summer. Fairy shrimp generally reach their population peak in the spring and disappear. At the same time, predacious beetles and another temporary pond crustacean, the clam shrimp, may appear. As the water warms, activity increases. New pond residents appear, either by hatching from dormant eggs or cysts or by migrating to the pond. Frogs and salamanders arrive in early spring, court, mate, deposit their gelatinous eggs, and depart. Fingernail clams are common beginning in late winter. Other organisms that inhabit these vernal pools include aquatic sow bugs, water fleas, ostracods, copepods, scuds, burrowing crayfish, and abundant plankton organisms. The pond dries out during the summer. Eggs of shrimp, cysts of flatworms, and dormant mollusks lie buried in the bottom mud. But for many animals the drying of the pond means death. Insect nymphs not yet mature and frogs and salamanders that fail to reach adult form before the pond dries perish. When the pond life subsides, mesophytic growths of willows, dogwoods, cattails, and sedges appear. Roughly nine months later the pond will fill once more and the cycle will start again.

## Restoration and Management of Lakes and Ponds

Lakes and ponds have been artificially built for a number of reasons, mostly for livestock and water supply but also for recreational purposes. In previously glaciated regions, natural lakes and ponds are common. In unglaciated regions, the majority of lakes and ponds have been created by humans. They are relatively easy to construct. Existing lakes and ponds can be enhanced or restored by making adjustments in the hydrology, planting native trees, shrubs, and/or herbaceous plants, and improving wildlife habitat by installing structures and leaving standing dead trees.

Lakes and ponds have the most basic hydrology; there is a basin that holds a certain amount of water, and the inflow and outflow of water are relatively balanced to create a somewhat stable water level. During dry periods, especially if a pond is used for irrigation, the water may become lower than normal, exposing the bottom. Water control structures are useful in some lakes and ponds as they allow the land manager to control the amount and duration of water in the basin.

Planting native aquatic plants in and adjacent to ponds and lakes can provide useful habitat for animals. Many seeds are blown in by wind (e.g., cattails) or carried in by waterfowl (e.g., sedges). Native wetland trees and shrubs can be used to enhance the margins of ponds and lakes. Emergent plants should be installed in the shallow water, or littoral, zone. Floating-leaved aquatic plants provide shade for aquatic organisms and prevent excessive growth of algae and invasive submerged plants such as water naiad or water nymph. The water levels are more constant in ponds and lakes, making planting easier there than in other wetland ecosystems. Some species, such as yellow pond lily and water lotus, are very aggressive and may have to be kept in submerged containers to limit growth. These two species have been known to completely take over shallow ponds. Cattails can also be aggressive under certain circumstances and should be monitored closely.

We recommend allowing vegetation to grow around the margins of ponds and lakes to a width of at least 6 feet. There should be, however, an area where one can access the water. Boardwalks make excellent access places and attractive paths. The wood should be treated with a copper-based wood preservative, because other types of wood preservative can poison fish and plants.

## Key Species by Region

### Southeastern Region

| | |
|---|---|
| *Acer rubrum* | Red maple |
| *Acorus calamus* | Calamus |
| *Alisma subcordatum* | American water plantain |
| *Azolla caroliniana* | Carolina mosquito fern |
| *Betula nigra* | River birch |
| *Cephalanthus occidentalis* | Common buttonbush |
| *Hibiscus moscheutos* | Crimson-eyed rose mallow |
| *Iris fulva* | Copper iris |

| | |
|---|---|
| *Iris prismatica* | Slender blue iris |
| *Iris virginica* | Virginia blue flag |
| *Orontium aquaticum* | Golden club |
| *Liquidambar styraciflua* | Sweet gum |
| *Magnolia grandiflora* | Southern magnolia |
| *Nuphar lutea* | Yellow pond lily |
| *Nymphaea odorata* | American white water lily |
| *Nymphoides aquatica* | Big floatingheart |
| *Nymphoides cordata* | Little floatingheart |
| *Peltandra virginica* | Green arrow-arum |
| *Pinus serotina* | Pond pine |
| *Pinus taeda* | Loblolly pine |
| *Pontederia cordata* | Pickerelweed |
| *Populus deltoides* | Eastern cottonwood |
| *Quercus lyrata* | Overcup oak |
| *Quercus nigra* | Water oak |
| *Quercus palustris* | Pin oak |
| *Quercus phellos* | Willow oak |
| *Ranunculus flabellaris* | Greater yellow water buttercup |
| *Sagittaria* spp. | Arrowhead, duck-potato |
| *Taxodium distichum* | Southern bald cypress |
| *Woodwardia virginica* | Virginia chain fern |

### Appalachian/Ozark Region

| | |
|---|---|
| *Acer rubrum* | Red maple |
| *Betula nigra* | River birch |
| *Cephalanthus occidentalis* | Common buttonbush |
| *Hibiscus moscheutos* | Crimson-eyed rose mallow |
| *Iris fulva* | Copper iris |
| *Liquidambar styraciflua* | Sweet gum |
| *Nuphar lutea* | Yellow pond lily |
| *Nymphaea odorata* | American white water lily |
| *Orontium aquaticum* | Golden club |

| | |
|---|---|
| *Peltandra virginica* | Green arrow-arum |
| *Pontederia cordata* | Pickerelweed |
| *Populus deltoides* | Eastern cottonwood |
| *Quercus bicolor* | Swamp white oak |
| *Sagittaria* spp. | Arrowhead, duck-potato |
| *Salix* spp. | Willows |
| *Thuja occidentalis* | Eastern arborvitae |
| *Woodwardia virginica* | Virginia chain fern |

### New England/Great Lakes Region

| | |
|---|---|
| *Acer rubrum* | Red maple |
| *Alisma subcordatum* | American water plantain |
| *Alnus* spp. | Alder |
| *Betula alleghaniensis* | Yellow birch |
| *Betula papyrifera* | Paper birch |
| *Caltha palustris* | Yellow marsh marigold |
| *Cephalanthus occidentalis* | Common buttonbush |
| *Hibiscus moscheutos* | Crimson-eyed rose mallow |
| *Iris versicolor* | Harlequin blue flag |
| *Nuphar lutea* | Yellow pond lily |
| *Nymphaea odorata* | American white water lily |
| *Orontium aquaticum* | Golden club |
| *Peltandra virginica* | Green arrow-arum |
| *Pontederia cordata* | Pickerelweed |
| *Populus balsamifera* | Balsam poplar |
| *Populus grandidentata* | Big-tooth aspen |
| *Quercus bicolor* | Swamp white oak |
| *Quercus macrocarpa* | Burr oak |
| *Quercus palustris* | Pin oak |
| *Sagittaria* spp. | Arrowhead, duck-potato |
| *Thuja occidentalis* | Eastern arborvitae |
| *Woodwardia virginica* | Virginia chain fern |

### Central Plains, Plateaus, and Deserts

| | |
|---|---|
| *Acer rubrum* | Red maple |
| *Betula papyrifera* | Paper birch |
| *Cephalanthus occidentalis* | Common buttonbush |
| *Fraxinus* spp. | Ash |
| *Hibiscus moscheutos* | Crimson-eyed rose mallow |
| *Pontederia cordata* | Pickerelweed |
| *Populus deltoides* | Eastern cottonwood |
| *Populus fremontii* | Fremont's cottonwood |
| *Prosopis* spp. | Mesquite |
| *Quercus bicolor* | Swamp white oak |
| *Quercus lyrata* | Overcup oak |
| *Quercus nigra* | Water oak |
| *Quercus palustris* | Pin oak |
| *Quercus phellos* | Willow oak |
| *Sagittaria* spp. | Arrowhead, duck-potato |
| *Salix* spp. | Willows |
| *Woodwardia virginica* | Virginia chain fern |

### Rocky Mountains Region

| | |
|---|---|
| *Acer grandidentatum* | Canyon maple |
| *Betula papyrifera* | Paper birch |
| *Fraxinus* | Ash |
| *Hibiscus moscheutos* | Crimson-eyed rose mallow |
| *Picea pungens* | Blue spruce |
| *Populus deltoides* | Eastern cottonwood |

### Intermountain Range

| | |
|---|---|
| *Acorus calamus* | Calamus |
| *Betula* | Birch |
| *Fraxinus* | Ash |
| *Hibiscus moscheutos* | Crimson-eyed rose mallow |
| *Lysichiton americanus* | Yellow skunk cabbage |

| *Mimulus* spp. | Monkeyflowers |
| *Platanus wrightii* | Arizona sycamore |
| *Ranunculus longirostris* | Long-beak water crowfoot |
| *Sagittaria* spp. | Arrowhead, duck-potato |

**West Coast Region**

| *Acer macrophyllum* | Big-leaf maple |
| *Alisma gramineum* | Narrow-leaf water plantain |
| *Alisma triviale* | Northern water plantain |
| *Hibiscus moscheutos* | Crimson-eyed rose mallow |
| *Limnanthes douglassii* | Douglas's meadow foam |
| *Lysichiton americanus* | Yellow skunk cabbage |
| *Nymphaea tetragona* | Pygmy water lily |
| *Populus balsamifera* | Balsam poplar |
| *Sagittaria* spp. | Arrowhead, duck-potato |

Nursery-grown wetland plants in containers and bare root plants are most commonly used for planting in and around ponds or lakes. The most important factors contributing to their success are water level and duration. There is an optimum range of water depth in which these aquatic plants will thrive. Some common pond plants and their optimal planting depths are listed in Table 4.2. This serves as a guideline for planting depths for a few common species. However, appropriate planting depths need to be determined on a site-specific basis utilizing knowledge of the regional flora. Although most lakes and ponds are disconnected from other wetland systems, exotic plants should be discouraged. The following exotic wetland species should not be used around lakes and ponds: purple loosestrife, exotic willows, yellow flag iris, reed canary grass, common reed, quackgrass, exotic water milfoils. Check with local experts for exotic pest species in your region (see Appendix B).

Some native wildlife may become pests in your wetland areas, such as white-tailed deer, muskrats, and Canada geese.

A greater variety of wildlife will be attracted to wetlands connected to forested areas or natural meadows. Islands and nesting platforms are useful in attracting and encouraging breeding birds to use managed wetlands. Improving the structural diversity of a wetland by providing perches, nesting cavities (natural and/or nest boxes), sunning logs (for turtles), rocks, snags and logs (for snakes), can be very beneficial to local wildlife. If pos-

**TABLE 4.2.** Planting Depths for Some Common Wetland Plants (Bailey, 1985)

| Species | |
|---|---|
| Skunk cabbage (*Symplocarpus foetidus*) | 0–6 inches |
| Buttonbush *(Cephalanthus occidentalis)* | 0–12 inches |
| River-scouring rush (*Equisetum fluviatile*) | 0–12 inches |
| Narrow-leaf cattail (*Typha angustifolia*) | 0–12 inches |
| Broad-leaf cattail (*Typha latifolia*) | 0–12 inches |
| Large-fruited burr reed (*Sparganium eurycarpum*) | 0–12 inches |
| Mud plantain (*Alisma plantago-aquatica*) | 0–12 inches |
| Pickerelweed (*Pontederia cordata*) | 0–12 inches |
| Water arum (*Peltandra virginica*) | 0–12 inches |
| Softstem bulrush (*Scirpus validus*) | 0–12 inches |
| Marsh marigold (*Caltha palustris*) | 0–12 inches |
| Lizard tail (*Saururus cernuus*) | 0–12 inches |
| Crowfoot (*Ranunculus septentrionalis*) | 0–12 inches |
| Duck potato (*Sagittaria latifolia*) | 0–24 inches |
| Water pepper (*Plygonum hydropiperoides*) | 6–15 inches |
| Common bladderwort (*Utricularia vulgaris*) | 6–24 inches |
| Milfoil (*Myriophyllum verticillatum*) | 6–24 inches |
| Water smartweed (*Polygonum amphibium*) | 12–24 inches |
| Yellow pond lily (*Nuphar luteum*) | 12–24 inches |
| American white water lily (*Nymphaea odorata*) | 12–24 inches |
| Coontail (*Ceratophyllum demersum*) | 12–24 inches |

sible, use structural materials on the site instead of hauling them away. Try to minimize artificial structures and encourage natural materials (see Figure 4-11).

Many managed areas now provide bat houses to encourage local bat populations, which keep insect populations in check. A single little brown bat can eat more than 1000 insects per hour. Bats consume many different kinds of insects (e.g., mosquitoes, beetles, moths). If bats are inhabiting a golf course, artificial bat houses may provide sites for daytime roosting. Bat houses are more likely to be used in areas lacking natural roost sites (hollow trees, loose pieces of bark, foliage of trees, abandoned buidlings). Although bat houses have met with mixed results, recent information suggests that design and placement are important factors in the installation of

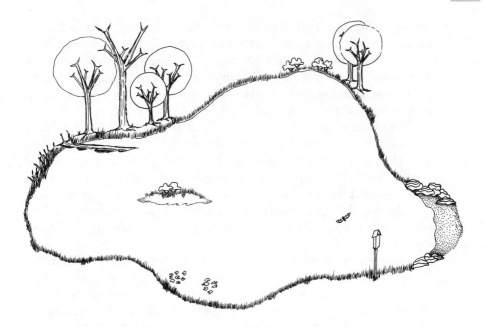

**Figure 4-11** Incorporating structural diversity for habitat improvement in managed wetlands.

bat houses. If the temperature in July is less than 80° Fahrenheit, bat houses should be placed in areas where they will receive 10 hours of direct sunlight each day. If temperatures average 80–100° Fahrenheit, the houses should receive at least 6 hours of sun daily. Bat houses should be mounted 15–30 feet high on a building or a pole (not on a tree) within 0.25 mile of fresh water.

In small ponds guppies, or mosquito fish, provide an effective control of mosquitoes. Mosquito fish are native to the southeastern United States, ranging from New Jersey south to Florida and west to Texas. Prolific live breeders, they give birth to as many as 200 fry every 3 weeks through the summer. In natural marshes and ponds, mosquito fish are food for larger fish, such as sunfish. If larger predatory fish are absent, mosquito fish can become abundant and may eat amphibian eggs and larvae. Mosquito fish should not be introduced into ponds that are being managed for salamanders.

Frogs and salamanders (amphibians) will gradually colonize a new pond or lake on their own; however, they can also be introduced. Introductions are generally most successful when the egg masses, rather than adults or young, are transplanted. If your goal is to create amphibian habitat, then predacious fish such as bluegill and bass should not be stocked.

Synthetic fertilizers used on adjacent turfgrasses may wash into ponds and streams, causing explosive growths of algae that rob the water of oxygen, thus killing fish and other organisms. It is important to keep in mind that although in these situations daytime oxygen levels may be very high, nighttime levels can be drastically lower. Algae problems can be dealt with by chemical, biological, and/or mechanical means. Chemicals that artificially shade the surface to control or kill algae are often harmful to other aquatic life and should therefore be used only as a last resort.

The key to keeping the pond water clear is controlling nutrient input and establishing a balance of plants and animals in the pond. The flowering higher plants are your most valuable aids in controlling algae. They compete for light, dissolved carbon dioxide, and nutrients in the water. Aquatic vegetation that shades the water surface, such as water lilies, can naturally reduce algae populations. Submerged aquatic plants can also help maintain the clarity of the water and provide extra oxygen for fish populations.

A buffer strip of grasses and sedges around a lake or a pond will reduce the amount of nutrients entering the wetland, thus decreasing algal growth. Grass carp can be introduced into ponds and lakes to control algae and other aquatic vegetation that is problematic. The sterile triploid grass carp can be used so that this species does not spread into adjacent waterways where it could reproduce. Always check with appropriate state agencies before introducing any fish species or other aquatic species into a waterway. Snails, tadpoles, and freshwater clams eat algae. Snails and tadpoles are scavengers, cleaning up leftover fish food and droppings. Algae and other nuisance aquatic vegetation can also be removed mechanically with the use of specially designed rakes or draglines. Often a combination of these methods is the best approach to effective algae control.

Glattstein (1994) offered the following suggestions for small pond maintenance:

- Limit pesticide and herbicide use in surrounding areas. If they are necessary, use only those that will not adversely affect water.

- Create a plunge pool, a deeper area in an entering stream where sediment is deposited before it enters the pond.

- To prevent soils from washing into the water, minimize land disturbance around the pond.

- Stabilize the pond edge by planting appropriate shrubs and herbaceous plants. Their roots stabilize the soil, and their uptake of nutrients keeps them out of the water, slowing eutrophication. Native species are recommended.

- Avoid lawn fertilizers, which result in nutrient loss to the water, and mowing, which produces grass clippings that end up in the water. Both increase the growth of algae and speed the aging of the pond.

- Combat the overgrowth of vigorous aquatic plants, which can take over a pond.

A completely mown and manicured lawn surrounding a wetland has an artificial look and allows for rapid runoff, enriching and aging a water body, as well as being visually unappealing. On the other hand, completely surrounding a pond with vegetation makes it unaccessible. Although this situation exists in nature, it limits a person's view of the water and conveys a feeling of being shut out. Piers, boardwalks, and/or observation decks make wetlands more accessible and easier to enjoy.

## MARSHES AND WET MEADOWS

### Physical Characteristics of Marshes and Wet Meadows

Marshes are relatively open areas, with emergent aquatic plants often dominating the understory and open water dominated by floating-leaved plants. Marshes and wet meadows vary in depth, ranging from saturated soil and shallow water to depths of several meters. The maximum tolerable depth for emergent vegetation is about 3 feet. Shallow freshwater marshes, those whose soil is under as much as 1 foot of water, are dominated by cattails, sedges, and rushes. Other plants of the shallows include arrowheads and pickerelweed. Wet meadows develop on soils raised high enough to prevent standing water from remaining throughout the growing season but still waterlogged within an inch or so of the surface. The substrate of marshes and wet meadows is soft muck, rich in decaying organic matter mixed with mineral soil. Wet meadow conditions can exist along a stream or in a roadside ditch, as well as in low-lying, poorly drained fields.

### Plants and Animals of Marshes and Wet Meadows

The vegetation of marshes and wet meadows is usually dominated by grasses and sedges. The emergent plants that in these wetlands are wandlike and flexible, able to bend before the stresses of wind and water. These plants have firm bases, as they send tough, fibrous rhizomes and roots into the soft ooze. This type of vegetation can tolerate submerged or waterlogged organic soil and form firm mats, called **tussocks,** in the ooze. Open water dominated by free-floating plants (such as duckweed and watermeal) and floating-leaved plants (such as yellow pond lily and white water lily) also may occur (see Figure 4-12).

**Figure 4-12** Wet meadows develop on soils raised enough to prevent standing water from remaining throughout the growing season, but still waterlogged within an inch or so of the surface. As with many wet meadows, this one at Amana Colonies Golf Course in Amana, Iowa, exists along a stream. Golf course managers should strive to maintain wet meadows for the diversity of wildlife species that are attracted to them. (Courtesy of Audubon International.)

The plant life of marshes and wet meadows supports a rich and abundant animal life. Snails, which are among the most common marsh animals, feed on ooze and dead animal matter and, in turn, are consumed by birds and fish. Birds add the most color to marshlands. Waterfowl, such as ducks and geese, are characteristic of marshes. Marshes of the prairie pot hole region are valuable for waterfowl as feeding and nesting areas during the spring and summer and as havens to find food and a place to rest during migration. The most typical mammalian member of the marsh community is the muskrat. This rodent uses cattails, sedges, and other plants to build its moundlike lodge and eats on their roots and leaves. Muskrats also make holes along the shores of ponds and lakes, which can lower water levels.

A marsh can have a large number of bird species that seem to make use of the extremely abundant resources without severe competition, and some that feed on different resources in different places in different ways, so that competition does not limit their presence (Weller 1994). The waterfowl (ducks, geese, and swans) are a good example. Swans and widgeons feed on submerged plants in water or on fine grasses along seasonally flooded shore-lines. Geese feed on drier sites on sedges and grasses; some feed on the tubers (snow geese), whereas others feed on stems and leaves (Canada geese). Many dabbling ducks are **omnivores,** consuming seeds and foliage, usually in fall and winter (Bossenmaier and Marshall 1958), and feeding more on invertebrates in the prebreeding period (especially the females, which need special nutrients for egg production) (Krapu 1974; Krapu and Reineke 1992).

Inland diving ducks feed on bottom organisms such as snails, clams, and midge larvae in water depths that require diving (Weller 1994). Sea ducks use different habitats and are almost purely animal feeders, taking some very large, hard objects such as mollusks (eiders) or fast-swimming but large prey such as fish (mergansers). Thus, the various groups are well segregated by their habitat selection as well as by their food, and many seem to feed side by side with little of the aggressiveness seen among potential competitors (Weller 1994).

Some birds are dense colony nesters; some nest in a loose colony; others remain solitary, but may cluster because of the patchiness of suitable habitat (Weller 1994). Egrets, ibises, eared grebes, and yellow-headed blackbirds are typical colony nesters. Nests of western grebes and some ducks may be found in clusters in suitable habitats.

Characteristic marsh animals include leopard frogs, American toads, mosquitoes, midges, yellow-headed blackbirds, red-winged blackbirds, American bitterns, rails, terns, coots, and grebes. Open mudflats may be frequented by killdeer or other shorebirds and waders. Frogs of several species use wet meadows adjacent to marshes. Red-winged blackbirds are fond of wet places with patches of dense shrubs, cattails, or other emergent plants. Bitterns and herons may catch meadow jumping mice as well as insects in such areas. Some bird species such as swamp sparrows and yellowthroats are in their prime habitat here; this is where they nest, although they may stray some distance into the uplands or into the marsh to forage (Weller 1994). Blackbirds may fly hundreds of meters from the marsh to seek insect foods for their nestlings. The mallard and blue-winged teal nest in the uplands or at the marsh edge but feed in the marsh during the breeding period (Weller 1994). They are plagued by such terrestrial predators as striped skunks, raccoons, and ground squirrels, but their persistent nesting behavior helps to compensate for high losses.

Mink and raccoons concentrate along the marsh edge and capture crayfish, mice, and frogs. Deer have well-defined trails leading to the marsh, where they drink; they find shelter in the willow thickets or in the reed or cattail beds, but prefer the drier sites for bedding down.

Swallows that feed over both land and marsh roost in the vegetation at night. The marsh is attractive to birds not only because of its food richness but also because it provides nesting, resting, and feeding sites protected from ground predators. Various bird groups have adapted anatomically to such aquatic situations to the extent that they are less effective on land (loons, grebes, inland diving ducks); others use upland as well as aquatic habitats and have added flexibility, but certain disadvantages too (dabbling ducks, some waders, rails); and numerous species use the marsh edge as the focal point of their feeding and breeding (swamp sparrows, sedge wrens, red-winged blackbirds) (Weller 1994).

The use of marsh and wet meadow habitats and foods varies seasonally, as influenced by needs for reproduction or food availability. Well-adapted aquatic species are limited to marshes or lakes year-round even if they migrate long distances, and they use few if any terrestrial foods (some inland diving ducks, grebes) (Weller 1994). Marsh-edge species also tend to seek out similar habitats all year, but they have greater flexibility, seeking food in uplands as well as in marsh areas (geese, blackbirds). In the spring, robins, song sparrows, woodcock, and snipe are common inhabitants of wet meadows and marshes in the eastern United States. In fall, winter, and spring, dabbling ducks, mallards, shovelers, and pintails commonly rest and nest in freshwater marshes.

In one North Dakota marsh, 37 species nest during the summer (Krapu and Duebbert 1974). A still larger number of migrants use these marshes during their annual stopovers. In a study of bird species using a southern shrub wetland (Louisiana), breeding birds numbered only 7 species, but 17 wintering species were found (Ortego et al. 1976). Like other birds, most marsh birds return in the spring to nest in last year's vegetation, but if this vegetation is missing for some reason, most birds probably move elsewhere.

Mammals inhabiting marshes include beavers, otters, muskrats, nutrias, mink, short-tailed weasels, least weasels, raccoons, meadow jumping mice, and short-tailed shrews. Beavers compensate for fluctuating water levels by damming streams and creating their own stable ponds. Otters adapt through maintenance of strong terrestrial behavior and their flexibility in using streams, lakes, or ponds, but marshes must have large fish or amphibians to attract them (Weller 1994). However, otters are very abundant in coastal fresh and salt marshes of the Gulf coast, where they feed on crayfish, crabs, and mammals as well as fish (Chabreck et al. 1982). The widespread muskrat and the nutria (introduced from South America) constitute the major herbivorous wetland specialists. They are both fairly adaptable and are found in a variety of aquatic and wetland habitats. Where plant material is abundant and easily obtained, herbivores such as muskrats and meadow jumping mice are common.

Marsh environments limit the kinds of fish that can live and, especially, reproduce there. Because of the shallower depths, reduced wind action, higher water temperature, reduced oxygen, and sometimes more turbid water, the larger fish are those that we associate with highly eutrophic systems: bullheads and introduced carp. Northern pike sometimes enter lakeshore marshes to breed and may prey on ducklings. For northern pike, this relationship of marsh to lake is so vital that fish populations decline when water levels prevent spawning and rearing in such areas (Forney 1968; Kleinert 1970). Brook sticklebacks and fathead minnows are presumably the major underwater omnivores and animal consumers in the marsh system (Peterka 1989). Some marshes are excellent fishing areas for bullheads, panfish, and, occasionally, bass. The introduction of carp in North America has produced serious and recurring problems in maintenance of marsh quality, as they muddy the water, dislodge vegetation, and feed on the eggs of other species (King and Hunt 1967; Robel 1961).

Marsh amphibians include salamanders, frogs, and toads. These animals can be major food items for birds, such as white pelicans, that use marshes and shallow lakes to gather food for their young (Lingle and Sloan 1980). Frogs, such as the common leopard frog, use both shallow aquatic areas and wet meadows. The bullfrog of warmer southern and eastern waters is found in deeper water and is a significant predator on larger prey items, taking other frogs and even ducklings. In the West, where bullfrogs have been introduced they are competing with native frogs, none of which are omnivorous. Toads are more terrestrial, turning up in very dry sites long distances from water, but in the spring, it is the marsh where they chorus, mate, and breed. Amphibians are prime food sources for all the larger predators such as mink, raccoons, herons, bitterns, and fish.

Reptiles characteristic of marshes are turtles, snakes, and alligators. Although painted and mud turtles are common, less often seen is the massive, predatory snapping turtle that slips slowly and silently bederneath its prey, including fish, frogs, and birds. Snakes are also relatively common in marshes, but less so than in swamps or river wetlands. In the northern marshes the only regular resident is the garter snake, which seems mainly to patrol the marsh edge, where it takes eggs and young from red-winged blackbird nests, but it does not fear water and is occasionally found basking on a muskrat lodge. In more southerly areas, numerous species of water snakes dominate, and there are also poisonous water moccasins. Water snakes feed on fish, frogs, and other vertebrates opportunistically. Southern marshes and other wetland types also are known for a large and feared freshwater reptile, the alligator. Each has its "hole," which seems to be dug out and retains water even in the drier periods.

Invertebrate marsh fauna include freshwater jellyfish and freshwater sponges, the true flies (midges, mosquitoes, and crane flies), mayflies, dragonflies, and damselflies, the true bugs (water striders, back swimmers, giant water bugs, and water boatmen), caddis flies, aquatic beetles (predaceous diving beetles and whirligig beetles), crustaceans, plankton water fleas such as daphnia, and the copepods such as cyclops, scuds, and side swimmers. Fairy shrimp can dominate wetlands of a more temporary nature. Also common are seed shrimp or ostracods, aquatic sow bugs, and several species of crayfish. Snails and other mollusks such as fingernail clams may be present as well.

In addition to being used as food and converting plant materials to animal protein, invertebrates break down plant material to a size and structure that allows bacteria and aquatic fungi to further process these products.

Butterflies are frequent marsh and wet meadow dwellers. They often congregate around areas that are moist but not saturated. Many wetland plants are host species that are used by butterflies and moths during their development, or life cycle. Many native wet meadow wildflowers are popular butterfly garden selections, such as milkweeds, Turk's cap lily, joe-pye weed, ironweed, and cardinal flower.

## Restoration and Management of Marshes and Wet Meadows

Marshes and wet meadows can be created in areas where they have not previously existed, or preexisting areas can be enhanced or restored. The best sites are those that historically had wetlands, which have been drained or otherwise diminished. These areas have hydric or somewhat poorly drained soils and are prime candidates for restoration. Earth-moving equipment is commonly used for contouring and should be used to create water depths associated with the desired plant communities. Islands, bays, and other structural features can be created during construction. Where such work is done in areas with rich seed banks, soil should be moved off-site and returned as topsoil to take advantage of both its organic content and its seed bank. Dams and levees are often built of borrowed soil taken from the waterside to create some deep water sites or to facilitate installation of water control structures. Modifying shallow wetlands to create open pools and deeper water can be done by dewatering and use of a bulldozer, by dragline movement of basin substrate, or by blasting with explosives (Strohmeyer and Fredrickson 1967; Mathiak 1965). Enhancement or restoration may involve adjusting the hydrology, planting native trees, shrubs, or herbaceous plants, removing exotic species, and/or improving wildlife habitat. Success should be determined based on the functions provided by the wetland and how they compare with those of natural systems. Often, the hydrology is measured using groundwater wells and staff gauges to determine the hydroperiods of the wetland. Vegetation is usually monitored to determine the survival of planted species, as well as the overall species composition of the wetland, to determine success (see Figure 4-13).

Two forces dramatically influence change in marsh vegetation and associated animal communities. The most crucial is changing water depth, which is the deciding influence as to where plants grow and what plant life forms (i.e., emergent or floating-leaved) dominate a particular marsh (Weller 1994). The second major influence on marsh vegetation is the activity of herbivores such as muskrats, introduced nutria, and, occasionally, beavers that "eat out" large areas of vegetation used for lodges and food (Weller 1994).

A marsh is relatively unattractive to birds unless emergent vegetation is standing in water. Stabilizing water at high levels is detrimental to marshes because it tends to create lake-like situations. At low water levels, marshes become too dense and more like terrestrial systems. Periodic drying and reflooding is generally beneficial, but erratic water-level changes at any time

**Figure 4-13** Willows are propagated in an on-site nursery for use in pond edges and wetland mitigation projects taking place at Saddle Rock Golf Course, City of Aurora Parks and Open Space Department, Aurora, Colorado. The willows and other wetland plants control erosion, cover unsightly cement drainage pipes, and filter and slow storm water from nearby residential roads as it enters creeks and wetlands on the golf course. (Courtesy of Audubon International.)

of the year should be avoided. Fluctuations that are too rapid may cause mortality of muskrats and ducks if such a change occurs during the breeding period. If muskrats become problematic, however, lowering the water level can be used to control their numbers.

Inland marshes fill and empty, fluctuating as they are affected by rainfall and evaporation. Water supplies are influenced by rainfall, but there is usually drainage into the marsh from an adjacent watershed, either from a stream or from groundwater below the soil surface. Water level management is generally feasible only when a water control structure has been constructed either to restore a marsh or to aid in water level stability. Water control structures can improve chances of successful marsh management in areas with modified stream flow, lowered water tables, or increased sedimentation due to wind or water erosion, or increased disturbance or consumption of vegetation because of high populations of wildlife or domestic livestock.

Increased eutrophication of open water areas can be a product of pollution with excessive nutrients. Management to correct the problem may involve upstream sediment and erosion control structures or changes in watershed cover plants, along with reduced chemical use.

Managers should strive to provide quality habitats with patchy, as opposed to continuous, cover. The opening of dense cover adds a diversity of plant life and invertebrate species and encourages bird use. In larger marshes, an approximately 50:50 cover-to-water ratio is ideal (Weller and Fredrickson 1974), but diversity can also result from a complex of marshes in different successional stages.

## Key Species by Region

### Southeast Region

| | |
|---|---|
| *Alisma subcordatum* | American water plantain |
| *Asclepias incarnata* | Swamp milkweed |
| *Bidens* spp. | Tickseed sunflower |
| *Cephalanthus occidentalis* | Common buttonbush |
| *Crinum americanum* | Seven sisters |
| *Dodecatheon meadia* | Eastern shooting star |
| *Eleocharis obtusa* | Blunt spike-rush |
| *Eupatorium fistulosum* | Trumpetweed |
| *Helianthus angustifolius* | Swamp sunflower |
| *Helianthus grosserratus* | Sawtooth sunflower |

| | |
|---|---|
| *Hibiscus moscheutos* | Crimson-eyed rose mallow |
| *Hymenocallis caroliniana* | Carolina spider lily |
| *Lobelia cardinalis* | Cardinal flower |
| *Lobelia siphilitica* | Great blue lobelia |
| *Rhexia* spp. | Meadow beauties |

### Appalachian/Ozark Region

| | |
|---|---|
| *Agalinus tenuifolia* | Slender-leaf false foxglove |
| *Alisma subcordatum* | American water plantain |
| *Asclepias incarnata* | Swamp milkweed |
| *Bidens aristosa* | Bearded beggar-ticks |
| *Bidens cernua* | Nodding burr-marigold |
| *Boltonia asteroides* | White doll's-daisy |
| *Carex* spp. | Sedge |
| *Cephalanthus occidentalis* | Common buttonbush |
| *Eleocharis* spp. | Spike-rush |
| *Eupatorium coelestinum* | Blue mistflower |
| *Eupatorium maculatum* | Spotted joe-pye weed |
| *Eupatorium perfoliatum* | Common boneset |
| *Helianthus angustifolius* | Swamp sunflower |
| *Hibiscus laevis* | Halbert-leaf rose mallow |
| *Hibiscus moscheutos* | Crimson-eyed rose mallow |
| *Iris brevicaulis* | Zigzag iris |
| *Iris virginica* | Virginia blue flag |
| *Juncus effusus* | Lamp rush |
| *Leersia virginica* | White grass |
| *Lobelia cardinalis* | Cardinal flower |
| *Lobelia siphilitica* | Great blue lobelia |
| *Nelumbo lutea* | American lotus |
| *Nuphar lutea* | Yellow pond lily |
| *Panicum virgatum* | Wand panic grass |
| *Polygonum amphibium* | Water smartweed |
| *Rudbeckia laciniata* | Green-head coneflower |
| *Rumex verticillatus* | Swamp dock |

| | |
|---|---|
| *Sagittaria latifolia* | Duck-potato |
| *Scirpus* spp. | Bulrush |
| *Sium suave* | Hemlock water parsnip |
| *Solidago rugosa* | Wrinkle-leaf goldenrod |
| *Sparganium eurycarpum* | Broad-fruit burr reed |
| *Spartina pectinata* | Freshwater cord grass |
| *Spiraea alba* | White meadowsweet |
| *Tripsacum dactyloides* | Eastern mock grama |
| *Typha latifolia* | Broad-leaf cattail |
| *Verbena hastata* | Simpler's-joy |
| *Vernonia arkansana* | Arkansas ironweed |
| *Vernonia gigantea* | Giant ironweed |

### New England/Great Lakes Region

| | |
|---|---|
| *Asclepias incarnata* | Swamp milkweed |
| *Aster novae-angliae* | New England aster |
| *Aster nova-belgii* | New Belgium aster |
| *Aster puniceus* | Purple-stem aster |
| *Bidens* spp. | Tickseed sunflower |
| *Chelone glabra* | White turtlehead |
| *Gentiana andrewsii* | Closed bottle gentian |
| *Gentianopis crinita* | Greater fringed gentian |
| *Geum rivale* | Purple avens |
| *Hibiscus moscheutos* | Crimson-eyed rose mallow |
| *Lobelia cardinalis* | Cardinal flower |
| *Lobelia siphilitica* | Great blue lobelia |
| *Monarda didyma* | Scarlet beebalm |
| *Rudbeckia laciniata* | Green-head coneflower |
| *Sanguisorba canadensis* | Canada burnet |
| *Spartina pectinata* | Freshwater cord grass |
| *Veronicastrum virginicum* | Culver's-root |
| *Vernonia gigantea* | Giant ironweed |
| *Vernonia novaboracensis* | New York ironweed |

## Central Plains, Plateaus, and Deserts

| | |
|---|---|
| *Asclepias incarnata* | Swamp milkweed |
| *Aster novae-angliae* | New England aster |
| *Aster puniceus* | Purple-stem aster |
| *Bidens* spp. | Tickseed sunflower |
| *Chelone obliqua* | Red turtlehead |
| *Dodecatheon pulchellum* | Dark-throat shooting star |
| *Gentiana andrewsii* | Closed bottle gentian |
| *Gentianopis crinita* | Greater fringed gentian |
| *Helianthus tuberosa* | Jerusalem artichoke |
| *Heliopsis helianthoides* | Smooth oxeye |
| *Hibiscus moscheutos* | Crimson-eyed rose mallow |
| *Iris versicolor* | Harlequin blueflag |
| *Lilium philidelphicum* | Wood lily |
| *Lilium michiganense* | Michigan lily |
| *Lobelia cardinalis* | Cardinal flower |
| *Lobelia siphilitica* | Great blue lobelia |
| *Lysichiton americanum* | Yellow skunk cabbage |
| *Parnassia glauca* | Grass-of-Parnassus |
| *Rhexia* spp. | Meadow beauty |
| *Sparganium eurycarpum* | Broad-fruit burr reed |
| *Spartina pectinata* | Freshwater cord grass |

## Rocky Mountains Region

| | |
|---|---|
| *Asclepias incarnata* | Swamp milkweed |
| *Calamagrostis canadensis* | Bluejoint |
| *Vahlodea atropurpurea* | Arctic hair grass |
| *Eupatorium maculatum* | Spotted joe-pye weed |
| *Eupatorium perfoliatum* | Common boneset |
| *Geum rivale* | Purple avens |
| *Heliopsis helianthoides* | Smooth oxeye |
| *Hibiscus moscheutos* | Crimson-eyed rose mallow |
| *Lobelia siphilitica* | Great blue lobelia |

| | |
|---|---|
| *Lysichiton americanus* | Yellow skunk cabbage |
| *Rudbeckia laciniata* | Green-head coneflower |
| *Verbena hastata* | Simpler's-joy |

### Intermountain Region

| | |
|---|---|
| *Asclepias incarnata* | Swamp milkweed |
| *Calamagrostis canadensis* | Bluejoint |
| *Carex* spp. | Sedges |
| *Darmera peltata* | Indian rhubarb |
| *Deschampsia cespitosa* | Tufted hair grass |
| *Eupatorium maculatum* | Spotted joe-pye weed |
| *Gentiana andrewsii* | Closed bottle gentian |
| *Gentianopis crinita* | Greater fringed gentian |
| *Geum rivale* | Purple avens |
| *Helianthus tuberosa* | Jerusalem artichoke |
| *Heliopsis helianthoides* | Smooth oxeye |
| *Hibiscus moscheutos* | Crimson-eyed rose mallow |
| *Lobelia siphilitica* | Great blue lobelia |
| *Lysichiton americanus* | Yellow skunk cabbage |
| *Rudbeckia laciniata* | Green-head coneflower |
| *Scirpus* spp. | Bulrushes |
| *Sparganium americanum* | Broad-fruit burr reed |
| *Spartina pectinata* | Freshwater cord grass |
| *Vernonia corymbosum* | Ironweed |
| *Verbena hastata* | Simpler's-joy |

### West Coast Region

| | |
|---|---|
| *Camassia leichtlinii* | Large camas |
| *Camassia quamash* | Small camas |
| *Darmera peltata* | Indian rhubarb |
| *Fritillaria camschatcensis* | Kamchatka missionbells |
| *Gentiana calycosa* | Ranier pleated gentian |
| *Geum rivale* | Purple avens |

| | |
|---|---|
| *Hibiscus moscheutos* | Crimson-eyed rose mallow |
| *Iris setosa* | Beach-head iris |
| *Iris tenax* | Tough-leaf iris |
| *Lilium columbianum* | Columbian lily |
| *Lysichiton americanus* | Yellow skunk cabbage |
| *Malus fusca* | Oregon crabapple |
| *Mimulus spp.* | Monkeyflowers |
| *Myrica gale* | Sweetgale |
| *Sisyrinchium bellum* | California blue-eyed grass |
| *Sisyrinchium californicum* | Golden blue-eyed grass |
| *Sisyrinchium idahoense* | Idaho blue-eyed grass |
| *Sparganium americanum* | American burr reed |
| *Spiraea douglasii* | Douglas's meadowsweet |

Wet meadows can be maintained by annual mowing. Mowing should be done in late fall or during early spring. The latter is preferable because it provides ample winter cover for wildlife and maintains a large insect population for fall-migrating birds, particularly kestrels and other hawks (see Figure 4-14).

Because so many plants and invertebrates of marshes survive as a result of tolerant seeds or eggs, and because these organisms are distributed by wind, birds, and probably other animals, diversity seems to come quickly to marshes (Weller 1994). A restoration site that is situated in a low area may have a seed bank representative of a marsh, indicating a former wetland. Once a water supply is returned to an area, it may be worthwhile to wait and see what germinates.

Several introduced weeds, such as water hyacinth, Eurasian water milfoil, hydrilla, and purple loosestrife, make it impossible to keep wetlands open without some type of control measure. The grass carp, or white amur, is widely used throughout the South for weed control. Some state agencies allow such introductions only in closed basins, but the use of such biological control agents has been successful in reducing populations of the exotic water weed hydrilla. Although natural reproduction of grass carp in lakes is unlikely (as it naturally spawns in streams), sterile hybrids have been developed for weed control efforts. Grass carp may compete with waterfowl and other fish in marshes, as it feeds on submerged water plants and invertebrates (Gasaway and Drda 1977). If the goal is to create natural habitat, grass carp should be avoided.

**Figure 4-14** This shrub-scrub thicket at Sand Ridge Golf Club in Chardon, Ohio, was once dominated by invasive buckthorn (*Rhamnus frangula*), which the club removed. The area now supports wet meadow vegetation that has established naturally, including boneset (*Eupatorium perfoliatum*) and joe-pye weed (*Eupatorium purpureum*). (Courtesy of Audubon International.)

Created, enhanced, or restored marshes and wet meadows will likely attract many types of wildlife, even if they are relatively small areas. The addition of structures such as boxes and houses can make these wetlands more attractive to particular species of bats, birds, and small mammals.

## FORESTED WETLANDS

### Physical Characteristics of Forested Wetlands

Forested wetlands are dominated by trees and have a relatively sparse, or sometimes nonexistent, shrub and herbaceous layer. The presence of water during the growing season often causes the trees to have widened bases (buttresses) or aboveground (adventitious) roots. Forested wetlands are often called swamps or bottomland hardwood forests. They are dominated by trees that are tolerant to flooding or inundation. Bottomland hardwood forests occur extensively on the floodplains of the larger southern river systems, especially in the Mississippi River drainage system and on the uplands of the coastal plain. They are shaded situations with standing water most of the growing season. They occur where there is a high water table—for example, bordering the banks of wide, slow-running streams or surrounding shallow lakes. The water levels fluctuate seasonally. Water levels are typically lowest in summer, especially in locations that are more dependent on rainfall. The swamp may appear dry, although there can be subterranean water in the root zone. Occasionally, some sites may have open water into summer and even into the winter dormant period (see Figure 4-15).

**Figure 4-15** Minimal management is needed in wooded wetlands, such as this one at Alpine Country Club in Demarest, New Jersey. Nesting boxes can be added to attract wood ducks, and golfers should be encouraged to stay out, even during seasonally dry periods. (Courtesy of Audubon International.)

The vegetation in shallow-water swamps ranges from shrubby willows, alders, and common buttonbush (these are discussed in the following section on shrub wetlands) to oaks and maples. Where water is nearly permanent throughout the year, willow thrives, together with common buttonbush, a shrub capable of growing in deep water. Alder is tolerant of permanent shallow-water areas and is common throughout North America. Shallow-water swamp forests include elm, silver maple, red maple, white pine, and northern white cedar. Common southern swamp associates are overcup oak and water hickory. In the deep South the understory of these swamps is usually a tangle of shrubs, vines, ferns, and palmetto.

Swamp vegetation must also be able to anchor itself in soft muck saturated with water. The root systems of trees are often massive, but they develop superficially and do not penetrate deeply. They spread widely and develop wide bases, or buttresses. These are exaggerated in deep-water swamp trees such as bald cypress and tupelo.

An outstanding feature of shallow-water swamps is the rapid and uneven elevation of the land. The floor of the swamp is a series of depressions and rises created by fallen logs and upturned roots. On the rises grow ferns, vines, shrubs, and more **mesic** trees. Logs and tree bases are covered with mosses, liverworts, lichens, and fungi. In spring and other periods of high water the depressions are small pools; in dry weather they are little hollows filled with mosses, liverworts, and marsh annuals. Thus, across the swamp there is rapid and marked differentiation of ecotones with varying moisture conditions and temperatures.

## Plants and Animals of Forested Wetlands

Swamps are important places with unique beauty. They provide a diversity of habitats for animals. Inhabitants range from aquatic and semiaquatic insects, turtles, snakes, alligators and crocodiles, ducks, and herons, to animals more closely associated with purely terrestrial situations, such as the deer, bear, and squirrel. Like the marsh, the swamp contains a richness of life often little appreciated by humans.

Barred owls frequent swamps year-round. Although they have been recorded eating screech owls and even long-eared owls, barred owls subsist mainly on mice, occasionally eating other mammals, birds, amphibians, insects, reptiles, and even fish (Caduto 1990). Barred owls usually nest in hollow trees or old red-shouldered hawk nests, often returning to the same nest for many years to lay, usually, two pure white eggs. Wooded swamps are the breeding grounds of thrushes, vireos, numerous flycatchers, and warblers. Pileated woodpeckers are also common inhabitants of forested wetlands. Squirrels, mice, and tree-nesting birds often inhabit old pileated woodpecker holes.

Floodplain swamps usually consist of bald cypress and water tupelo and upland swamps are often dominated by black gum and pond cypress, but all four species may grow in mixed stands. In shallower water, sweet bay, slash pine, and pond pine are common associates. The deep-water swamps lack herbaceous plants but support abundant **epiphytes,** plants that grow perched on other plants. Outstanding among these are **bromeliads** such as Spanish moss.

## Restoration and Management of Forested Wetlands

Forested wetlands can be created in areas where they did not previously exist, and previously existing areas may be enhanced or restored. The hydrology is the most important factor to consider in the restoration and management of forested wetlands. If the hydrologic condition is too wet or too dry, it can prove detrimental to the desired tree species. A dry period is necessary at times to allow tree roots to breath and new tree seedlings to germinate and become established.

Forested wetlands are typically seasonally or temporarily flooded, usually in the spring. Most do not have standing water year-round; however, some contain shallow water throughout the growing season. In some situations, a water control device may be useful for management of forested wetlands.

Forested wetlands are characterized by an obvious overstory layer, or canopy, formed by the dominant trees. Several species of shrubs and herbaceous plants are also characteristic of forested wetlands.

## Key Species by Region

### Southeastern Region

| | |
|---|---|
| *Acer rubrum* | Red maple |
| *Acorus calamus* | Calamus |
| *Carex stricta* | Uptight sedge |
| *Cephalanthus occidentalis* | Common buttonbush |
| *Chamaecyparis thyoides* | Atlantic white cedar |
| *Fraxinus pennsylvanica* | Green ash |
| *Ilex opaca* | American holly |
| *Lindera benzoin* | Spicebush |

| | |
|---|---|
| *Liquidambar styraciflua* | Sweet gum |
| *Lyonia lucida* | Shinyleaf |
| *Nyssa aquatica* | Water tupelo |
| *Nyssa sylvatica* | Black tupelo |
| *Onoclea sensibilis* | Sensitive fern |
| *Orontium aquaticum* | Golden club |
| *Osmunda cinamomea* | Cinnamon fern |
| *Osmunda regalis* | Royal fern |
| *Peltandra virginica* | Green arrow-arum |
| *Pinus serotina* | Pond pine |
| *Quercus lyrata* | Overcup oak |
| *Quercus michauxii* | Swamp chesnut oak |
| *Quercus nigra* | Water oak |
| *Quercus palustris* | Pin oak |
| *Quercus phellos* | Willow oak |
| *Sparganium americanum* | American burr reed |
| *Taxodium ascendens* | Pond cypress |
| *Taxodium distichum* | Southern bald cypress |

### *Appalachian/Ozark Region*

| | |
|---|---|
| *Acer rubrum* | Red maple |
| *Acorus calamus* | Calamus |
| *Chamaecyparis thyoides* | Atlantic white cedar |
| *Clethra alnifolia* | Coastal sweet pepperbush |
| *Cornus racemosa* | Gray dogwood |
| *Cornus sericea* | Red osier |
| *Ilex glabra* | Inkberry |
| *Ilex verticillata* | Common winterberry |
| *Lindera benzoin* | Spicebush |
| *Lysimachia terrestris* | Swampcandles |
| *Matteuccia struthiopteris* | Ostrich fern |
| *Nyssa sylvatica* | Black tupelo |
| *Onoclea sensibilis* | Sensitive fern |

| | |
|---|---|
| *Orontium aquaticum* | Golden club |
| *Osmunda cinamomea* | Cinnamon fern |
| *Osmunda regalis* | Royal fern |
| *Peltandra virginica* | Green arrow-arum |
| *Symplocarpus foetidus* | Skunk cabbage |
| *Viburnum edule* | Squashberry |

### New England/Great Lakes Region

| | |
|---|---|
| *Acer rubrum* | Red maple |
| *Acorus calamus* | Calamus |
| *Alnus incana* | Speckled alder |
| *Betula papyrifera* | White birch |
| *Chamaecyparis thyoides* | Atlantic white cedar |
| *Clethra alnifolia* | Coastal sweet pepperbush |
| *Cornus racemosa* | Gray dogwood |
| *Cornus sericea* | Redosier |
| *Ilex glabra* | Inkberry |
| *Ilex laevigata* | Smooth winterberry |
| *Ilex verticillata* | Common winterberry |
| *Larix laricina* | American larch |
| *Lindera benzoin* | Spicebush |
| *Lysimachia terrestris* | Swampcandles |
| *Matteuccia struthiopteris* | Ostrich fern |
| *Nyssa sylvatica* | Black tupelo |
| *Onoclea sensibilis* | Sensitive fern |
| *Orontium aquaticum* | Golden club |
| *Osmunda cinamomea* | Cinnamon fern |
| *Osmunda regalis* | Royal fern |
| *Peltandra virginica* | Green arrow-arum |
| *Picea mariana* | Black spruce |
| *Quercus bicolor* | Swamp white oak |
| *Symplocarpus foetidus* | Skunk cabbage |
| *Thuja occidentalis* | Eastern arborvitae |
| *Viburnum edule* | Squashberry |

### Central Plains, Plateaus, and Deserts

| | |
|---|---|
| *Acer rubrum* | Red maple |
| *Betula papyrifera* | Paper birch |
| *Cephalanthus occidentalis* | Common buttonbush |
| *Cornus racemosa* | Gray dogwood |
| *Cornus sericea* | Red osier |
| *Cornus foemina* | Stiff dogwood |
| *Ilex glabra* | Inkberry |
| *Ilex vomitoria* | Yaupon |
| *Lindera benzoin* | Spicebush |
| *Lysimachia terrestris* | Swampcandles |
| *Nyssa sylvatica* | Black tupelo |
| *Onoclea sensibilis* | Sensitive fern |
| *Osmunda cinamomea* | Cinnamon fern |
| *Osmunda regalis* | Royal fern |
| *Populus heterophylla* | Swamp cottonwood |
| *Quercus bicolor* | Swamp white oak |
| *Quercus lyrata* | Overcup oak |
| *Quercus nigra* | Water oak |
| *Quercus palustris* | Pin oak |
| *Quercus phellos* | Willow oak |
| *Quercus virginiana* | Live oak |
| *Salix pedicellaris* | Waxy bog willow |
| *Salix serissima* | Autumn willow |
| *Symplocarpus foetidus* | Skunk cabbage |
| *Viburnum edule* | Squashberry |

### Rocky Mountains Region

| | |
|---|---|
| *Acorus calamus* | Calamus |
| *Betula papyrifera* | Paper birch |
| *Cornus sericea* | Red osier |
| *Fraxinus* spp. | Ash |
| *Onoclea sensibilis* | Sensitive fern |

| *Populus* spp. | Cottonwood, aspen |
| *Salix pedicellaris* | Waxy bog willow |
| *Salix serissima* | Autumn willow |
| *Viburnum lentago* | Nanny-berry |

### Intermountain Region

| *Acorus calamus* | Calamus |
| *Betula* spp. | Birch |
| *Cornus sericea* | Red osier |
| *Fraxinus* spp. | Ash |
| *Onoclea sensibilis* | Sensitive fern |
| *Platanus wrightii* | Arizona sycamore |
| *Salix pedicellaris* | Waxy bog willow |
| *Salix serissima* | Autumn willow |
| *Viburnum lentago* | Nanny-berry |

### West Coast Region (Northern Portion)

Red alder (*Alnus rubra*) and western arborvitae (*Thuja plicata*) are characteristic of swamps on the coastal plain of the northern portion of the West Coast.

| *Abies amabilis* | Pacific silver fir |
| *Athyrium felix-femina* | Subarctic lady fern |
| *Alnus rubra* | Red alder |
| *Blechnum spicant* | Deerfern |
| *Carex obnupta* | Slough sedge |
| *Cornus canadensis* | Canadian bunchberry |
| *Gaultheria shallon* | Salal |
| *Lysichiton americanus* | Yellow skunk cabbage |
| *Maianthemum dilatatum* | Two-leaf false Solomon's seal |
| *Menziesia ferruginea* | Fool's-huckleberry |
| *Oenanthe sarmentosa* | Pacific water-dropwort |
| *Picea sitchensis* | sitka spruce |
| *Pinus contorta* | lodgepole pine |

| *Pinus monticola* | western white pine |
| *Rubus spectabilis* | salmon raspberry |
| *Salix hookeriana* | coastal willow |
| *Spiraea douglassii* | Douglas's meadowsweet |
| *Stachys mexicana* | Mexican hedge-nettle |
| *Thuja plicata* | western arborvitae |
| *Tolmiea menziesii* | piggyback-plant |
| *Tsuga heterophylla* | western hemlock |
| *Vaccinium ovalifolium* | oval-leaf blueberry |
| *Vaccinium ovatum* | evergreen blueberry |
| *Vaccinium parvifolium* | red blueberry |

If a forested wetland is being created, planting bare root seedlings/saplings is usually the most effective and economic method of establishing the desired tree species. Moderate success has also been achieved using seeds (i.e., acorns, nuts, cones).

Forested wetlands may be flooded by adjacent streams or lakes or simply by rainfall and surface runoff. If they are too dry, upland species will invade them, and if they are too wet, the trees will die. A proper hydrologic regime must be maintained. Periodic monitoring of water levels and vegetation is useful for determining the success of a created, enhanced, or restored forested wetland.

Forested wetlands are attractive to a variety of wildlife. Leaving dead timber standing provides habitat for cavity-nesting birds and small mammals. Forested wetlands should provide the three basic requirements for wildlife—food, water, and cover, or shelter—and adequate space for the species you wish to attract.

## SHRUB WETLANDS

### Physical Characteristics of Shrub Wetlands

Shrub wetlands are dominated by woody shrubs such as willows, alders, and common buttonbush. They are often intermediate between marshes and wet meadows and forested wetlands. They may represent a successional, or seral, stage between a meadow and a forested wetland. There is, however, usually some environmental factor or natural disturbance that prevents the growth of trees and maintains the shrub vegetation. Shrub wetlands are frequently or continuously flooded wetlands.

## Plants and Animals of Shrub Wetlands

A shrub wetland is dominated by shrubs or small trees and may be somewhat open or a dense thicket. Birds are attracted to shrub thickets for the protection they offer as well as the food many shrubs provide. Some common scrub swamp plants in the Northeast include red osier dogwood and silky dogwood, swamp rose, pussy willow, winterberry, spicebush, sweet pepperbush, elderberry, and swamp azalea. Beneath the shrubs there is frequently a rich community of ferns and herbs; jewelweed, royal fern, cinnamon fern, and sensitive fern are just a few. Deer seek cover in shrub wetlands, and their browsing can be problematic in areas where deer "yard," or gather, during the winter.

## Restoration and Management of Shrub Wetlands

Shrub wetlands can be created, enhanced, or restored. They are among the simplest wetland types to restore and manage. Shrub wetlands are wetter than forested wetlands and often occur next to wet meadows or marshes. The correct inflow and outflow of water can be monitored by measuring water levels and observing the condition of the vegetation. The hydrology of shrub wetlands does not require dry periods, as in forested wetlands. In fact, the additional water is one reason that trees do not invade shrub wetlands. Water control structures are often useful in managing shrub wetlands. They do not have to be mechanical structures, but can consist of earthen berms with overflow areas and or small check dams. However, unless the appropriate natural hydrology is intact, hydrologic alterations will be necessary to maintain the appropriate water budget.

## Key Species by Region

### Southeastern Region

| | |
|---|---|
| *Alnus serrulata* | Brookside alder |
| *Cephalanthus occidentalis* | Common buttonbush |
| *Chamaecyparis thyoides* | Atlantic white cedar |
| *Cliftonia monophylla* | Buckwheat tree |
| *Cornus amomum* | Silky dogwood |
| *Cyrilla racemiflora* | Swamp titi |
| *Decodon verticillatus* | Swamp loosestrife |
| *Fothergilla gardenii* | Dwarf witch-alder |
| *Fothergilla major* | Mountain witch-alder |

| | |
|---|---|
| *Gordonia lasianthus* | Loblolly bay |
| *Ilex decidua* | Deciduous holly |
| *Magnolia virginiana* | Sweet bay |
| *Myrica cerifera* | Southern bayberry |
| *Salix* spp. | Willows |
| *Sambucus canadensis* | American elderberry |
| *Spiraea tomentosa* | Steeplebush |

### Appalachian/Ozark Region

| | |
|---|---|
| *Alnus serrulata* | Brookside alder |
| *Amelanchier canadensis* | Canadian serviceberry |
| *Cephalanthus occidentalis* | Common buttonbush |
| *Cornus amomum* | Silky dogwood |
| *Leitneria floridana* | Corkwood |
| *Sambucus canadensis* | American elderberry |
| *Sanguisorba canadensis* | Canadian burnet |
| *Spiraea alba* | White meadowsweet |
| *Spiraea tomentosa* | Steeplebush |
| *Viburnum lentago* | Nanny-berry |

### New England/Great Lakes Region

| | |
|---|---|
| *Alnus incana* | Speckled alder |
| *Amelanchier canadensis* | Canadian serviceberry |
| *Aronia melanocarpa* | Black chokeberry |
| *Betula* spp. | Birch |
| *Cephalanthus occidentalis* | Common buttonbush |
| *Cornus racemosa* | Gray dogwood |
| *Cornus sericea* | Red osier |
| *Ilex verticillata* | Common winterberry |
| *Rhododendron viscosum* | Clammy azalea |
| *Salix bebbiana* | Long-beak willow |
| *Salix candida* | Sage willow |
| *Salix discolor* | Tall pussy willow |
| *Salix pellita* | Satiny willow |

| *Sambucus canadensis* | American elderberry |
| *Sambucus racemosa* | Red elderberry |
| *Sanguisorba canadensis* | Canadian burnet |
| *Sorbus americana* | Mountain ash |
| *Thuja occidentalis* | Eastern arborvitae |
| *Viburnum lentago* | Nanny-berry |

### Central Plains, Plateaus, and Deserts

| *Alnus incana* | Speckled alder |
| *Alnus serrulata* | Brookside alder |
| *Alnus viridis* | Sitka alder |
| *Amelanchier alnifolia* | Saskatoon serviceberry |
| *Amorpha fruticosa* | False indigo-bush |
| *Cephalanthus occidentalis* | Common buttonbush |
| *Cornus racemosa* | Gray dogwood |
| *Cornus foemina* | Stiff dogwood |
| *Salix bebbiana* | Long-beak willow |
| *Salix candida* | Sage willow |
| *Salix discolor* | Tall pussy willow |
| *Salix pellita* | Satiny willow |
| *Sambucus canadensis* | American elderberry |

### Rocky Mountain Region

| *Alnus incana* | Speckled alder |
| *Alnus viridis* | Sitka alder |
| *Amelanchier alnifolia* | Saskatoon serviceberry |
| *Rubus* spp. | Blackberries, raspberries |
| *Salix bebbiana* | Long-beak willow |
| *Salix candida* | Sage willow |
| *Salix drummondiana* | Drummond's willow |
| *Salix planifolia* | Tea-leaf willow |
| *Sambucus racemosa* | Red elderberry |
| *Viburnum lentago* | Nanny-berry |

### Intermountain Region

| | |
|---|---|
| *Alnus incana* | Speckled alder |
| *Alnus viridis* | Sitka alder |
| *Amelanchier alnifolia* | Saskatoon serviceberry |
| *Cornus sericea* | Red osier |
| *Salix amygdaloides* | Peach-leaf willow |
| *Salix bebbiana* | Long-beak willow |
| *Salix candida* | Sage willow |
| *Sambucus racemosa* | Red elderberry |
| *Viburnum lentago* | Nanny-berry |

### West Coast Region

| | |
|---|---|
| *Alnus rubra* | Red alder |
| *Amelanchier alnifolia* | Saskatoon serviceberry |
| *Ribes* spp. | Currants |
| *Salix drummondiana* | Drummond's willow |
| *Salix eriocephala* | Missouri willow |
| *Salix pedicellaris* | Waxy bog willow |
| *Salix serissima* | Autumn willow |
| *Sambucus racemosa* | Red elderberry |

Wetland shrubs are usually planted as bare root seedlings or saplings. Cuttings may be used in some cases.

Shrub wetlands are attractive to many species of birds because of the density of vegetation and the food provided by many shrubs.

# BOGS

## Physical Characteristics of Bogs

Bogs are found mostly in the northern United States; however, some occur further south on mountaintops or along the coastal plain. Bogs develop in areas where surface drainage is impeded and soil and water temperatures are low. Bog waters are low in available nitrogen, potassium, and phosphorus, inasmuch as these nutrient elements are tied up in **peat,** or undecomposed plant matter. These waters have high carbon dioxide content and possess traces of hydrogen sulfide. Some bog wetlands may actually draw water from lower levels by capillary action in the organic substrate.

Sphagnum mosses accumulate and create a spongy, quaking terrain that may be several feet thick. Sphagnum contributes to the acidic growing conditions. The varied species of soil bacteria responsible for the decomposition of organic material cannot live in such an acidic environment, so dead bog vegetation does not decay but rather accumulates as peat. Bogs are unique environments with species adapted to low oxygen and nutrient levels and acidic conditions. A bog often begins forming at the edge of a pond or lake, with sphagnum moss and sedges forming at the edge of the pond or lake and creating an open mat.

## Plants and Animals of Bogs

Many spectacular orchids grow in bogs, such as the rose pogonia, grass pink, and swamp pink. In addition to these beautiful orchids, unique carnivorous (insect-eating) plants such as pitcher plants and sundews inhabit many bogs. Sphagnum dominates a large portion of a bog. It is a common moss in wet areas and is especially important in bogs. Each species of sphagnum has its own requirements for sunlight, water chemistry, and pH. Sphagnum is less common in the grass-sedge bogs of the South, where acidity is caused by mineral compounds, not accumulating peat. Other conspicuous plants are buckbean and water willow, which commonly grow at the edge of the bog mat. Cranberry is a low, creeping plant native to northern bogs. Leatherleaf is a common bog shrub. Other common shrubs include sweetgale, sheep laurel, bog laurel, bog rosemary, and Labrador tea. Sweetgale is able to thrive in nutrient-poor bog soils by fixing nitrogen from the air. As the peat accumulates, taller shrubs and trees take root in the bog mat, black spruce and larch in the north and Atlantic white cedar in the coastal plain. Deciduous trees such as red maple do not grow well in a bog until the peat is firm and has begun to decompose (Caduto 1990).

Animals that inhabit bogs are water shrews and masked shrews, along with white-tailed deer, otters, and minks. Water shrews are good swimmers. They can run on the water surface as well as walk along the bottom while submerged. They are primarily nocturnal; they eat fish eggs, aquatic insects such as mayfly nymphs, and caddis flies and can even catch small fish. The southern bog lemming is a common mammal found in bogs.

The bird communities of bogs are not as diverse as those of other wetland types. Black and ring-necked ducks, northern waterthrushes, golden-crowned kinglets, and song, swamp, and white-throated sparrows are common (Caduto 1990). Other inhabitants include cedar waxwings and several species of warbler, such as the palm warbler, common yellowthroat, yellow-rumped warbler, parula, and magnolia warbler. Wood frogs and pickerel frogs are common inhabitants of bog environments.

## Restoration and Management of Bogs

Bogs can be created in areas where they did not previously exist, but this process is often difficult, costly, and ineffective. Many bogs that have been disturbed are prime candidates for enhancement or restoration. The natural conditions under which bog communities develop must be properly maintained. All bogs are successional communities, gradually being invaded by woody plants in the absence of disturbance. Depending on management goals, the encroachment of woody vegetation may have to be cut back to keep the bog open. This discussion is not meant to discourage permitting natural succession but, rather, to illustrate different management options.

Should the water levels or the vegetation of existing bogs be disturbed, the health and well-being of the bog are compromised. The first step is to ensure that the sphagnum is well established. Sphagnum is the most satisfactory growing medium for bog plants. Bogs must be designed with suitable conditions for the sphagnum. Most bogs have no water flow, but some do have a little water flow. Although bogs are most prevelant in glaciated areas, they also occur on mountaintops, in coastal areas, in sandy places, and even on some disturbed sites.

## Key Species by Region

### Southeastern Region

| | |
|---|---|
| *Acorus americanus* | Sweet flag |
| *Calopogon tuberosus* | Tuberous grass-pink |
| *Carex* spp. | Sedges |
| *Chamaecyparis thyoides* | Atlantic white cedar |
| *Drosera* spp. | Sundews |
| *Eriocaulon* spp. | Pipeworts |
| *Osmunda cinnimomea* | Cinnamon fern |
| *Osmunda regalis* | Royal fern |
| *Pinus* spp. | Pines |
| *Pogonia ophioglossoides* | Snake-mouth orchid |
| *Polygala lutea* | Orange milkwort |
| *Rhexia* spp. | Meadow beauties |

| | |
|---|---|
| *Symplocarpus foetidus* | Skunk cabbage |
| *Thelypteris palustris* | Eastern marsh fern |
| *Vaccinium* spp. | Blueberries, cranberries |
| *Xyris* spp. | Yellow-eyed grasses |

### Appalachian/Ozark Region

| | |
|---|---|
| *Acorus americanus* | Sweet flag |
| *Caltha palustris* | Yellow marsh marigold |
| *Chamaecyparis thyoides* | Atlantic white cedar |
| *Chamaedaphne calyculata* | Leatherleaf |
| *Coptis trifolia* | Three-leaf goldthread |
| *Cypripedium reginae* | Showy lady's slipper |
| *Osmunda cinnimomea* | Cinnamon fern |
| *Osmunda regalis* | Royal fern |
| *Menyanthes trifoliata* | Buckbean |
| *Parnassia asarifolia* | Kidney-leaved grass-of-Parnassus |
| *Platanthera* spp. | Fringed and fringeless orchids |
| *Pogonia ophioglossoides* | Snake-mouth orchid |
| *Symplocarpus foetidus* | Skunk cabbage |
| *Vaccinium* spp. | Blueberries, cranberries |
| *Xyris* spp. | Yellow-eyed grasses |

### New England/Great Lakes Region

| | |
|---|---|
| *Andromeda polifolia* | Bog-rosemary |
| *Betula glandulosa* | Scrub birch |
| *Calamagrostis canadensis* | Bluejoint |
| *Carex* spp. | Sedges |
| *Chamaecyparis thyoides* | Atlantic white cedar |
| *Chamaedaphne calyculata* | Leatherleaf |
| *Coptis trifolia* | Three-leaf goldthread |
| *Cypripedium reginae* | Showy lady's slipper |
| *Drosera rotundifolia* | Round-leaf sundew |
| *Eriophorum* spp. | Cotton grasses |
| *Helonias bullata* | Swamp pink |

| | |
|---|---|
| *Iris versicolor* | Harlequin blue flag |
| *Juncus stygius* | Moor rush |
| *Kalmia polifolia* | Bog laurel |
| *Ledum groenlandicum* | Rusty Labrador tea |
| *Menyanthes trifoliata* | Buckbean |
| *Osmunda cinnimomea* | Cinnamon fern |
| *Osmunda regalis* | Royal fern |
| *Pogonia ophioglossoides* | Snake-mouth orchid |
| *Sarracenia purpurea* | Purple pitcher plant |
| *Sphagnum* spp. | Sphagnum moss |
| *Symplocarpus foetidus* | Skunk cabbage |
| *Thuja occidentalis* | Eastern arborvitae |
| *Vaccinium angustifolium* | Late lowbush blueberry |
| *Vaccinium* spp. | Blueberries, cranberries |

### Central Plains and Plateaus

| | |
|---|---|
| *Acorus americanus* | Sweet flag |
| *Arethusa bulbosa* | Dragon's mouth |
| *Calamagrostis canadensis* | Bluejoint |
| *Calla palustris* | Water dragon |
| *Calopogon tuberosus* | Tubercus grass-pink |
| *Caltha palustris* | Yellow marsh marigold |
| *Eriphorum* spp. | Cotton grasses |
| *Platanthera* spp. | Fringed and fringeless orchids |
| *Salix* spp. | Willows |
| *Sphagnum* spp. | Sphagnum moss |
| *Vaccinium* spp. | Blueberries, cranberries |

### Rocky Mountain Region

| | |
|---|---|
| *Acorus americanus* | Sweet flag |
| *Alnus incana* | Speckled alder |
| *Alnus viridis* | Sitka alder |
| *Betula* spp. | Birches |
| *Calamagrostis canadensis* | Bluejoint |

| | |
|---|---|
| *Calla palustris* | Water dragon |
| *Caltha palustris* | Yellow marsh marigold |
| *Carex* spp. | Sedges |
| *Chamaedaphne calyculata* | Leatherleaf |
| *Eriphorum* spp. | Cotton grasses |
| *Kalmia polifolia* | Bog laurel |
| *Ledum groenlandicum* | Rusty Labrador tea |
| *Lysichiton americanus* | Yellow skunk cabbage |
| *Menyanthes trifoliata* | Buckbean |
| *Platanthera* spp. | Fringed and fringeless orchids |
| *Salix* spp. | Willows |
| *Sphagnum* spp. | Sphagnum moss |
| *Thelypteris palustris* | Eastern marsh fern |
| *Vaccinium* spp. | Blueberries, cranberries |

### West Coast Region

| | |
|---|---|
| *Alnus incana* | Speckled alder |
| *Alnus viridis* | Sitka alder |
| *Caltha palustris* | Yellow marsh marigold |
| *Carex* spp. | Sedges |
| *Chamaedaphne calyculata* | Leatherleaf |
| *Darlingtonia californica* | Cobraplant |
| *Eriphorum* spp. | Cotton grasses |
| *Gentiana calycosa* | Ranier pleated gentian |
| *Kalmia polifolia* | Bog laurel |
| *Ledum groenlandicum* | Rusty Labrador tea |
| *Lysichiton americanus* | Yellow skunk cabbage |
| *Menyanthes trifoliata* | Buckbean |
| *Myrica gale* | Sweetgale |
| *Picea* spp. | Spruces |
| *Platanthera* spp. | Fringed and fringeless orchids |
| *Salix pedicellaris* | Waxy bog willow |
| *Thelypteris palustris* | Eastern marsh fern |
| *Vaccinium* spp. | Blueberries, cranberries |

As a general rule, most bog orchids are not commercially available. Horticulturists are beginning to understand the requirements of bog orchids, so they may be more readily available in the future. Be cautious of using plants that may have been dug from the wild. In addition to the ethical implications, these plants often die after a season or two. Do not gather plants from the wild.

Bogs gradually progress (over a very long period of time) from open bogs with peat moss and herbaceous plants, to shrub bogs, and then to forested bogs. Bog areas often are a complex of these three cover types. In the absence of natural disturbances such as fire, cutting and selective removal of trees or shrubs may be required to prevent encroachment that will accelerate the drying of the bog. This process happens naturally over hundreds of years.

# Golf Courses and Wetlands

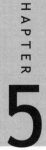

## PAST AND PRESENT ROLES OF WETLANDS ON GOLF COURSES

Golf has come a long way since its origins as an unpretentious game, shaped by the natural elements of the landscapes from which it grew in Scotland. There is little question that golf course architecture in general, and the preservation and management of wetlands on golf courses in particular, have been through many transformations since then.

As the game has evolved in the United States in the last 50 years or more, golf course design and construction have typically caused the plowing and leveling of natural features of the landscape to create a uniform surface on which a golf ball can travel virtually unhindered. Natural grass species have been replaced with less tolerant, domesticated cultivars (Tietge 1992). These turfgrass species receive intense chemical and mechanical management. Pest resistance to chemical control, potential groundwater contamination, animal, bird, and fish deaths, and occasional human health effects have changed the regulatory and management perspectives for both agricultural and turfgrass systems (Tietge 1992). This has resulted in stricter permitting and licensing regulations for many turfgrass and agricultural chemicals, as well as stricter permitting requirements for constructing new golf courses.

Wetlands, too, historically have been viewed as something to eliminate in the development of a golf course. Golf course lakes, ponds, and streams generally have been changed from thriving habitats into manicured "water features." And golf course superintendents received little or no training on how to manage them, other than how to eliminate plants and wildlife.

In recent years, however, increasing governmental regulation and public scrutiny, changing attitudes within the golf industry, and both criticism from and collaboration with the environmental community have led the golf industry to take a closer look at its stance on environmental issues. The central question facing the golf community today is how to move the industry forward in a way that not only *does no harm*, but that may actually *do some good* in terms of integrating environmental attributes, including fully functioning wetlands, into golf course design and management.

Environmental education and certification programs for golf courses, such as those offered by Audubon International, Wildlife Links research sponsored by the United States Golf Association and administered by the National Fish and Wildlife Foundation, and seminars and training offered by industry groups have led to significant improvements in environmental management on golf courses. Golf course superintendents, architects, owners, and managers are increasingly taking action to become better stewards of golf course lands. Efforts to showcase natural elements of the landscape and incorporate natural habitats as part of the golf course design are more and more common.

## OPPORTUNITIES FOR INTEGRATING WETLANDS ON GOLF COURSES

Viewing wetlands as assets rather than liabilities is a first step in properly protecting and managing them. There are many opportunities to protect and showcase wetlands both on established courses and in new golf course developments.

## Wetlands on Existing Golf Courses

As commercial, industrial, and suburban development continues to extend farther into agricultural and rural lands, larger blocks of wildlife habitat are often lost or fragmented. As a result, smaller, disconnected pieces of forest, wetland, and other natural communities remain to serve the needs of wildlife populations.

When managed properly, golf courses in urban and suburban settings can serve as valuable "island reserves" of open space and wildlife habitat, sustaining a diversity of species. Courses located in more rural areas can strive to complement nearby natural areas to form larger, contiguous blocks of habitat (see Figure 5-1).

**Figure 5-1** The Club at Seabrook Island, Johns Island, South Carolina. When golf courses are built in wetland environments extraordinary care must be taken to minimize negative impacts from construction and maintenance. A commitment to good environmental stewardship on the part of club managers, superintendents, maintenance staff, and golfers is key to ensuring the long-term success of environmentally sensitive management. (Courtesy of Audubon International.)

Many different groups of wildlife inhabit golf course wetland communities, including ducks and geese, wading birds, songbirds, raptors, a variety of small and large mammals, bats, butterflies, dragonflies and damselflies, snakes, lizards, turtles, fish, frogs, and salamanders. The ability of golf course wetlands to provide food, shelter, water, and breeding sites is directly related to several factors:

- Overall size of habitat areas
- Quality of wetland habitat, including water quality
- Diversity and structure of the existing native plant community
- Disturbance or intrusion caused by people
- Disturbance caused by invasive plant and wildlife species
- Proximity to and connectedness with adjacent habitat areas

Golf course superintendents can sustain a diversity of wildlife species in wetlands by keeping several key principles in mind (Harker et al. 1999):

1. **The bigger the better.** The larger the wetland area, the greater its ability to sustain a diversity of species. The exception to this rule is vernal pools, which, by definition, are small, seasonal wetlands. These small wetlands are extremely valuable to amphibians because of their small size and lack of fish predators. Many reptiles and amphibians use seasonal wetlands for breeding (Gibbons 2001).

2. The more types of plants in a wetland, the more types of food and cover sources it will offer throughout the year.

3. Increasing structural diversity increases wildlife diversity. Structural elements include submergent and emergent aquatic plants, shoreline herbaceous plants, shrubs, and trees, and rocks, fallen limbs or logs, and tree snags.

4. Species survival depends on maintaining minimum population levels. The golf course in general must provide food, cover, and water, as well as areas for reproduction where wildlife species can mate and raise their young. When species cannot successfully reproduce, their population numbers decline.

5. The less disturbance by golfers and maintenance activities the better. Signs, roped boundaries, or designation as an "Environmentally Sensitive Area" may be needed to keep golfers from searching for stray balls.

6. Wildlife corridors that connect smaller wetlands with larger wetlands or other types of habitats will improve species diversity.

Corridors may connect habitat patches within the golf course (e.g., from woods to a wetland on the course) or from the golf course to neighboring habitats (e.g., from golf course wetlands to woods on an adjacent parcel of land).

## New Golf Course Developments

Rather than meeting minimal regulatory requirements for wetland protection, enlightened architects, developers, and managers seek to protect not just the land that is wet, but a functioning wetland system. When integrated into the golf course design, the wetland system can hold storm water runoff, filter nutrients and pollutants, trap sediments, and attract wildlife, while offering golfers a naturally scenic round of golf.

In the design phase of development, wetland features and functions should be considered along with routing plans. Developers must evaluate opportunities to

- Protect existing wetlands.
- Improve the functioning of degraded wetland systems. The hydrology is usually reestablished in a former wetland that has been drained.
- Enhance existing wetlands by removing and replacing exotic, invasive plants with desirable wetland vegetation.
- Create new wetlands.
- Design small wetlands that will be part of the drainage and water filtering system on the course.
- Connect wetlands with other types of wildlife habitat. This may include creating natural corridors that link habitats throughout the property or designing golf layouts that leave habitats, such as woods, adjacent to wetlands.
- Educate golfers about the need to protect wetlands on-site.

Information about significant habitat features and plant and wildlife species, as well as previous disturbances to wetlands on-site, should be recorded during initial site surveys and wetland delineation. Architects and developers, along with project consultants, can then use this information to route the golf course in a way that takes advantage of the site's natural features and protects or enhances wetlands and other wildlife habitats.

**Figure 5-2** A nature preserve and interpretative boardwalk at
Pelican Preserve in Fort Myers, Florida, covers approximately 40
acres. The boardwalk treats visitors to a walk through four distinct plant communities, including live oak/sable palm,
bay/gum/cypress, freshwater maidencane, and emergent marsh.
Pelican Preserve provides a trail guide, a kiosk, and several viewing stations to educate patrons about wildlife and plants of the
preserve. (Courtesy of Audubon International.)

## Golfer and Community Education

Wetlands on golf courses can be showcased as unique golf course features. Educational signage, displays, tours, and boardwalk trails have been employed successfully by golf courses to educate golfers about the value of wetlands. Consider using one or more of these methods to highlight your course's wetlands:

- Photographs and text can be combined to create an informational display that shows the types of wildlife and plants that rely on the wetland. Appropriate locations for such a display may include the clubhouse, pro shop, or halfway house.

- A brief description about the course's wetlands and golfer etiquette for protecting such areas can be included in a yardage book.

- Attractive signage can direct golfers to respect wetland boundaries, or it can go much further by including information about the value of wetlands.

- Constructing a boardwalk trail that takes walkers or carts through a wetland can be an elaborate, yet worthwhile project. The boardwalk should avoid, as much as possible, removing vegetation and disturbing reproductive sites. Stations along the trail can be created to invite people to stop and observe specific features of the wetland. An accompanying trail guide can be picked up and dropped off at each end of the wetland boardwalk (Fig. 5-2).

## Environmental Management Planning

In every aspect of golf course management, from planning and construction to pesticide and fertilizer application, aquatic and terrestrial species should be integral factors in the plan. Fortunately, a healthy functioning wetland does not need "management" per se. However, when located on a golf course, wetlands will benefit from a number of best management practices. The simple self-assessment checklist provided on page 153 can be used as a guide to basic environmental management practices for wetlands.* Golf courses can adapt these general guidelines with site-specific practices that account for regional influences and site characteristics (see Figures 5-3 and 5-4).

**Figure 5-3** Golfers searching for stray balls can damage plants and compact wetland soils. Signs like this one at Fawn Lake Country Club in Spotsylvania, Virginia, help to delineate the wetland boundary and underscore the need for golfers to stay out. (Courtesy of Audubon International.)

**Figure 5-4** In 2001, a local scout troop assisted staff from the Parks and Open Space Department in Aurora, Colorado, to plant a mitigated wetland on Murphy Creek Golf Course, one of the city's public courses. The mitigation site occurs within a formerly dry channel of East Murphy Creek and replaced 0.09 acres of wetlands that were impacted by golf course construction. (Courtesy of Audubon International.)

| Self-Assessment Checklist for Managing Wetlands on Golf Courses* | | | |
|---|---|---|---|

| **Wetland Delineation** | Yes | No | N/A |
|---|---|---|---|
| **1.** Have boundaries been delineated for each wetland present on site? | ☐ | ☐ | ☐ |
| **2.** Has a basic description of the type(s) of wetland(s) present been written and kept on file? | ☐ | ☐ | ☐ |
| **3.** Is the Army Corps of Engineers contacted when wetlands are to be altered? | ☐ | ☐ | ☐ |
| **Water Quality Protection** | | | |
| **4.** Have physical and chemical baseline parameters been established for water quality (e.g., temperature, pH, turbidity, dissolved oxygen)? | ☐ | ☐ | ☐ |
| **5.** Are no-mow buffer zones or shoreline plantings incorporated around wetland areas to slow and filter runoff? | ☐ | ☐ | ☐ |
| **6.** Is the mowing height raised to create a turf filter strip surrounding wetland areas that border golf play, where more extensive plantings of aquatic/shoreline vegetation cannot be incorporated? | ☐ | ☐ | ☐ |
| **7.** Are no-spray or limited-spray practices and non-chemical weed and disease control methods employed near wetlands? | ☐ | ☐ | ☐ |
| **8.** Is a comprehensive, integrated pest management program in place to keep turfgrass in a vigorous and healthy state and minimize the need for chemical control measures? | ☐ | ☐ | ☐ |
| **9.** Are best management practices (BMPs) employed to apply chemical products in a manner that minimizes harmful environmental impacts to people, water, and nontarget wildlife? | ☐ | ☐ | ☐ |

*Note: The Self-Assessment Checklist includes general practices that protect and enhance wetlands; more specific lists of environmentally sensitive management practices for golf courses are available from Audubon International, the Michigan State Environmental Stewardship Program, and several U.S. state and Canadian provincial golf course superintendent associations.

|  | Yes | No | N/A |
|---|---|---|---|
| **10.** Are BMPs employed to reduce the potential for nutrient loading to water bodies? (These may include the use of slow-release fertilizers, spoon feeding, filtering drainage through vegetative or mechanical filters, and fertigation.) | ☐ | ☐ | ☐ |
| **11.** Is a covered boom used to minimize chemical spray drift near water bodies? | ☐ | ☐ | ☐ |
| **12.** Are chemicals properly stored and handled, and equipment properly maintained, to reduce the potential for negative environmental impacts to water sources and wetlands? | ☐ | ☐ | ☐ |
| **13.** Are maintenance facility structures, including fuel and chemical storage structures, equipment storage, wash pad, and mix-load areas, adequate to ensure that chemicals do not contaminate water sources or wetlands? | ☐ | ☐ | ☐ |
| **14.** Are proper safeguards in place to contain spills? | ☐ | ☐ | ☐ |
| **15.** Are chemical containers and other waste materials disposed of in a manner that eliminates potential on-site or off-site contamination of water bodies? | ☐ | ☐ | ☐ |
| **16.** When aquatic weed management is required, are physical solutions employed first, (e.g., priority is given to hand or mechanical removal, use of sterile grass carp, etc.), rather than seeking chemical solutions? | ☐ | ☐ | ☐ |
| **17.** When chemical weed management is necessary, are least-toxic EPA-approved products chosen and applied according to label directions? | ☐ | ☐ | ☐ |
| **18.** Are water body management companies selected that comply with the course's request for environmentally sensitive best management practices? | ☐ | ☐ | ☐ |
| **19.** Do wetlands on-site fulfill their intended functions and values? (Not all functions and values apply to all wetlands.) | ☐ | ☐ | ☐ |

|  | Yes | No | N/A |
|---|---|---|---|
| a. Groundwater recharge | ☐ | ☐ | ☐ |
| b. Groundwater discharge | ☐ | ☐ | ☐ |
| c. Flood flow alteration | ☐ | ☐ | ☐ |
| d. Sediment stabilization | ☐ | ☐ | ☐ |
| e. Sediment/toxicant retention | ☐ | ☐ | ☐ |
| f. Nutrient removal/transformation | ☐ | ☐ | ☐ |
| g. Wildlife diversity/abundance | ☐ | ☐ | ☐ |
| h. Aquatic diversity/abundance | ☐ | ☐ | ☐ |
| i. Uniqueness/heritage | ☐ | ☐ | ☐ |
| j. Recreation | ☐ | ☐ | ☐ |
| **20.** For new golf developments: Have hydrologic conditions on-site been preserved to enable protected wetlands to remain viable? (Hydrologic pathways include groundwater discharge and recharge, surface water runoff and flooding, storm water flow, drainage, and tidal flow.) | ☐ | ☐ | ☐ |

**Wetland Wildlife Management**

| | Yes | No | N/A |
|---|---|---|---|
| **21.** Has a survey of wildlife present in and around the golf course wetlands been compiled? | ☐ | ☐ | ☐ |
| **22.** Are yearly updates to the wildlife survey added to note changes in species diversity, as well as reproductive successes of species relying on the wetlands? | ☐ | ☐ | ☐ |
| **23.** Has a survey of plants present in the golf course wetlands been compiled? | ☐ | ☐ | ☐ |
| **24.** Are yearly updates to the plant survey added to note changes in diversity? | ☐ | ☐ | ☐ |

| | Yes | No | N/A |
|---|---|---|---|
| **25.** Is plant diversity maintained in and around wetlands (e.g., submergent and emergent aquatic plants; shoreline herbaceous plants, shrubs, and trees)? | ☐ | ☐ | ☐ |
| **26.** Are structural elements added to enhance wildlife cover (e.g., rock piles, fallen limbs or logs, tree snags)? | ☐ | ☐ | ☐ |
| **27.** Are wetland and upland habitats connected when possible? | ☐ | ☐ | ☐ |
| **28.** Are natural corridors present to connect wetlands with larger blocks of wildlife habitat on and off the property? | ☐ | ☐ | ☐ |
| **29.** Is woodland the understory, including leaf litter, downed limbs, and shrub layers, left intact in wooded areas adjacent to wetlands to provide amphibian habitat? | ☐ | ☐ | ☐ |
| **30.** Are suitable ecotones (transition zones) established in wildlife corridors or wetland-upland boundaries? (*Note:* Ecotones are areas of high biological diversity.) | ☐ | ☐ | ☐ |
| **31.** Are newly constructed or renovated ponds designed to promote bird and amphibian habitats—that is, with gently sloping shoreline banks, shallow water margins (less than 2 feet of water) created along the pond edge, and vegetation, rather than riprap, used to stabilize shorelines? | ☐ | ☐ | ☐ |
| **32.** Is trash and maintenance debris (e.g., clippings, brush, leaves, etc.) kept out of wetland areas? | ☐ | ☐ | ☐ |
| **33.** Are exotic-invasive plants kept in check or removed to prevent their spread or takeover of wetlands? | ☐ | ☐ | ☐ |

| | Yes | No | N/A |
|---|---|---|---|
| **Staff and Golfer Awareness** | | | |
| 34. Are maintenance staff, including seasonal employees, trained and familiar with management strategies that protect wetland areas? | ☐ | ☐ | ☐ |
| 35. Are golfers aware of wetland boundaries and asked to refrain from searching for lost balls in wetland areas? | ☐ | ☐ | ☐ |
| 36. Are signs used to call attention to wetland areas? | ☐ | ☐ | ☐ |
| 37. Are carts kept out of wetland areas? | ☐ | ☐ | ☐ |
| 38. Are other methods employed to educate golfers or community members about the value of golf course wetlands? | ☐ | ☐ | ☐ |

# Common and Scientific Names of Organisms

## CLASSIFICATION SYSTEM FOR ORGANISMS

### MONERA
Bacteria

### PLANTS
Fungi
Algae
Dinoflagellates
Mosses and liverworts
Ferns and fern allies
Gymnosperms (cone-bearing plants)
Angiosperms (flowering plants)

### ANIMALS
**Invertebrates** (animals without a backbone)
Arthropods (insects, crustaceans, spiders, mites)
Mollusks (snails, clams, and mussels)
Protozoans (single-celled animals)
Sponges
Hydras and jellyfishes
Rotifers
Moss animals (bryozoans)
Worms
Water bears (tardigrades)

**Vertebrates** (animals with a backbone)
Reptiles and amphibians
Fish
Birds
Mammals

## ORGANISMS MENTIONED IN TEXT

### MONERA
Bacteria

### PLANTS
Fungi
Algae

| | |
|---|---|
| Blue-green algae | Cyanobacteria |
| Diatoms | Chrysophyta |
| Muskgrass | *Chara* spp. |
| Stonewort | *Nitella* spp. |

Dinoflagellates
Mosses and liverworts

| | |
|---|---|
| Sphagnum | *Sphagnum* spp. |
| Water moss | *Fontinalis* spp. |

Ferns and fern allies

Gymnosperms (cone-bearing plants)

| | |
|---|---|
| Bald cypress | *Taxodium distichum* |
| Eastern arborvitae | *Thuja occidentalis* |
| Northern white cedar | *Chamaecyparis thyoides* |
| Pines | *Pinus* spp. |
| Pond cypress | *Taxodium ascendens* |
| Pond pine | *Pinus serotina* |
| Slash pine | *Pinus elliotii* |
| White pine | *Pinus strobus* |

Angiosperms (flowering plants)

| | |
|---|---|
| Alders | *Alnus* spp. |
| American white water lily | *Nymphaea odorata* |
| Arrowhead | *Sagittaria* spp. |
| Bayberry | *Myrica pensylvanica* |
| Black tupelo | *Nyssa syvatica* |
| Black needle rush | *Juncus roemerianus* |
| Bladderwort | *Utricularia* spp. |
| Bulrushes | *Scirpus* spp. |

| Common buttonbush | *Cephalanthus occidentalis* |
|---|---|
| Carolina fanwort | *Cabomba caroliniana* |
| Carolina sea-lavender | *Limonium carolinianum* |
| Cattail | *Typha* spp. |
| Chairmaker's bulrush | *Scirpus americanus* |
| Coastal salt grass | *Distichlis spicata* |
| Common reed | *Phragmites australis* |
| Coontail | *Ceratophyllum denersum* |
| Cranberry | *Vaccinium* spp. |
| Dogwoods | *Cornus* spp. |
| Duck-potato | *Sagittaria latifolia* |
| Duckweed | *Lemna* spp. |
| Eelgrass | *Zostera mariana* |
| Elm | *Ulmus* spp. |
| Glasswort | *Salicornia virginica* |
| Groundsel | *Baccharis halmifolia* |
| Hardstem bulrush | *Scirpus acutus* |
| Heaths | Ericaceae (ericads) |
| Horned pondweed | *Zannichellia palustris* |
| Hydrilla | *Hydrilla verticillata* |
| Lesser duckweed | *Lemna minor* |
| Maple | *Acer* spp. |
| Marsh elder | *Iva frutescens* |
| Marsh hay cord grass | *Spartina patens* |
| Mosquito fern | *Azolla caroliniana, A. mexicana* |
| Oak | *Quercus* spp. |
| Overcup oak | *Quercus lyrata* |
| Pacific cord grass | *Spartina foliosa* |
| Oalmetto | *Sabal palmetto* |
| Pickerelweed | *Pontederia cordata* |
| Pin oak | *Quercus palustris* |
| Pondweed | *Potamogeton* spp. |
| Purple loosestrife | *Lythrum salicaria* |
| Red maple | *Acer rubrum* |
| Rice cut-grass | *Leersia oryzoides* |
| River bulrush | *Scirpus fluviatilis* |
| Riverweed | *Podostemum ceratophyllum* |
| Rose mallow | *Hibiscus palustris* |
| Rushes | *Juncus* spp. |
| Sago pondweed | *Potamogeton pectinatus* |
| Saltwater cord grass | *Spartina alterniflora* |
| Saltwort | *Salicornia* spp. |

| | |
|---|---|
| Sea blite | *Suaeda maritima* |
| Sedges | *Carex* spp., *Cyperus* spp. |
| Silver maple | *Acer saccharinum* |
| Softstem bulrush | *Scirpus validus* (= *S. tabernaemontani*) |
| Spanish moss | *Tillandsia usneoides* |
| Spearscale | *Atriplex patula* |
| Spike-rush | *Eleocharis* spp. |
| Star duckweed | *Lemna trisulca* |
| Swamp tupelo | *Nyssa biflora* |
| Sweet bay | *Magnolia virginiana* |
| Three-square bulrush | *Scirpus americanus* |
| Tupelo | *Nyssa* spp. |
| Water crowfoot | *Ranunculus trichophyllus, R. subrigidus, R. longirostris* |
| Water hickory | *Carya aquatica* |
| Water hyacinth | *Eichhornia crassipes* |
| Water lilies | *Nymphaea* spp. |
| Water meal | *Wolffia* spp. |
| Water milfoil | *Myriophyllum* spp. |
| Water nymph | *Najas* spp. |
| Water shield | *Brasenia schreberi* |
| Water tupelo | *Nyssa aquatica* |
| Waterweed | *Elodea* spp. |
| White grass | *Leersia virginica* |
| Widgeon grass | *Ruppia maritima* |
| Wild celery | *Vallisneria americana* |
| Willow oak | *Quercus phellos* |
| Willows | *Salix* spp. |
| Yellow pond lily | *Nuphar luteum* |

## ANIMALS

**Invertebrates** (animals without a backbone)

Arthropods (insects, crustaceans, spiders, mites)

| | |
|---|---|
| Alderfly | Sialidae, *Sialis* spp. |
| Aquatic sow bug | Isopoda |
| Back swimmer | Notonectidae |
| Blue crab | *Callinectes sapidus* |
| Burrowing crayfish | *Cambarus* spp. |
| Burrowing mayfly | Ephemeroptera, *Hexagenia* and *Ephemera* spp. |
| Caddis fly | Trichoptera |

| | |
|---|---|
| Clam shrimp | Ostracoda |
| Crane fly | Tipulidae, *Tipula* spp. |
| Crayfish | *Cambarus* spp., *Orconectes* spp. |
| Cyclops | Copepoda |
| Damselfly | Zygoptera |
| Daphnia | *Daphnia* spp. |
| Dobsonfly | *Corydalus* spp. |
| Dragonfly | Anisoptera |
| Fairy shrimp | Anostraca |
| Fiddler crabs | *Uca pugilator, U. pugnax* |
| Fish fly | Megaloptera, *Chauliodes* spp. |
| Giant water bug | *Belostoma* spp., *Lethoserus* spp. |
| Greenhead fly | *Tabinus* spp. |
| Isopods | Isopoda |
| Mayfly | Ephemeroptera |
| Midges | Chironomidae |
| Mosquito | Culicinae |
| Ostracods | Ostracoda |
| Phantom midge | Chaoborinae |
| Predaceous diving beetle | *Dytiscus* spp. |
| Salt marsh mosquito | *Aedes sollicitans* |
| Scuds | Amphipoda |
| Seed shrimp | Ostracoda |
| Side swimmers | Amphipoda |
| Springtails | Collembola |
| Stone fly | Plecoptera |
| Water boatmen | Corixidae |
| Water flea | Cladocera |
| Water scorpion | Nepidae |
| Water strider | *Gerris* spp. |
| Whirligig beetle | *Dineutes* spp. |

**Mollusks** (snails, clams and mussels)

| | |
|---|---|
| Fingernail clams | *Sphaerium* spp. |
| Freshwater clams | Pelecypoda |
| Freshwater mussels | Pelecypoda |
| Marsh periwinkle | *Littorina* spp. |
| Oyster | *Crassostrea* spp., *Ostrea* spp. |
| Pulmonate marsh snail | *Melampus* spp. |
| Razor clam | *Ensis directus* |
| Ribbed mussel | *Modiolus demissus* |
| Snails | Gastropoda |

Protozoans (single-celled animals)

| | |
|---|---|
| Amoeba | *Amoeba* spp. |
| Rhizopods | *Rhizopoda* |
| Vorticella | *Vorticella* spp. |

Sponges

| | |
|---|---|
| Freshwater sponges | Porifera, *Spongilla lacustris* and *Heteromeyenia tubisperma* |

Hydras and jellyfishes

| | |
|---|---|
| Freshwater jellyfish | Coelenterata, *Craspedacusta sowerbyi* |
| Hydras | Coelenterata |

Rotifers

| | |
|---|---|
| Rotifers | Rotifera |

Moss animals (bryozoans)

| | |
|---|---|
| Moss animals | Bryozoa |

Worms

| | |
|---|---|
| Annelid worms | Annelida |
| Bloodworm (phantom midge larvae, *see* Arthropods) | |
| Earthworms | Annelida |
| Flatworms | Platyhelmithes |
| Leeches | Hirudinea |
| Roundworms | Nematoda |
| Tube worm | *Tubifex* spp. |

Water bears (tardigrades)

| | |
|---|---|
| Water bears | *Tardigrada* |

**Vertebrates** (animals with a backbone)

Amphibians

| | |
|---|---|
| American toad | *Bufo americanus* |
| Amphibians | Amphibia |
| Dusky salamander | *Desmognathus fuscus* |
| Giant bullfrog | *Rana catesbeiana* |
| Green frog | *Rana clamitans* |
| Leopard frog | *Rana pipiens* |
| Mud puppy | *Necturus maculosus* |
| Pickerel frog | *Rana palustris* |
| Red-spotted newt | *Notopthalmus viridescens* |
| Spotted salamander | *Ambystoma maculatum* |
| Spring peeper | *Hyla crucifer* |
| Two-lined salamander | *Eurycea bislineata* |
| Wood frog | *Rana sylvatica* |

## Reptiles

| | |
|---|---|
| American alligator | *Alligator mississipiensis* |
| Bog turtle | *Clemmys muhlenbergii* |
| Diamondback terrapin | *Malaclemys* spp. |
| Eastern painted turtle | *Chrysemys picta* |
| Garter snake | *Thamnophis sirtalis* |
| Mud turtle | *Kinosternon subrubrum* |
| Reptiles | *Reptilia* |
| Snapping turtle | *Chelydra serpentina* |
| Water moccasin (cottonmouth) | *Agkistrodon piscivorous* |
| Water snake | *Natrix sipedon* |

## Fish

| | |
|---|---|
| Bass | *Micropterus* spp. |
| Brook stickleback | *Culaea inconstans* |
| Bullheads | *Ameiurus* spp. |
| Carp | *Cyprinus carpio* |
| Catfish | *Ictalurus* spp. |
| Chain pickerel | *Esox niger* |
| Crappie | *Pomoxis* spp. |
| Fathead minnow | *Pimephales promelas* |
| Flounder | *Pleuronectidae* |
| Four-spined stickleback | *Apeltes quadracus* |
| Grass carp (white amur) | *Ctenopharyngodon idella* |
| Grass pickerel | *Esox americanus* |
| Guppy | *Lebistes reticulatus* |
| Killifish (mummichogs) | *Fundulus heteroclitus* |
| Minnows | *Cyprinidae* |
| Mosquito fish | *Gambusia affinis* |
| Muskellunge (muskie) | *Esox masquinongy* |
| Northern pike | *Esox lucius* |
| Salmon | *Salmo* spp. |
| Silversides | *Labidesthes* spp., *Menidia* spp. |
| Sucker | *Catostomidae* |
| Sunfish | *Lepomis* spp. |
| Trout | *Salmo* spp., *Salvelinus* spp. |

## Birds

| | |
|---|---|
| American bittern | *Botaurus lentiginosus* |
| American coot | *Fulica americana* |
| American robin | *Turdus migratorius* |
| American white pelican | *Pelecanus erythrorhynchos* |
| American widgeon | *Anas americana* |

| American woodcock | *Scolopax minor* |
| Bald eagle | *Haliaeetus leucocephalus* |
| Barred owl | *Strix varia* |
| Belted kingfisher | *Ceryle alcyon* |
| Black skimmer | *Rynchops niger* |
| Black tern | *Chlidonias niger* |
| Blue-winged teal | *Anas discors* |
| Brown pelican | *Pelecanus occidentalis* |
| Bufflehead | *Bucephala albeola* |
| Canada goose | *Branta canadensis* |
| Canvasback | *Aythya valisneria* |
| Caspian tern | *Sterna caspia* |
| Cattle egret | *Bubulcus ibis* |
| Clapper rail | *Rallus longirostris* |
| Common goldeneye | *Bucephala clangula* |
| Common merganser | *Mergus merganser* |
| Common snipe | *Gallinago gallinago* |
| Common tern | *Sterna hirundo* |
| Common yellowthroat | *Geothlypis trichas* |
| Eared grebe | *Podiceps nigricollis* |
| Eiders | *Somateria* spp. |
| Falcons | *Falco* spp. |
| Glossy ibis | *Plegadis falcinellus* |
| Great blue heron | *Ardea herodias* |
| Great egret | *Casmerodius albus* |
| Grebes | Podicipedidae |
| Green-backed heron | *Butorides striatis* |
| Gulls | *Larus* spp. |
| Hawks | *Buteo* spp. |
| Hooded merganser | *Lophodytes cucullatus* |
| Killdeer | *Charadrius vociferus* |
| Least bittern | *Ixobrychus exilis* |
| Least tern | *Sterna antillarum* |
| Little blue heron | *Egretta caerulea* |
| Loons | *Gavia* spp. |
| Louisiana waterthrush | *Seiurus motacilla* |
| Mallard | *Anas platyrhynchos* |
| Marsh wren | *Cistothorus palustris* |
| Northern pintail | *Anas acuta* |
| Northern shoveler | *Anas clypeata* |
| Northern waterthrush | *Seiurus noveboracensis* |
| Osprey (fish eagle) | *Pandion haliaetus* |

| Pied-billed grebe | *Podilymbus podiceps* |
| Purple gallinule | *Porphyrula martinica* |
| Redhead | *Aythya americana* |
| Red-winged blackbird | *Agelaius phoeniceus* |
| Ring-necked duck | *Aythya collaris* |
| Ruddy duck | *Oxyura jamaicensis* |
| Sandpipers | Scolopacidae |
| Scaups | *Aythya affinis, A. marila* |
| Seaside sharp-tailed sparrow | *Ammospiza caudacuta* |
| Seaside sparrow | *Ammospiza maritima* |
| Sedge wren | *Cistothorus platensis* |
| Snow goose | *Chen caerulescens* |
| Snowy egret | *Egretta thula* |
| Song sparrow | *Melospiza melodia* |
| Spotted sandpiper | *Actitus macularia* |
| Swamp sparrow | *Melospiza georgiana* |
| Swans | Cyginae |
| Virginia rail | *Rallus limicola* |
| Water ouzel (dipper) | *Cinclus mexicanus* |
| Western grebe | *Aechmophorus occidentalis* |
| White ibis | *Eudocimus albus* |
| Willet | *Catotrophorus semipalmatus* |
| Yellow-headed blackbird | *Xanthocephalus xanthocephalus* |

## Mammals

| American beaver | *Castor canadensis* |
| Black bear | *Ursus americanus* |
| Eastern chipmunk | *Tamias striatus* |
| Least weasel | *Mustela nivalis* |
| Little brown bat | *Myotis lucifugus* |
| Meadow jumping mouse | *Zapus hudsonius* |
| Mink | *Mustela vison* |
| Muskrat | *Ondatra zibethicus* |
| Nutria | *Myocastor coypus* |
| Raccoon | *Procyon lotor* |
| River otter | *Lutra canadensis* |
| Short-tailed shrew | *Blarina brevicauda* |
| Southern bog lemming | *Synaptomys cooperi* |
| Squirrels | *Sciurus* spp. |
| Striped skunk | *Mephitis mephitis* |
| Water shrew | *Sorex palustris* |
| White-tailed deer | *Odocoileus virginianus* |

# Wetland Resources

## Nongovernmental Resources

**Association of State Wetland Managers**
P.O. Box 269
1434 Helderberg Trail
Berne, NY 12023-9746

**Audubon International**
46 Rarick Road
Selkirk, NY 12158
www.audubonintl.org

**The Conservation Fund**
1800 N. Kent St., Suite 1120
Arlington, VA 22209-2109
www.conservationfund.org

**Ducks Unlimited**
One Waterfowl Way
Memphis, TN 38120
www.ducks.org

**Envirolink — Environmental Resources**
http://envirolink.org

**Environmental Law Institute**
www.eli.org

**Izaak Walton League of America**
Save Our Streams Program
707 Conservation Lane
Gaithersburg, MD 20878-2983
http://www.iwla.org

**Land Trust Alliance**
1331 H Street NW, Suite 400
Washington, DC 20005
www.ita.org

**National Association of Conservation Districts**
509 Capitol Court NE
Washington, DC 20002-4946
http://www.nacdnet.org

**National Audubon Society**
700 Broadway
New York, NY 10003
http://www.audubon.org

**National Wildlife Federation**
11100 Wildlife Center Drive
Reston, VA 20190
www.nwf.org

**National Wildlife Federation — Wetlands**
www.nwf.org/wetlands

**The Nature Conservancy**
International Headquarters
1815 N. Lynn St.
Arlington, VA 22209
http://nature.org

**Sierra Club**
National Headquarters
730 Polk St.
San Francisco, CA 94109
http://www.sierraclub.org

**Society for Ecological Restoration**
University of Wisconsin–Madison
Arboretum
1207 Seminole Highway
Madison, WI 53711
www.ser.org

**Society of Wetland Scientists**
P.O. Box 1897
Lawrence, KS 66044-8897
http://www.sws.org

**Terrene Institute**
http://www.terrene.org

**Trout Unlimited**
National Headquarters
1500 Wilson Blvd., Suite 310
Arlington, VA 22209-2310
(703) 522-0200
http://www.tu.org

**Trust for Public Land**
116 New Montgomery St., 4th Floor
San Francisco, CA 94105
(415) 495-4014
www.tpl.org

**Wetlands International**
www.wetlands.org

**Wetlands Regulation Center**
http://www.wetlands.com

**Wildlife Habitat Council**
8737 Colesville Rd., Suite 800
Silver Spring, MD 20910
http://www.wildlifehc.org

## Governmental Resources

**U.S. DEPARTMENT OF AGRICULTURE**
http://www.usda.gov

**U.S. Forest Service**
National Headquarters
P.O. Box 96090
Washington, DC 20090-6090
www.fs.fed.us

Region 1 — Northern Region
Federal Building
P.O. Box 7669
Missoula, MT 59807

Region 2 — Rocky Mountain Region
740 Sims Street
Lakewood, CO 80225

Region 3 — Southwestern Region
Federal Building
507 Gold Ave., SW
Albuquerque, NM 87102

Region 4 — Intermountain Region
Federal Building
324 25th St.
Ogden, UT 84401

Region 5 — California Office
630 Sansome St.
San Francisco, CA 94111

Region 6 — Pacific Northwest Region
333 SW First Ave.
Box 3623
Portland, OR 97208

Region 7—does not exist

Region 8—Southern Region
1720 Peachtree Rd. NW, Suite 800
Atlanta, GA 30367

Region 9—Northeastern Region
310 West Wisconsin Ave.,
   Room 500
Milwaukee, WI 53203

Region 10—Alaska Region
Federal Offic Building
Box 21628
Juneau, AK 99802-1628

**Natural Resources
Conservation Service (NRCS)
(formerly the Soil Conservation
Service)**
National Headquarters
P.O. Box 2890
Washington, DC 20013
www.nrcs.usda.gov
NRCS has wetland contacts and
state conservationists in each state.

**NRCS Wetland Science Institute**
www.pwrc.usgs.gov/wli

**U.S. DEPARTMENT OF
COMMERCE**

**National Marine Fisheries
Service—Regional Habitat
Offices**
National Headquarters
Silver Spring Metro Center 3
1315 East-West Hwy
Silver Spring, MD 20910
www.nmfs.nuaa.gov

Northeast Region Habitat &
Protected Resources Division
One Blackburn Drive
Gloucester, MA 01930-2298

Southeast Region Habitat
Conservation District
9721 Executive Center Drive
St. Petersburg, FL 33702

Southwest Region Habitat
Conservation Division
501 W. Ocean Blvd., Suite 4200
Long Beach, CA 90802-4213

Northwest Region Habitat
Conservation Branch
7600 Sand Point Way NE
Seattle, WA 98115

Pacific Islands
1601 Kapiolani Blvd.
Honolulu, HI 96814

Alaska Region Protected Resources
Management Division
P.O. Box 21668
Juneau, AK 99802-1668

**U.S. ARMY CORPS OF
ENGINEERS**
National Office
20 Massachusetts Ave., NW
Washington, DC 20314-1000

Institute for Water Resources
7701 Telegraph Rd.
Alexandria, VA 22315
www.usace.army.mil

Great Lakes Ohio River Division
Federal Office Bldg.
550 Main St.
Cincinnati, OH 45201

Mississippi Valley Division
P.O. Box 80
Vicksburg, MS 39180-0080

Northwestern Division
12565 West Center Rd.
Omaha, NE 68144

North Atlantic Division
90 Church St.
New York, NY 10007-9998

Pacific Ocean Division
Building 230
Fort Shafter, HI 96858-5440

South Atlantic Division
77 Forsyth St., SW, Room 322
Atlanta, GA 30303-3490

South Pacific Division
333 Market St.
San Francisco, CA 94111-2206

## U.S. DEPARTMENT OF THE INTERIOR

### Fish and Wildlife Service

National Headquarters
1849 C St., NW
Washington, DC 20240
(202) 208-5634 (general
    information)
www.fws.gov

National Wetlands Inventory
www.nwi.fws.gov

Region 1 — Pacific Regional
    Office
Eastside Federal Complex
911 NE 11th Ave.
Portland, OR 97232-4181
California, Hawaii and the Pacific
Islands, Idaho, Nevada, Oregon,
Washington

Region 2 — Southwest Regional
    Office
500 Gold Ave., SW, Room 3018
Albuquerque, NM 87102
Arizona, New Mexico, Oklahoma,
Texas

Region 3 — Great Lakes–Big Rivers
    Regional Office
Federal Building
1 Federal Drive
Fort Snelling, MN 55111
Iowa, Illinois, Indiana, Michigan,
Minnesota, Missouri, Ohio,
Wisconsin

Region 4 — Southeast Regional
    Office
1875 Century Blvd.
Atlanta, GA 30345
Alabama, Arkansas, Florida,
Georgia, Kentucky, Louisiana,
Mississippi, North Carolina, Puerto
Rico, South Carolina, Tennessee,
the Virgin Islands

Region 5 — Northeast Regional
    Office
300 Westgate Center Drive
Hadley, MA 01035
Connecticut, Delaware, Maine,
Maryland, Massachusetts, New
Hampshire, New Jersey, New York,
Pennsylvania, Rhode Island,
Vermont, Virginia, West Virginia

Region 6 — Mountain–Prairie
    Regional Office
134 Union Blvd.
P.O. Box 25486
Denver, CO 80225
Colorado, Kansas, Montana, North
Dakota, Nebraska, South Dakota,
Utah, Wyoming

Region 7 — Alaska Regional Office
1011 E. Tudor Rd.
Anchorage, AK 99503

### Geological Survey

National Center
Reston, VA 22092
www.usgs.gov

## National Wetlands Center
www.nwrc.gov

## National Park Service
National Headquarters
1849 C St., NW
Washington, DC 20013-7127
http://www.nps.gov/

Alaska Region
2525 Gambell St., Room 107
Anchorage, AK 99503

National Capital Region
1100 Ohio Drive, SW
Washington, DC 20242

Northeast Region
U.S. Custom House
200 Chestnut St., 5th Floor
Philadelphia, PA 19106
Connecticut, Delaware, Maine,
Maryland, Massachusetts, New
Hampshire, New Jersey, New York,
Pennsylvania, Rhode Island,
Vermont, Virginia, West Virginia

Midwest Region
1709 Jackson St.
Omaha, NE 68102
Illinois, Indiana, Iowa, Kansas,
Michigan, Minnesota, Missouri,
Nebraska, Ohio, Wisconsin

Intermountain Region
12795 Alameda Parkway
Denver, CO 80225
Colorado, Idaho, Montana, North
Dakota, South Dakota, Utah,
Wyoming

Southeast Region
100 Alabama St. SW
Atlanta, GA 30303
Alabama, Florida, Georgia,
Kentucky, Mississippi, North
Carolina, Puerto Rico, South

Carolina, Tennessee, the Virgin
Islands

Southwest Region
P.O. Box 728
Santa Fe, NM 87504
Arkansas, Louisiana, New Mexico,
Oklahoma, Texas

Pacific West Region
600 Harrison St., Suite 600
San Francisco, CA 94107
Arizona, California, Hawaii,
Nevada, Oregon, Washington

Rivers, Trails, and Conservation
Assistance Program
P.O. Box 37127
Washington, DC 20013

## U.S. ENVIRONMENTAL PROTECTION AGENCY
National Headquarters
401 M St., SW
Washington, DC 20460
http://www.epa.gov

Region 1
John F. Kennedy Bldg.
Boston, MA 02203
Connecticut, Maine, Massachusetts,
New Hampshire, Rhode Island,
Vermont

Region 2
290 Broadway, 26th Floor
New York, NY 10007-1866
New Jersey, New York, Puerto
Rico, Virgin Islands

Region 3
1650 Arch St.
Philadelphia, PA 19103-2029
Delaware, District of Columbia,
Maryland, Pennsylvania, Virginia,
West Virginia

Region 4
Atlanta Federal Center
61 Forsyth St., SW
Atlanta, GA 30303-3104
Alabama, Florida, Georgia,
Kentucky, Mississippi, Ohio,
Wisconsin

Region 5
77 West Jackson Blvd.
Chicago, IL 60604
Illinois, Indiana, Michigan,
Minnesota, Ohio, Wisconsin

Region 6
1445 Ross Ave.
12th Floor, Suite 1200
Dallas, TX 75270
Arkansas, Louisiana, New Mexico,
Oklahoma, Texas

Region 7
726 Minnesota Ave.
Kansas City, KS 66101
Iowa, Kansas, Missouri, Nebraska

Region 8
999 18th St., Suite 500
Denver, CO 80202-2405
Colorado, Montana, North Dakota,
South Dakota, Utah, Wyoming

Region 9
75 Hawthorne St.
San Francisco, CA 94015
Arizona, California, Hawaii,
Nevada, America Samoa, Trust
Territories of the Pacific, Guam,
Northern Marianas

Region 10
Water Management Division
12000 Sixth Ave.
Seattle, WA 98101
Alaska, Idaho, Oregon, Washington

Surf your watershed
http://www.epa.gov/surf

Wetlands Division
http://www.epa.gov/wetlands

# Wetland
# Regulatory Issues **C**

Various state and federal laws are used to protect wetlands. The primary federal laws for protecting wetlands are Section 404 of the 1977 Clean Water Act, which is jointly administered by the U.S. Army Corps of Engineers and the U.S. Environmental Protection Agency with consultation from the U.S. Fish and Wildlife Service and state water agencies, and the Swampbuster Provision of the Food Security Act (which denies federal subsidies to any farm owner who knowingly converts wetlands to farmland). A wetland subject to regulation is called a *jurisdictional wetland*. The U.S. Army Corps of Engineers developed a regulatory definition of wetlands used in the Section 404 permitting process. The legal definition included in that regulation is as follows:

> The term "wetlands" means those areas that are inundated or saturated by surface or ground water at a frequency and duration sufficient to support, and that under normal circumstances do support, a prevalence of vegetation typically adapted for life in saturated soil conditions. Wetlands generally include swamps, marshes, bogs, and similar areas.

Delineation of wetland boundaries is a critical part of the regulatory process. The delineation methods include three criteria: hydrology, soils, and vegetation. Wetland hydrology includes the presence of water, either at the surface or within the root zone. Hydrologic conditions can vary throughout the year from standing water to dry. Wetland soils have characteristics distinct from those of upland soils. Soil scientists have identified a series of hydric soils. Wetland plants (hydrophytes) are specifically adapted to wet conditions. They include facultative wetland plants that can live in either wet or dry conditions and obligate wetland plants that are able to live only in a wet environment. Experts should be consulted for the technical, regulatory delineation of wetlands. The government's approach to delineation is contained in a single manual, *Federal Manual for Identifying and Delineating Jurisdictional Wetlands.*

The "no net loss" concept has become an important part of wetland conservation in the United States. This concept was formulated by the National Wetlands Policy Forum in 1987. The one overall objective recommended by the forum was

> To achieve no overall net loss of the nation's remaining wetlands base and to create and restore wetlands, where feasible, to increase the quantity and quality of the nation's wetland resource base.

In addition to the requirements of the federal 404 permit, states have the power to restrict the discharges of "dredged or fill material" into wetlands. This state process is called the 401 certification process. A 404 permit cannot be issued unless the state certifies that the permit meets water quality standards through the 401 process. It is during the 404 permit review process that the 401 certification review by the state occurs. Figure C-1 shows the 404 permitting process. Table C-1 provides addresses for Corps division offices.

---

**TABLE C-1.** Regional Offices of the U.S. Army Corps of Engineers

| | | |
|---|---|---|
| Missouri River Division<br>P.O. Box 103 Downtown Station<br>Omaha, NE 68101 | Ohio River Division<br>P.O. Box 1159<br>Cincinnati, OH 45201 | New England Division<br>424 Trapelo Road<br>Waltham, MA 02254 |
| Pacific Ocean Division Building<br>230, Fort Shafter<br>Honolulu, HI 96858 | North Atlantic Division<br>90 Church Street<br>New York, NY 10007 | South Atlantic Division<br>77 Forsyth Street,<br>SW Atlanta, GA 30303 |
| North Central Division<br>536 S. Clark Street<br>Chicago, IL 60605 | South Pacific Division 630<br>Sansome Street, Room 1218<br>San Francisco, CA 94111 | Southwestern Division<br>1114 Commerce Street<br>Dallas, TX 75242 |
| Lower Mississippi Valley Division<br>P.O. Box 80<br>Vicksburg, MS 39180 | North Pacific Division<br>P.O. Box 2870<br>Portland, Oregon 97208 | |

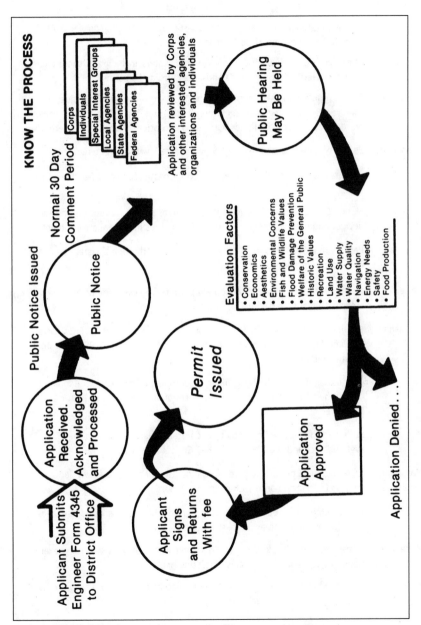

**Figure C-1** Corps of Engineers Permit Review Process (*Source:* U.S. Army Corps of Engineers.)

**TABLE C-2.** States with Wetland Protection Programs

| State | Program |
|---|---|
| Alabama | Permits are required for activities in coastal zone (dredging, dumping, etc.) that alter tidal movement or damage flora and fauna. |
| Alaska | State agencies regulate use of coastal land, waters, including offshore areas, estuaries, wetlands, tide flats, islands, sea cliffs, and lagoons. |
| California | Permit required for development up to 1000 yards of mean high tide; coastal zone regulated by regional regulatory boards; prohibits siting coastal-dependent developments in wetlands with some exceptions that must be permitted. |
| Connecticut | Permit required for all regulated activity; state inventory required. |
| Delaware | Permits required for all activities; has both Coastal Zone and Beach Protection Acts. |
| Florida | Florida Coastal Zone Management Act requires permit for erosion-control devices and excavations or erections of structures in coastal environments. |
| Georgia | Permits required for work in coastal salt marshes through Coastal Marshlands Protection Program. |
| Hawaii | County authorities issue development permits for development of coastal areas with state oversight. |
| Louisiana | State and/or local permits required for activity in coastal wetlands. Coastal Wetland Planning, Protection and Restoration Act passed in 1990 to restore coastal wetlands. |
| Maine | Permits required for dredging, filling, or dumping into coastal wetlands. Comprehensive coastal/fresh water protection in Protection of Natural Resources Act. |
| Maryland | State permits required for activity in coastal wetlands based on the Tidal Wetlands Act and the Chesapeake Bay Critical Area Act. |
| Massachusetts | State and local permits required for fill or alteration of coastal wetlands. Permits from local conservation commissioners. |
| Michigan | Permit required for development in high rule erosion areas, flood risk areas, and environmental areas of coastal Great Lakes. |
| Mississippi | Permits required for dredging and dumping, although there are many exemptions through Coastal Wetlands Protection Act. |
| New Hampshire | Permit required for dredge and fill in or adjacent to fresh- and saltwater wetlands; higher priority usually given to saltwater marshes. |
| New Jersey | Permit required for dredging and filling; agriculture and Hackensack meadowlands exempted. |

| New York | Permits required for tidal wetland alteration by the Tidal Wetlands Act. |
| North Carolina | State permit required for coastal wetland excavation or fill of estuarine waters, tidelands, or salt marshes. |
| Oregon | Local zoning requirements on coastal marshes and estuaries with state review. |
| Rhode Island | Coastal wetlands designated by order and use limited; permits required for filling, aquaculture, development activity on salt marshes. |
| South Carolina | Permits required for dredging, filling, and construction in coastal waters and tidelands including salt marshes. |
| Virginia | Wetlands Act requires permits for all activities in coastal counties with some exemptions; also 1988 Chesapeake Bay Preservation Act. |
| Washington | Shoreline Management Act requires local governments to adopt plans for shorelines, including wetlands; state may regulate if local government fails to do so. |

*Sources:* After Zinn and Copeland 1982; Kusler 1979; Want 1990; Meeks and Runyon 1990 (from Mitsch and Gosselink 1993).

Individual states have developed their own laws for the protection of coastal wetlands and inland wetlands. The federal Coastal Zone Management Act of 1972 created a grant program for states to develop plans for coastal management. Table C-2 provides a list of states with coastal wetland protection programs (Mitsch and Gosselink 1993).

State programs relating to the protection of inland wetlands vary considerably. Table C-3 lists states that have comprehensive wetland laws for inland waters (Mitsch and Gosselink 1993). It is recommended that the U.S. Army Corps of Engineers and the state agency responsible for water be contacted about current wetland regulations.

The most comprehensive definition of wetlands was adopted by the U.S. Fish and Wildlife Service. This is an important ecological definition and is widely accepted by wetland scientists. The U.S. Army Corps of Engineers definition is the regulatory definition. The definition and a full classification of wetlands is presented in *Classification of Wetlands and Deep Water Habitats of the United States* by Cowardin et al. (1979):

Wetlands are lands transitional between terrestrial and aquatic systems where the water table is usually at or near the surface or the land is covered by shallow water.... Wetlands must have one or more of the following three attributes: (1) at least periodically, the land supports predominantly hydrophytes, (2) the substrate is predomi-

**TABLE C-3.** States That Have Comprehensive Wetland Laws for Inland Waters

| State | Law |
|---|---|
| Connecticut | Inland Wetlands and Watercourses Act |
| Delaware | The Wetlands Act |
| Florida | Henderson Wetlands Protection Act of 1984 |
| Maine | Protection of Natural Resources Act |
| Maryland | Chesapeake Bay Critical Area Act |
| Massachusetts | Wetland Protection Act |
| Michigan | Goemaere-Anderson Wetland Protection Act |
| Minnesota | The Wetland Conservation Act of 1991 |
| New Hampshire | Fill and Dredge in Wetlands Act |
| New Jersey | Freshwater Wetlands Protection Act of 1987 |
| New York | Freshwater Wetlands Act |
| North Dakota | No Net Wetlands Loss Bill of 1987 |
| Oregon | Fill and Removal Act<br>Comprehensive Land Use Planning Coordination Act |
| Rhode Island | Freshwater Wetlands Act |
| Vermont | Water Resources Management Act |
| Wisconsin | Water Resources Development Act<br>Shoreland Management Program |

*Sources:* Want 1990; Meeks and Runyon 1990 (from Mitsch and Gosselink 1993).

nantly undrained hydric soil, and (3) the substrate is nonsoil and is saturated with water or covered by shallow water at some time during the growing season of each year. The term "wetland" includes a variety of areas that fall into one of five categories: (1) areas with hydrophytes and hydric soils, such as those commonly known as marshes, swamps, and bogs; (2) areas without hydrophytes but with hydric soils—for example, flats where drastic fluctuation in water level, wave action, turbidity, or high concentration of salts may prevent the growth of hydrophytes; (3) areas with hydrophytes but non-hydric soils, such as margins of impoundments or excavations where hydrophytes have become established but hydric soils have not yet developed; (4) areas without soils but with hydrophytes such as the seaweed-covered portion of rocky shores; and (5) wetlands without soil and without hydrophytes, such as gravel beaches or rocky shores without vegetation.

The definitions of wetlands do not include drained hydric soils that have the hydrology so altered that they will not support wetland plants. These areas of hydric soils are good candidates for restoration if the wetland hydrology is reestablished.

# Glossary

**Aerobic**  Refers to life or a process occurring only in the presence of free oxygen.

**Allochthonous**  Refers to deposits of material that originated elsewhere, e.g., plant materials from adjacent areas that are washed into a stream.

**Anaerobic**  Refers to life or activity in the absence of free oxygen.

**Autochthonous**  Refers to local origin, e.g., deposits produced within a lake.

**Basin**  A depression in the surface of the land used for holding water.

**Benthic**  Refers to the bottom of any body of water.

**Benthos**  Organisms that live on the bottom of the ocean or bodies of fresh water, from the water's edge down to the greatest depths.

**Brackish**  Water of mild salinity; occurs where fresh water and salt water meet as a river empties into the ocean.

**Biodiversity**  The variety of living organisms present in an area.

**Bromeliads**  Members of the vascular plant family Bromeliaceae; includes the pineapple.

**Compensation depth**  The depth of water at which photosynthesis balances respiration and beyond which light penetration is so low that it is no longer effective.

**Decomposers**  Organisms (such as bacteria and fungi) that break down plant and animal remains into forms once again usable by producers.

**Desmid**  Class of the Chlorophyta (green algae), whose members are distinguished by their distinctively symmetrical cells, anatomically complex plastids, and the lack of free-swimming forms.

**Diatom**  A class of golden-brown algae (Chrysopohyta) that is unicellular or colonial nonflagellate algae having delicately sculptured silica cell walls divided into two overlapping halves.

**Diversity**   The variety, number, and distribution of species within a community.

**Dystrophic**   A type of lake or pond that contains brown water with much humic material in solution and with a small bottom fauna characterized by pronounced oxygen consumption. See *eutrophic* and *oligotrophic.*

**Ecotone**   The juncture of two or more different kinds of ecosystems, a place that possesses the qualities of several types of ecosystems.

**Epilimnion**   The upper thermal layer that forms in lakes during the summer when warmer, less dense water is buoyed by the colder water below. See *metalimnion* and *hypolimnion.*

**Epiphyte**   A plant that has no roots in the soil and lives above the ground surface, supported by another plant or object. It obtains its nutrients from the air, rainwater, and organic debris on its support plant.

**Eutrophic**   Refers to a productive body of water, high in organic matter and mineral nutrients (e.g., phosphate and nitrate) and often exhibiting seasonal oxygen deficiency.

**Eutrophication**   The overfertilization of an aquatic ecosystem, resulting in high levels of production and decomposition. Eutrophication can hasten the aging process in a pond or lake as a result of the rapid buildup of organic remains.

**Evapotranspiration**   The sum total of water lost from the land by evaporation and plant transpiration.

**Habitat**   The kind of environment in which a certain organism normally lives.

**Heath**   Collectively, the vascular plants belonging to the Ericaceae family; these include many evergreen shrubs such as blueberry, cranberry, leatherleaf, and maleberry.

**Hummocks**   Mounds within a wetland that are slightly higher than adjacent ground.

**Hydric soil**   Soil that is typical of and developed under wetland conditions.

**Hydrophyte**   A plant that is adapted to living either in waterlogged soil or partly or wholly submerged in water.

**Hydrosere**   A pioneer plant community that develops in water when the depth is decreased by silting.

**Hypolimnion**   The lower, colder thermal layer that forms in lakes during the summer when the warmer, less dense water rises toward the surface, leaving the colder, denser water below. See *epilimnion* and *metalimnion.*

**Larva**   An immature stage in the development of an animal that usually undergoes major changes before changing into an adult form.

**Lentic**   Of still waters.

**Limnetic**   Pertaining to the open water zone of a lake that lies beyond the littoral zone and extends down to the depth at which light levels are at least 1 percent of the available sunlight at the surface. See *littoral*.

**Littoral**   The shoreline zone of a lake where sunlight penetrates to the bottom and is sufficient to support rooted plant growth. See *limnetic*.

**Lotic**   Of flowing waters.

**Mesic**   Moist, e.g., mesic forest.

**Metalimnion**   A thermal layer that forms in lakes during the warm season, intermediate between the upper warm layer (epilimnion) and the colder layer beneath (hypolimnion).

**Microhabitats**   Habitats or homes on a very small scale, such as the underside of a leaf.

**Motile**   Exhibiting or capable of movement.

**Neap tides**   The lowest tides during a month, occurring at about the time of the moon's first and last quarters.

**Nekton**   The strong swimming animals in water, e.g., fish.

**Nymph**   The interim stage of development, between egg and adult, among insects that undergo incomplete metamorphosis.

**Oligotrophic**   Refers to ponds or lakes that are low in content of basic nutritive substances for plants, lacking a distinct stratification of dissolved oxygen in summer or winter.

**Omnivore**   An animal that eats both plant and animal food.

**Peat**   Organic soil composed of fibrous, spongy, partially decomposed organic matter. Peat forms under conditions where decomposition is incomplete, such as in wetlands. Peat is the typical soil of bogs.

**Periphyton**   Algae that are attached to substrates or to living things.

**Physiognomy**   The appearance of vegetation as determined by the life form of the dominant plants, e.g., grassland, pine forest.

**Phytoplankton**   Plankton that is composed of tiny plants and plant matter that consists largely of algae. These plants are major sources of production in aquatic systems.

**Plankton**   Minute suspended organisms; some contain chlorophyll (phytoplankton), others are motile (zooplankton), and some have characteristics of both types, making them difficult to classify.

**Pool**   The slower moving sections of a stream where the topographical gradient is slight. See *riffle*.

**Protozoans**   Tiny unicellular organisms.

**Rheotropism**   The response of an organism to a current.

**Richness**   The number of species in an area; if an area has a large number of species, it is said to be "species rich."

**Riffle**   Fast moving section of a stream characterized by high dissolved oxygen levels and higher topographic gradients. See *pool*.

**Rill erosion**   The removal of soil by running water, resulting in the formation of shallow channels (rills) that can be smoothed completely by cultivation in the normal manner.

**Seepage**   (1) The water that passes through or emerges from the ground along a line or surface, in contrast to a spring, where the water emerges from a localized spot. (2) The process by which water passes through the soil.

**Sessile**   An organism that is attached to an object or is fixed in place, e.g., barnacles.

**Spring**   A concentrated flow of groundwater rising from an opening in the ground surface.

**Stomata**   Small or microscopic openings found on the surface layer (epidermis) of cells of plant leaves or stems, through which gas exchange occurs with the surrounding environment.

**Substrate**   The base or substance on which an organism is growing.

**Thermocline**   A layer in a thermally stratified body of water within which the temperature decreases rapidly with increasing depth, usually at a rate greater than 12° Celsius per meter of depth.

**Transpiration**   The loss of water in vapor form from a plant, mostly through the stomata and lenticels.

**Tussocks**   A plant form that is tufted, bearing many stems, arising as a large, dense cluster from the crown, e.g., *Carex stricta*, uptight sedge.

**Vernal pool**   A temporary pond that exists only during the wet season of spring and dries up later, in the growing season.

**Zooplankton**   Plankton that is composed of tiny animals and animal matter such as eggs, larvae, and other immature stages of insects and crustaceans.

# Bibliography and References

Amos, W. H. 1967. *The Life of the Pond*. New York: McGraw-Hill.

Andrews, W. A. 1972. *Freshwater Ecology*. Englewood Cliffs, NJ: Prentice-Hall.

Anonymous. 1988a. "Building the Links at Spanish Bay." *Landscape Management* 27(1): 58–60.

Anonymous. 1988b. "The Making of a Great Course." *Landscape Management* 27(1): 44–48.

Anonymous. 1988c. "A Peaceful Co-existence: Bonita Bay Golf Course." *Grounds Maintenance* 23(2): 110–111.

Anonymous. 1990a. "Permit Problems Getting Serious, Say Architects." *Florida Green* (summer): 16–18.

Anonymous. 1990b. "Survey Indicates Environmental Standardization Needed." *Golf and Sportsturf* 6(7): 7.

Bailey, C. A. 1985. "Planting of Sanctuary Marsh (Ohio)." *Restoration and Management Notes*. 3(1): 53–54.

Balogh, J. C., and W. J. Walker, eds. 1992. *Golf Course Management and Construction*. Boca Raton: Lewis Publishers.

Beecher, W. J. 1942. *Nesting Birds and Vegetative Substrate*. Chicago: Chicago Ornithological Society.

Bossenmaier, E. F., and W. H. Marshall. 1958. *Field-feeding by Waterfowl in Southwestern Manitoba*. Wildlife Monograph 1. Wildlife Society.

Caduto, M. J. 1990. *Pond and Brook: A Guide to Nature in Freshwater Environments*. Hanover: University Press of New England.

Chabreck, R. H., J. E. Holcombe, R. G. Linscombe, and N. E. Kinler. 1982. "Winter foods of River Otters from Saline and Fresh Environments in Louisiana." *Proceedings of the Annual Conference of the South East Association of Fish and Wildlife Agencies* 36: 1–20.

Coker, R. E. 1968. *Streams, Lakes, Ponds*. New York: Harper & Row.

Cowardin, L. M., V. Carter, F. G. Golet, and E. T. LaRoe. 1979. *Classification of Wetlands and Deep Water Habitats of the United States.* Washington, DC: U.S. Fish and Wildlife Service Publication FWS/OBS-79/31.

Credland, P., and G. Stranding. 1976. *The Living Waters: Life in Lakes, Rivers, and Seas.* New York: Doubleday.

Dye, P. 1989. "Golf Course Architects Adapt to Environmental Challenges." *SportsTURF* 5(5): 29.

Ernst, C. H., and R. W. Barbour. 1972. *Turtles of the United States.* Lexington, KY: University Press of Kentucky.

Forney, J. L. 1968. "Production of Young Northern Pike in a Regulated Marsh." *New York Fish and Game* 15: 143-154.

Frayer, W. E., et al. 1983. *Status and Trends of Wetlands and Deep Water Habitats of the Conterminous United States.* Washington, DC: United States Fish and Wildlife Service.

Gasaway, R. D., and T. F. Drda. 1977. "Effects of Grass Carp Introduction on Waterfowl Habitat." *Transactions of the North American Wildlife and Natural Resources Conference* 42: 73-85.

Gibbons, J. Whitefield. 2001. *Enhancing Amphibian and Reptile Biodiversity on Golf Courses Through Use of Seasonal Wetlands.* USGA 2001 Turfgrass and Environmental Research Summary. Far Hills, NJ: United States Golf Association.

Glattstein, J. 1994. *Waterscaping: Plants and Ideas for Natural and Created Water Gardens.* Pownal, VT: Storey Communications.

Goldman, C. R., and A. J. Horne. 1983. *Limnology.* New York: McGraw-Hill.

Golet, F. C., and J. S. Larsen. 1974. *Classification of Freshwater Wetlands in the Glaciated Northeast.* Washington, DC: U.S. Fish and Wildlife Service. Resource Publication 116.

Good, R. E., D. F. Whigham, and R. L. Simpson, eds. 1978. *Freshwater Wetlands: Ecological Processes and Management Potential.* New York: Academic Press.

Gore, A. J. P. 1983a. "Mires: Swamp, Bog, Fen, and Moor." In *Ecosystems of the World.* Vol. 4A. General studies, ed. New York: Elsevier Scientific Publishing.

Gore, A. J. P. 1983b. "Mires: Swamp, Bog, Fen, and Moor." In *Ecosystems of the World.* Vol. 4B. Regional studies, ed. New York: Elsevier Scientific Publishing.

Greeson, P. E., J. R. Clark, and J. E. Clark. 1979. *Wetland Functions and Values: The State of Our Understanding.* Minneapolis: American Water Resources Association.

Grue, C. E., W. J. Fleming, D. G. Busby, and E. F. Hill. 1983. "Assessing Hazards of Organophosphate Pesticides to Wildlife. In *Transactions of the 48th North American Wildlife and Natural Resources Conference,* edited by

Hammer, D. A., ed. 1989. *Constructed Wetlands for Wastewater Treatment: Municipal, Industrial and Agricultural.* Chelsea: Lewis Publishers.

Harker, D., G. Libby, K. Harker, S. Evans, and M. Evans. 1999. *Landscape Restoration Handbook,* 2nd ed. Boca Raton, FL: Lewis Publishers.

Hasler, A. D. 1969. "Cultural Eutrophication is Reversible." *Bioscience* 19: 425–431.

Hotchkiss, N. 1972. *Common Marsh, Underwater and Floating-Leaved Plants of the United States and Canada.* New York: Dover Publications.

Hutchins, R. E. 1966. *Insects.* Englewood Cliffs, NJ: Prentice-Hall.

Hynes, H. B. N. 1970. *The Ecology of Running Waters.* Liverpool, U.K.: Liverpool University Press.

Jones, P. 1988. "Innovative Construction: A model of Cooperation." *Golf Course Management* 56(11): 6–16.

Jones, R. T., Jr. 1989. "A Challenging Environmental Issue: Use of Wetlands in Golf Course Design. *Golf Course Management* 57(7): 6–16.

Kadlec, R. H., and J. A. Kadlec. 1979. "Wetlands and Water Quality." In *Wetland Functions and Values: The State of Our Understanding*, edited by P. E. Greeson, J. R. Clark, and J. E. Clark. Minneapolis: American Water Resources Association.

Kelting, R. W., and W. T. Penfound. 1950. "The Vegetation of Stock Pond Dams in Central Oklahoma." *American Midland Naturalist* 44: 69–75.

King, D. R., and G. S. Hunt. 1967. "Effect of Carp on Vegetation in a Lake Erie Marsh." *Journal of Wildlife Management* 31: 181–188.

Klein, R. D. 1990. *Protecting the Aquatic Environment from the Effects of Golf Courses.* Maryland Line, MD: Community and Environmental Defense Associates.

Kleinert, S. J. 1970. *Production of Northern Pike in a Managed Marsh.* Lake Ripley: Wisconsin Department of Natural Resources. Report 49.

Klots, E. B. 1966. *The New Fieldbook of Freshwater Life.* New York: G. P. Putnam's Sons.

Knighton, M. D., ed. *Water Impoundments for Wildlife: A Habitat Management Workshop.* St. Paul, MN: U.S. Forest Service North Central Forest Experiment Station. Technical Report NC-100.

Koskimies, J. 1957. "Terns and Gulls as Features of Habitat Recognition for Birds Nesting in Their Colonies." *Ornis Fennica* 34: 1–6.

Krapu, G. L. 1974. "Feeding Ecology of Pintail Hens during Reproduction." *Auk* 91: 278–290.

Krapu, G. L., and H. F. Duebbert. 1974. "A Biological Survey of Kraft Slough." *Prairie Naturalist* 6: 33–55.

Krapu, G. L., and K. J. Reinecke. 1992. Foraging Ecology and Nutrition." In *Ecology and Management of Breeding Waterfowl*, edited by B. D. J. Batt et al. Minneapolis: University of Minnesota Press.

Kusler, J. A. 1979. *Strengthening State Wetland Regulation.* Washington, DC: U.S. Fish and Wildlife Service Publication FWS/OBS-79/98.

Kusler, J. A., and Kentula, M. E., eds. 1990. *Wetland Creation and Restoration: The Status of the Science.* Covelo, CA: Island Press.

Larsen, J. A. 1982. *Ecology of Northern Lowland Bogs and Conifer Forests.* New York: Academic Press.

Lingle, G. R., and N. F. Sloan. 1980. "Food Habits of White Pelicans during 1976 and 1977 at Chase Lake National Wildlife Refuge, North Dakota." *Wilson Bulletin* 92: 123–125.

Livingston, R. J., and O. L. Loucks. 1979. "Productivity, Trophic Interactions, and Food Web Relationships in Wetlands and Associated Systems." In *Wetland Functions and Values: The State of Our Understanding*, edited by P E. Greeson, J. R. Clark, and J. E. Clark. Minneapolis: American Water Resources Association.

Lokemoen, J. T., and R. O. Woodward. 1992. "Nesting Waterfowl and Water Birds on Natural Islands in the Dakotas and Montana." *Wildlife Society Bulletin* 20: 163–171.

Mackey, D. 1987. "Golf Course Design Maximizes Grass Potential." *Seed World* 125(12): 71–71.

Madhun, Y. A., and V. H. Freed. 1990. "Impact of Pesticides on the Environment." In *Pesticides in the Soil Environment: Processes, Impacts, and Modeling*, edited by H. H. Cheng. Madison, WI: Soil Science Society of America. Book Series No. 2.

Maffei, E. J. 1978. Golf Course as Wildlife Habitat. *Transactions of the Northeast Section of the Wildlife Society* 35: 120–129.

Magee, D. W. 1981. *Freshwater Wetlands: A Guide to Common Indicator Plants of the Northeast*. Amherst: University of Massachusetts Press.

Mathiak, H. 1965. *Pothole Blasting for Wildlife*. Madison: Wisconsin Conservation Department. Publication 352.

Meeks, G., and L. C. Runyon. 1990. "Wetlands Protection and the States." National Conference of State Legislatures, Denver, CO, 26p.

Mitsch, W. J., and Gosselink, J. G. 1993. *Wetlands*. New York: Van Nostrand Reinhold.

Moore, P. D., and D. J. Bellamy. 1974. *Peatlands*. New York: Springer-Verlag.

National Research Council. 1992. *Restoration of Aquatic Ecosystems*. Washington, DC: National Academy Press.

Niering, W. A. 1966. *The Life of the Marsh: The North American Wetlands*. New York: McGraw-Hill.

Odum, E. P. 1971. *Fundamentals of Ecology*. Philadelphia: W. B. Saunders.

Ortega, B., R. B. Hamilton, and R. E. Noble. 1976. "Bird Usage by Habitat Types in a Large Freshwater Lake." *Proceedings of the South East Fish and Game Conference* 13: 627–633.

Peacock, C. H., A. H. Bruneau, and S. P. Spak. 1990. "Protecting a Valuable Resource: Preservation of Wetlands from a Technical Perspective." *Golf Course Management* 58(11): 6–16.

Pennak, R. W. 1978. *Freshwater Invertebrates of the United States*. New York: John Wiley & Sons, Inc.

Pennak, R. W., and E. D. Van Gerpen. 1947. "Bottom Fauna Production and Physical Nature of a Substrate in a Northern Colorado Trout Stream." *Ecology* 28: 42–48.

Perterka, J. J. 1989. "Fishes in Northern Prairie Wetlands." In *Northern Prairie Wetlands*, edited by A. G. van der Valk. Ames: Iowa State University Press.

Prescott, G. W. 1969. *How to Know the Aquatic Plants*. Dubuque, IA: William C. Brown.

Reichholf, J. 1976. "The Possible Use of the Aquatic Bird Communities as Indicators for the Ecological Conditions of Wetlands." *Landschaft Stadt* 8: 125–129.

Reid, G. K. 1961. *Ecology of Inland Waters and Estuaries*. New York: D. Van Nostrand.

Reid, G. K., and H. S. Zim. 1967. *Pond Life*. New York: Golden Press.

Robel, R. J. 1962. "Changes in Submersed Vegetation Following a Change in Water Level." *Journal of Wildlife Management* 26: 221–224.

Salvesen, D. 1990. *Wetlands: Mitigating and Regulating Development Impacts*. Washington, DC: The Urban Land Institute.

Scott, J. 1992. *Field and Forest: A Guide to Native Landscapes for Gardeners and Naturalists*. New York: Walker and Co.

Selcraig, B. 1993. "Green Fees." *Sierra* (July/August): 71–77, 86–87.

Shaw, S. P., and C. G. Fredine. 1956. *Wetlands of the United States*. Washington, DC: Government Printing Office. U.S. Fish and Wildlife Circular 39.

Smith, R. L. 1966. *Ecology and Field Biology*. New York: Harper & Row.

Stone, W. B. 1979. "Poisoning of Wild Birds by Organophosphate and Carbamate Pesticides." *New York Fish and Game Journal* 26(1): 37–47.

Stone, W. B., and P. B. Gradoni. 1985. "Recent Poisonings of Wild Birds by Diazinon and Carbofuran." *Northeastern Environmental Science* 4(3/4): 160–164.

Stone, W. B., and H. Knoch. 1982. "American Brant Killed on Golf Courses by Diazinon." *New York Fish and Game Journal* 29(2): 95–96.

Strohmeyer, D. L., and L. H. Fredrickson. 1967. "An Evaluation of Dynamited Potholes in Northwest Iowa." *Journal of Wildlife Management* 31: 525–532.

Temple, T. 1983. "The Marsh Makers of St. Michael's." *EPA Journal* 9(2): 9–12.

Tietge, R. M. 1992. "Wildlife and golf courses." In *Golf Course Management and Construction*, edited by J. C. Balogh and W. J. Walker. Boca Raton: Lewis Publishers.

Tiner, R. W., Jr. 1984. *Wetlands of the United States: Current Status and Recent Trends*. Washington, DC: U.S. Department of the Interior Fish and Wildlife Service.

Usinger, R. L. 1967. *The Life of Rivers and Streams*. New York: McGraw-Hill.

Vermeer, K. 1968. "Ecological Aspects of Ducks Nesting in High Densities among Larids." *Wilson Bulletin* 80: 78–83.

Verry, E. S. 1985. "Selection of Water Impoundment Sites in the Lake States." In *Water Impoundments for Wildlife: A Habitat Management Workshop*, edited by M. D. Knighton, 31–38. St. Paul, MN: United States Forest Service. North Central Forest Experiment Station Technical Report NC-100. 136 pages.

Want, W. L. 1990. *Law of Wetlands Regulation* (release #1/7/90). New York: Clark-Boardman Company, Ltd.

Weller, M. W. 1972. "Ecological Studies of Falkland Islands' Waterfowl." *Wildfowl* 23: 25–44.

Weller, M. W. 1978a. "Management of Freshwater Marshes for Wildlife." In *Freshwater Wetlands, Ecological Processes and Management Potential,* edited by R. E. Good, D. D. Whigham, and R. L. Simpson. New York: Academic Press.

Weller, M. W. 1994. *Freshwater Marshes.* Minneapolis: University of Minnesota Press.

Weller, M. W., and L. H. Frederickson. 1974. "Avian Ecology of a Managed Glacial Marsh." *The Living Bird* 12: 269–291.

Weller, M. W., and C. E. Spatcher. 1965. *Role of Habitat in the Distribution and Abundance of Marsh Birds.* Iowa State University Agriculture and Home Economics Experiment Station. Special Report No. 43.

Wetzel, R. G. 1975. *Limnology.* Philadelphia: Saunders.

Wharton, C. H. 1970. *Southern River Swamp: A Multiple Use Environment.* Atlanta: School of Business Administration, Georgia State University.

White, D. H., K. A. King, C. A. Mitchell, E. F. Hill, and T. G. Lamont. 1979. "Parathion Causes Secondary Poisoning in a Laughing Gull Breeding Colony." *Bulletin of Environmental Contamination and Toxicology* 23: 281–284.

Wilson, W. H. W. 1984. *Landscaping with Wildflowers and Native Plants.* San Ramon: Ortho Books.

Wolf, R. B., L. C. Lee, and R. R. Sharitz. 1986. "Wetland Creation and Restoration in the United States from 1970 to 1985: An Annotated Bibliography." Special issue. *Wetlands* 6(1): 1–88.

Zinkl, J. G., J. Rathert, and R. R. Hudson. 1978. "Diazinon Poisoning in Wild Canada Geese." *Journal of Wildlife Management* 43(2): 406–408.

Zinn, J. A., and C. Copeland. 1982. *Wetland Management.* Washington, DC: Congressional Research Service, The Library of Congress. 149 pp.

# About the Authors

Gary Libby, ecologist with EcoTech, Inc., of Frankfort, Kentucky, received his B.A. in biology from Berea College, Berea, Kentucky, and is completing a M.S. in biology and applied ecology at Eastern Kentucky University, Richmond, Kentucky. Gary worked as a botanist with the Kentucky State Nature Preserves Commission for two years.

Donald Harker is president and co-founder of Communities by Choice, an organization dedicated to sustainable community development. Don received his B.S. in biology from Austin Peay State University, Clarksville, Tennessee, and his M.S. degree in biology from the University of Notre Dame, South Bend, Indiana, where he studied "killer" bees in Brazil.

Don has been a naturalist, farmer, and environmental consultant. He spent over ten years in Kentucky state government as Director of the Kentucky Division of Water, and Director of the Kentucky Division of Waste Management. Don's consulting and research have taken him to Alaska, Mexico, Venezuela, Ecuador, Brazil, Costa Rica, Bahamas, and throughout the United States.

Kay Harker, manager of the Planning and Program Coordination branch of the Kentucky Department for Environmental Protection, received her B.S. and M.S. degrees in biology from Austin Peay State University, Clarksville, Tennessee, and has completed all the course work toward a Ph.D. in biology at the University of Kentucky, Lexington, Kentucky.

Since 1985, Kay has worked for the Kentucky Department for Environmental Protection on solid waste, hazardous waste, and water issues. Kay has also been a naturalist, college teacher, and high school teacher. She is an avid gardener.

Jean MacKay serves as the director of education services for Audubon International, a not-for-profit, 501(c) (3), environmental education organization located in Selkirk, New York. Audubon International works to educate, assist, and inspire millions of people from all walks of life to protect and sustain the land, water, wildlife, and natural resources around them. Since 1991, thousands of golf courses throughout the United States and in more than two dozen countries worldwide have been enrolled in Audubon International's Cooperative Sanctuary Program for Golf Courses and Audubon Signature Program for sites undergoing development.

# Index

ACE, *see* U.S. Army Corps of Engineers
Acidity, 96, 139
Acorns, 42
Aerobic, 97, 183
Aesthetics, 5–7, 22, 40, 73, 87, 88
Aggradation, 53
Alabama, 178
Alaska, 178
Alder flies, 78
Alders, 30, 128, 133, 134
Algae. *See also* Plankton
  classification of, 159, 160
  and fertilizers, 111–112
  in flowing-water systems, 72, 77
  in lakes/ponds, 95–97, 99, 101
  and snails, 59
  and vegetation zones, 30
Algal bloom, 89
Alligators, 117, 128
Allochthonous, 183
Alpine Country Club (Demarest, New
  Jersey), 127
Amana (Iowa), 114
Amana Colonies Golf Course (Amana,
  Iowa), 114
American bitterns, 101, 115
American coots, 101
American goldfinch, 79
American toads, 115
American white water lily, 30, 110
Amphibians:
  classification of, 160, 164
  conservation of, 102–103
  habitat for, 148
  introduction of, 111
  in lakes/ponds, 101–103
  in marshes/wet meadows, 117
Anaerobic, 97, 183
Angiosperms, 159–162
Animals:
  bog, 139–140

classification system for, 159–160
  estuarial, 66–67
  forested-wetland, 128–129
  in lakes/ponds, 99–104
  lotic, 77–79
  in marshes/wet meadows, 114–118
  shrub-wetland, 135
Annelid worms, 100
Appalachian region:
  bog plants for, 141
  flowing-water plants for, 80–81
  forested-wetland plants for, 130–131
  lake and pond plants for, 106–107
  marsh/wet meadow plants for,
    121–122
  shrub-wetland plants for, 136
Aquatic beetles, 117
Aquatic sow bugs, 104, 118
Aquifers, 4
Arborvitae, 133
Arrowheads, 19, 57, 104, 113
Arthropods, 159, 162–163. *See also*
  Crustaceans; Insects
Articulated concrete, 80
Ash (tree), 20, 30
Aspen Golf Club (Carbondale, Colorado),
  73
Association of State Wetland Managers,
  169
Atlantic coast, 7, 69
Atlantic white cedar, 139
Attached algae, *see* Periphyton
Audubon Cooperative Sanctuary
  Program, 5, 18, 28
Audubon International, 32, 48, 146, 153,
  169
Audubon Signature Program, 19, 33, 38,
  44, 48, 52, 54
Aurora (Colorado), 119, 152
Autochthonous, 183
Awareness, staff and golfer, 157

Back swimmers, 78, 101, 117
Bacteria, 118, 139, 159, 160
Balance, 27
Bald cypress, 30, 128, 129
Bald eagles, 21, 48, 101
Bank stabilization, 8, 42, 45
    pond, 90–92, 112
    stream, 79–80, 86–88
Bare root seedlings/saplings, 42, 134, 138
Barred owls, 128
Barrier beaches, 62
Basins, 183
Bass, 101, 111, 117
Bats, 43, 110
Bat houses, 27, 43, 110–111
Bays, 93, 118
Bayberry, 66
Beach Protection Act (Delaware), 178
Bear, 128
Beauty, 5
Beavers, 59, 116, 119
Bedrock, 72, 77, 78
Bee balm, 73, 79
Beetles, 104, 110, 117
Belted kingfishers, 101
Benches, 40
Benthic organisms, 65, 78, 97, 98, 100,
    183
Benthos, 98, 183
Berlin (Maryland), 62
Berms, 42, 49–51, 135
Best management practices (BMPs), 48
Big Canoe (Georgia), 14
Big Canoe Golf Course (Big Canoe,
    Georgia), 14
Big cord grass, 68
Biodiversity, 5, 11, 183
Bioengineering, 79–80
Biological control agents, 125
Birch, 79
Birds:
    in bogs, 139–140
    classification of, 160, 165–167
    enhancement of habitats for, 22
    in lakes/ponds, 94, 101
    in marshes/wet meadows, 114–117
Bitterns, 101, 115, 117
Blackberry Patch Golf Course (Coldwater,
    Michigan), 17
Blackbirds, 115, 116
Black ducks, 101, 139
Black gum, 129
Black Lake Golf (Onaway, Michigan), 28
Blacklick Woods Golf Course
    (Reynoldsburg, Ohio), 8

Black needle rush, 66, 68
Black rush, 89
Black spruce, 139
Black willow, 40
Bladderwort, 30, 110
Blasting, 118
Bloodworm, 100
Bloom, algal, 89
Blue crab, 67
Bluegill, 111
Blue-green algae, 72, 96, 101
Blue-winged teal, 115
BMPs (best management practices), 48
Boardwalks, 17, 105, 113, 150, 151
Bog laurel, 139
Bog rosemary, 139
Bogs, 11, 138–144
    physical characteristics of, 138–139
    plants/animals in, 139–140
    plants by region for, 140–143
    restoration/management of, 140
Bolivia (North Carolina), 10
Bonita Bay Group, 54, 56, 57
Botanical gardens, 45
Bottomland hardwood forests, 10, 72. *See
    also* Forested wetlands
Box elder, 79
Brackish water, 62, 63, 183
Branch packing, 80
Brazilian pepper, 55–57
Breeding grounds, 128, 148
Bridges, 22, 73
Broad-leaf cattail, 110
Bromeliads, 129, 183
Brook salamanders, 78
Brookside alder, 30
Brook sticklebacks, 117
Brush mattresses, 80
Bryozoans, *see* Moss animals
Buckbean, 139
Buckthorn, 23
Buffer areas, 15, 18–19, 27
    and flowing-water systems, 73, 79
    illustrations of, 28, 44
    and lakes/ponds, 92, 112
    reasons for using, 34, 43
    at Sand Ridge Golf Club, 23, 24
    for sedimentation control, 53
Bullfrog, 117
Bullheads, 101, 117
Bulrushes, 15, 19, 30, 57, 110
Burning, 40, 53
Burrowing crayfish, 95, 104
Bush honeysuckles, 85
Butterfield Creek, 86–87

Butterflies, 118
Buttonbush, 30, 40, 57, 86, 110, 128, 134
Buttresses, 126, 128

Cabbage palm, 54
Caddis flies, 78, 117, 139
Caesar weed, 55
California, 5–7, 38, 69, 95, 178
Canada geese, 59, 109, 115
Canopy, 129
Carbondale (Colorado), 73
Carbon dioxide, 112, 138
Cardinals, 79
Cardinal flower, 23, 79, 118
Carnivorous plants, 139
Carolina fanwort, 30
Carolina National Golf Club (Bolivia, North Carolina), 10
Carp, 78, 93, 112, 117, 125
Cart paths, 17, 46, 52
Catfish, 78, 101
Cattails, 9, 15, 30, 40
    in estuaries, 66
    illustration of, 44
    in lakes/ponds, 101, 104, 105, 110
    in marshes/wet meadows, 113–115
Cavity-nesting birds, 134
Cedars, 128, 139
Cedar waxwings, 79, 101, 139
Central Plains region:
    bog plants for, 142
    flowing-water plants for, 82–83
    forested-wetland plants for, 132
    lake and pond plants for, 108
    marsh/wet meadow plants for, 123
    shrub-wetland plants for, 137
Certification process, 176
Chagrin River, 21
Chagrin River Land Conservancy, 22
Chairmaker's bulrush, 30
Chardon (Ohio), 20, 126
Check dams, 135
Chemical drift, 73
Chesapeake Bay Critical Area Act (Maryland), 178, 180
Chesapeake Bay Preservation Act (Virginia), 179
Cinnamon fern, 135
Cladocerans, 100
Clams, 67, 77, 100, 104, 112, 115, 118
Clam shrimp, 104
Clapper rail, 67
Clarity of water, 112
Classification of Wetlands and Deep Water Habitats of the United States, 179

Classification system for organisms, 159–160
Clay subsoil, 42
Clean Water Act, 25, 175
Climbing hemp vine, 55
Closed gentian, 20
The Club at Mediterra (Florida), 54–58
The Club at Seabrook Island (Johns Island, South Carolina), 147
Clubhouses, 151
Coastal salt grass, 65, 66, 68
Coastal Wetland Planning, Protection and Restoration Act (Louisiana), 178
Coastal Wetlands Protection Act (Mississippi), 178
Coastal Zone Act (Delaware), 178
Coastal Zone Management Act (federal), 179
Coastal Zone Management Act (Florida), 178
Coconut (coir) fiber mats, 71, 85, 86
Coldwater (Michigan), 17
Colony nesters, 115
Color, soil, 16
Colorado, 44, 73, 119, 152
Columbia River basin, 69
Common bladderwort, 110
Common buttonbush, 128, 134
Common mergansers, 101
Common reed, 23, 53, 71, 109
Common yellowthroat, 139
Compensation depth, 183
Compost, 57, 91
Comprehensive Land Use Planning Coordination Act (Oregon), 180
Concrete, articulated, 80
Cone-bearing plants, see Gymnosperms
Connecticut, 178, 180
The Conservation Fund, 169
Conservation of wetlands, 13–34
    and adjacent areas, 31–34
    buffers for, 18–19
    and delineation of wetlands, 16
    on golf courses, 20, 23–25, 27–29
    and identification of wetlands, 14–15
    with natural landscaping, 27–29
    and permits, 25, 26
    and protection of wetlands, 15, 17
    SRGC case study of, 20–23
    and transitions, 31–34
    vegetation zones in, 29–31
Consultants, 45
Container-grown stock, 42
Contaminants, 17
Controlled burn, 53

Convection currents, 88–89
Coontail, 30, 110
Coots, 30, 101, 115
Copepods, 101, 104, 118
Copper-based wood preservative, 105
Cord grass, 57, 66, 68
Cornelias (Oregon), 46
Corridors, 27, 54, 148–149
    for amphibians, 103
    rivers/streams as, 34, 88
    wetland-upland, 23, 32–33
Cost:
    of exotic-species removal, 58
    of SRGC wetland creation, 23
Cottonwood, 40
Country Club of Virginia (Richmond), 3
County extension agents, 45
Cover, 103, 120
Cover-to-water ratio, 120
Crabs, 67, 116
Cranberries, 11, 139
Crane flies, 117
Crayfish, 115, 116, 118
Creating wetlands, *see* Wetland restoration
Creeks, 7–9. *See also* Flowing-water systems
Crocodiles, 128
Crowfoot, 110
Crustaceans, 65, 77, 99, 100, 104, 117
Cultural eutrophication, 96
Currents, 7–8
    convection, 88–89
    ocean, 62
    stream, 74, 78
    tidal, 66
Cuticle, 99
Cutting, selective, 85
Cuttings, 138
Cuyahoga River, 21
Cyclops, 118
Cypress, 2, 30, 48, 54, 57, 128, 129

Dabbling ducks, 101, 115, 116
Dahoon holly, 57
Dams:
    beaver, 59
    check, 135
    man-made, 93, 118
Damselflies, 78, 101, 117
Daphnia, 118
Daylilies, 73
Dead timber, 29, 43, 85, 88, 105, 109, 128, 134
Decaying organic matter, 72, 78, 113
Decomposed plant material, 16

Decomposers, 96, 97, 183
Decomposition, 88, 139
Deed restrictions, 17
Deep-water swamp forests, 10
Deer, 59, 94, 109, 115, 128, 135, 139
Degradation, 53
Delaware, 178, 180
Delineation of wetlands, 16, 175–176
Demarest (New Jersey), 127
Depressions, 64–65, 128
Depth:
    of light penetration, 97
    planting, 109, 110
    of water, 43, 119
    of water level, 31
Deserts:
    flowing-water plants for, 82–83
    forested-wetland plants for, 132
    lake and pond plants for, 108
    marsh/wet meadow plants for, 123
    shrub-wetland plants for, 137
Desmid, 99, 183
Detritus feeders, 78, 100
Diamondback terrapin, 67
Diatoms, 30, 72, 99, 101, 184
Dillsburg (Pennsylvania), 73
Dinelli, F. Dan, 90
Dinoflagellates, 159, 160
Dipper, 78
Diptera, 78
Displays, 41, 62, 93, 151
Disturbance:
    by golfers/maintenance, 148
    and nuisance vegetation, 56
    and phragmite, 71
Diversity, 40, 184
    of birds, 51
    enhancement of, 22
    in estuaries, 71
    exotic species' effect on, 56
    in lakes/ponds, 96, 97
    muck resulting in, 57
    of plants, 31
    of plants and animals, 29
    of species, 147, 148
    and wet meadows, 114, 125
Diving beetles, 78, 101, 117
Diving birds, 101
Diving ducks, 116
Dobsons, 78
Dog fennel, 55
Dogwoods, 104, 135
Downy rose myrtle, 55
Draglines, 112, 118
Dragonflies, 78, 94, 101, 117

Drainage, 11, 138
Dredged material, 176
Drift, 73
Drinking water, 97
Duck boxes, 27, 43
Duck potato, 110
Ducks, 30, 40, 94
    bog, 139
    dabbling, 101, 115, 116
    diving, 116
    forested-wetland, 128
    in marshes/wet meadows, 114–116, 120
    ring-necked, 101, 139
    ruddy, 101
    sea, 115
    wood, 40, 43, 78, 101, 127
Ducks Unlimited, 39, 41, 169
Duckweed, 30, 78, 113
Dusky salamanders, 78
Dwarf saltwater cord grass, 65, 66
Dystrophic lakes, 96, 184
Dystrophication, 96

Eagles, 21, 48, 101
Eagle's Landing Golf Course (Berlin, Maryland), 62
Eared grebes, 115
Easements, 17, 22, 48
Eastern bluebird, 79
Eastern painted turtles, 101
"Eat outs," 104, 119
Eco-Park, 48
Ecotones, 23, 30–31, 184
Education, 149, 150
Eelgrass, 99
Effluent, 72
Efts, 101
Eggs, 104, 111, 139
Egrets, 40, 67, 101, 115
Eiders, 115
Elderberry, 79, 135
Electric fences, 59
Elevation, 57, 66, 68, 128
Elm, 128
Emergent plants, 29–31
    in lakes/ponds, 98, 101, 105
    in marshes/wet meadows, 113, 115
Energy, 72, 99
Engineered watercourses, 79
Envirolink—Environmental Resources, 169
Environmental education and certification programs, 146
Environmental Law Institute, 169

"Environmentally Sensitive Area" designations, 148
Environmental management planning, 151–157
Environmental Protection Agency, 15
Environmental Stewardship Program (Michigan), 153
Epilimnion, 98, 184
Epiphytes, 129, 184
Erosion, 42, 64, 65, 68, 73, 79–80, 86, 91
Erosion control fabric, 91
Estero (Florida), 48, 49
Estuaries, 7, 62–71
    physical characteristics of, 62–65
    plants/animals of, 65–67
    plant species by region for, 69–71
    restoration/management of, 67–68
Etiquette, 151
Eubanks & Associates, Inc., 86, 87
Eurasial water milfoil, 125
Eutrophication, 31, 95, 97, 112, 120, 184
Eutrophic systems, 95–97, 117, 184
Evapotranspiration, 184
Evening grosbeak, 79
Excavation, 40
Exotic species, 17, 27
    awareness of, 45
    control of, 53–58
    and flowing-water systems, 85
    and lakes/ponds, 105, 109
    removal of, 23, 40
    streamside, 85
Explosives, 118

Facultative wetlands plants, 16
Fairy shrimp, 95, 104, 118
Fall overturn, 89, 94
Falls, 77
Farms, 175
Fascines, live, 80
Fathead minnows, 117
Fawn Lake Country Club (Spotsylvania, Virginia), 152
*Federal Manual for Identifying and Delineating Jurisdictional Wetlands*, 176
Federal subsidies, 175
Fencing, 17, 27, 40, 56, 59
Fern allies, 159, 160
Ferns, 30, 128, 135, 159, 160
Fertilizers, 4, 6, 18, 31, 111–112
Fescue, 43
Fiddler crab, 67
Filamentous green algae, 99

Fill and Dredge in Wetlands Act (New Hampshire), 180
Fill and Removal Act (Oregon), 180
Fill material, 25, 176
Filter feeders, 78
Filter strips, 18
Filter wetlands, 23
Finches, 79
Fingernail clams, 104, 118
First-order streams, 74, 76
Fish:
    bog, 139
    classification of, 160, 165
    estuarial, 65
    in flowing-water systems, 78
    in lakes/ponds, 96, 98, 99, 101
    in marshes/wet meadows, 114–117
    sources for obtaining, 59
    spawning beds for, 93
Fish and wildlife resources agencies, 45
Flatworms, 100, 104
Flies, 117
Floating-leaved plants, 30, 31, 98–99, 101, 105, 113
Flooding:
    and flowing-water systems, 4–5, 72, 74, 79
    of forested wetlands, 134
    of shrub wetlands, 134
Floodplain swamps, 129
Flood zones, 74
Florida, 4, 25, 28, 33, 48–52, 54–58, 89, 150, 178, 180
Flounder, 67
Flowering plants, *see* Angiosperms
Flowing-water systems, 4–5, 71–88
    classification of, 74, 76
    as corridors, 34
    exotic species in, 85
    features of, 75
    physical characteristics of, 71–77
    plants/animals of, 77–79
    plant species by region for, 80–85
    restoration/management of, 79–80
    stabilization of banks in, 86–88
Floyd, Raymond, 48
Flycatchers, 128
Food chains, 27, 96–97, 99, 100
Food Security Act, 175
Food web, 67
Forested bogs, 144
Forested wetlands, 9–10, 126–134
    physical characteristics of, 126–128
    plants/animals of, 128–129

plant species by region for, 129–134
    restoration/management of, 129
Fort Myers (Florida), 150
Four-spined sticklebacks, 67
Fragmentation, 32–34, 52
Free-floating plants, 30, 98, 113
Fremont cottonwood, 40
Fresh water, 7
Freshwater clams, 112
Freshwater jellyfish, 117
Freshwater mussels, 77, 78
Freshwater sponges, 117
Freshwater Wetlands Act (New York), 180
Freshwater Wetlands Act (Rhode Island), 180
Freshwater Wetlands Protection Act of 1987 (New Jersey), 180
Frogs:
    bog, 140
    introduction of, 111
    in lakes/ponds, 95, 101–104
    in marshes/wet meadows, 115, 117
    movement of, 32
    sources for obtaining, 59
Frogwatch USA, 102
Fungi, 118, 128, 159, 160

Gainesville (Virginia), 24
Garter snakes, 117
Gaylord (Michigan), 53
Geese, 30, 59, 101, 109, 114–116
Gentian, 20
Georgia, 14, 178
Giant reed, 40, 85
Giant water bugs, 117
Gillen, Dan, 26
Glaciated regions, 9, 11, 104, 140
Glassworts, 65, 66
Glattstein, J., 112
Glenview (Illinois), 90–94
Goemaer-Anderson Wetland Protection Act (Michigan), 180
Golden-crowned kinglets, 139
Goldfinches, 79
Golf courses, 145–157
    and education, 150–151
    environmental management of, 151–157
    new, 149
    roles of wetlands on, 145–146
    and wetland regulations, 25
    wetlands on existing, 147–149
Gopher tortoises, 48
Governmental resources, 170–174

Grapevine, 55
Grass carp, 93, 112, 125
Grasses, 2, 113
Gravel, 77, 78
Great blue herons, 21, 40, 101
Great egrets, 40
Great Lakes region, 178
  bog plants for, 141–142
  flowing-water plants for, 81
  forested-wetland plants for, 131
  lake and pond plants for, 107
  marsh/wet meadow plants for, 122
  shrub-wetland plants for, 136–137
Grebes, 101, 115, 116
Green algae, 72, 99
Green ash, 30
Green-backed herons, 101
Greenhead fly, 67
Grosbeak, 79
Groundsel, 66–68
Ground squirrel, 115
Groundwater, 77
Groundwater wells, 118
Gulf Coast, 7, 69
Gulls, 67
Gum, 2
Guppies, 111
Gymnosperms, 159, 160

Habitats, 1, 3, 5, 18, 184
  amphibian-breeding, 102
  and buffer areas, 18–19
  enhancement of, 21
  shrub-wetland, 11
  wildlife, 147
Hackensack meadowlands, 178
Halfway Creek, 48, 49
Halfway houses, 151
Hand weeding, 73
Hardstem bulrush, 30
Hawaii, 178
Hawks, 125
Haymaker Golf Course (Steamboat
  Springs, Colorado), 44
Heaths, 11, 184
Heavy metals, 5
Hellbenders, 78
Henderson Wetlands Protection Act of
  1984 (Florida), 180
Herbicides, 18, 85, 112
Herbs, 135
Herons, 21, 40, 67, 101, 115, 117, 128
Hickory, 52, 128
Honeybrook Golf Club (Pennsylvania), 19

Hooded mergansers, 40
Horned pondweed, 30
Humic materials, 96
Hummingbirds, 79
Hummocks, 9, 184
Hydras, 99, 101, 159, 164
Hydric soil, 15, 16, 42, 180–181, 184
Hydrilla, 125
Hydrogen sulfide, 97, 100, 139
Hydrological cycle, 2, 3
Hydrology, 15
  disturbance of, 71
  of estuaries, 68
  of forested wetlands, 129
  of lakes/ponds, 105
  of marshes/wet meadows, 118
  and restoration, 41–42
  of shrub wetlands, 135
  wetland, 15
  and wetlands delineation, 16, 175
Hydrophytes, 15, 16, 184
Hydrosphere, 185
Hypolimnion, 98, 185

Ibis, 67, 115
Ice, 94
IGM at the Habitat (Malabar, Florida), 28
Illinois, 31, 36, 86–88, 90–94
Inland Wetlands and Watercourses Act
  (Connecticut), 180
Insects:
  and bats, 110
  bog, 139
  in flowing-water systems, 77, 78
  forested-wetland, 128
  in lakes/ponds, 101, 104
  in marshes/wet meadows, 115, 125
Intermountain region:
  flowing-water plants for, 83–84
  forested-wetland plants for, 133
  lake and pond plants for, 108–109
  marsh/wet meadow plants for, 124
  shrub-wetland plants for, 138
Interpretive panels, 41
Intertidal flats, 66
Invertebrates, 159, 162–164
Iowa, 114
Iron, 16
Ironweed, 118
Irrigation, 6, 9, 21–23
"Island reserves," 147
Islands, 62, 109, 118
Isopods, 100
Izaak Walton League of America, 169

Jellyfishes, 117, 159, 164
Jewelweed, 79, 135
Joe-pye weed, 118
Johns Island (South Carolina), 147
Joint planting, 80
Jumping meadow mice, *see* Meadow jump-
    ing mice
"Jump starting," 52, 56–57
Juncos, 79
Jurisdictional wetlands, 20, 23, 24, 37, 42,
    175

Kestrels, 125
Killdeer, 101, 115
Kingbirds, 101
Kinglets, 139
Kings Beach (California), 5–7
Kiosks, 150

Labrador tea, 139
Lagoons, 62
Lake Honda, 38–41
Lakes and ponds, 9, 88–113
    aesthetics/water quality improvement
        case study of, 90–94
    and amphibian conservation, 102–103
    case study of enhancements to, 90–94
    creation of shallow, 42
    maintenance of, 112–113
    physical characteristics of, 88–97
    plants/animals of, 97–104
    plant species by region for, 105–109
Landscaping, natural, 27–29
Land Trust Alliance, 169
Larch, 139
Large-fruited burr reed, 110
Larva, 77–78, 100, 101, 115, 185
Laurel, 139
Laurie, David, 5
Leaf litter, 72
Least weasels, 116
Leatherleaf, 139
Leaves, 98–101
Lemming, 139
Lemon bacopa, 57
Lentic systems, 4, 185
Leopard frogs, 115, 117
Lesser duckweed, 30
Lesser yellowlegs, 101
Levees, 40, 118
Lichens, 128
Light, 9, 88, 96, 98
Lillifish, 67
Limited-spray zones, 18

Limnetic zones, 98, 99, 185
Littoral zones, 98–100, 185
Live cribwalls, 80
Live fascines, 80
Liverworts, 128, 159, 160
Live stakes, 80
Livestock, 27, 54
Lizard tail, 110
Long-eared owls, 128
Loons, 116
Lost Key Golf Course (Perdido Key,
    Florida), 33, 52
Lotic systems, 4–5, 72, 185
Louisiana, 116, 178
Louisiana waterthrushes, 78
Love vine, 55

Machinery, 42, 91, 118
Mackay, Jean, 32
Magnolia warbler, 140
Main channels (estuaries), 64
Maine, 178, 180
Maintenance:
    disturbance during, 148
    and exotic-species removal, 57
    of lakes and ponds, 112–113
    money reserved for, 43
Mallards, 101, 115, 116
Mammals, 160, 167
Management:
    of bogs, 140
    of estuaries, 67–68
    of flowing-water systems, 79–80
    of forested wetlands, 129
    of lakes and ponds, 104–105
    of marshes and wet meadows, 118–120
    principles of wetland, 148–149
    self-assessment checklist for, 153–157
    of shrub wetlands, 135
    wildlife, 155–156
Man-made lakes and ponds, 9, 104–105
Maples, 30, 57, 79, 128, 139
Marquis, Kraig, 48
Marshes and wet meadows, 9, 113–126
    physical characteristics of, 113
    plants/animals of, 113–118
    plant species by region for, 120–126
    restoration/management of, 118–120
Marsh elder, 66, 67
Marsh hay cord grass, 66
Marshmallow, 23
Marsh marigold, 73, 110
Marsh periwinkle, 67
Marsh wrens, 101

Maryland, 62, 178, 180
Masked shrews, 139
Massachusetts, 178, 180
Mayflies, 78, 117, 139
Meadow jumping mice, 67, 115, 116
Meanders, 68, 74, 79
Melaleuca, 54–57
Mergansers, 40, 101, 115
Mesic forests, 9, 128, 185
Mesotrophic, 96
Metalimnion, 98, 185
Mice, 115, 128, 129
Michigan, 17, 28, 53, 153, 178, 180
Microelevations, 66
Microhabitats, 30, 68, 185
Midges, 78, 100, 115, 117
Migration, 114
Milfoils, 30, 109, 110, 125
Milkweeds, 118
Mink, 104, 115–117, 139
Minnesota, 180
Minnows, 117
Mires, 11
Mississippi, 178
Mississippi River drainage system, 127
Mitigated wetlands, 152
Mitigation, 24
Mitigation agreement, 20
Mole salamanders, 78
Mollusks, 77, 104, 115, 118, 159, 163. See
    also Clams; Mussels; Snails
Monera, 159, 160
Mosquitoes, 67, 94, 99, 110, 115, 117
Mosquito ferns, 30
Mosquito fish, 111
Moss animals, 159, 164
Mosses, 128, 139, 159, 160
Moths, 110, 118
Motile organisms, 65, 185
Mountain streams, 74
Mountaintops, 11
Mowing, 18, 23, 28, 112–113
Muck, 16, 42, 56–57, 128
Mudflats, 115
Mud plantain, 110
Mud puppies, 78
Mud turtles, 101, 117
Muhly grass, 57
Mulch, 57
Mummichogs, 67
Murphy Creek Golf Course (Aurora,
    Colorado), 152
Muskegs, 11
Muskies, 78

Muskrats, 59, 104, 109, 114, 116, 119, 120
Musk turtles, 101
Muskwort, 30, 99
Mussels, 67, 77, 78, 104

NAAMP (North American Amphibian
    Monitoring Program), 102
Narrow-leaf cattail, 110
National Association of Conservation
    Districts, 169
National Audubon Society, 169
National Fish and Wildlife Foundation,
    146
National Park Service, 173
National Wetlands Center, 173
National Wetlands Policy Forum, 176
National Wildlife Federation, 169
National Wildlife Federation—Wetlands,
    169
Native plants, 23, 24, 27, 31, 43, 45
Native plant societies, 45
Natural landscaping, 27–29
Natural Resources Conservation Service
    (NRCS), 15, 39, 42, 171
Nature centers, 45
The Nature Conservancy, 45, 170
Nature trails, 40, 48
NAWCA, see North American Wetlands
    Conservation Act
Neap tides, 66, 185
Nekton, 98, 99, 185
Nesting, 115, 116
Nesting boxes, 43, 71, 127
Nesting platforms, 27, 71, 109
New England:
    bog plants for, 141–142
    flowing-water plants for, 81
    forested-wetland plants for, 131
    lake and pond plants for, 107
    marsh/wet meadow plants for, 122
    shrub-wetland plants for, 136–137
New Hampshire, 178, 180
New Jersey, 127, 178, 180
Newts, 101
New York, 179, 180
Nitrogen, 5, 89, 95, 96, 138
"No net loss," 176
No Net Wetlands Loss Bill of 1987
    (North Dakota), 180
Nongovernmental resources, 169–170
Non-native species:
    of plants, see Exotic species
    of wildlife, 59
Nonpersistent emergent plants, 30

North American Amphibian Monitoring Program (NAAMP), 102
North American Wetlands Conservation Act (NAWCA), 39, 41
North Carolina, 10, 179
North Dakota, 116, 180
Northern juncos, 79
Northern pike, 117
Northern waterthrushes, 78, 139
Northern white cedar, 128
North Lake Tahoe (California), 5
North Shore Country Club (Glenview, Illinois), 90–94
No-spray zones, 18, 73
NRCS, *see* Natural Resources Conservation Service
NRCS Wetland Science Institute, 171
Nurseries, 45
Nutria, 59, 104, 116, 119
Nutrients, 5, 27
  in bogs, 138, 139
  in flowing water, 72, 74
  in lakes/ponds, 89, 94–96, 99, 112
  seasonal levels of, 94
Nymphs, 30, 78, 105, 139, 185

Oak, 40, 48, 52, 128
Oats, 86
Obligate wetlands plants, 16
Observation decks, 113
Observation turnouts, 40–41
Odors, 16, 97
Ohio, 8, 20, 126
Old Brockway Golf Course (Kings Beach, California), 5–7
Old Marsh Golf Club (Palm Beach Gardens, Florida), 4
Oligotrophic, 96, 185
Oligotrophy, 96
Oller, Alicia, 54
Olympia Fields (Illinois), 36, 86–88
Olympia Fields Country Club (Olympia Fields, Illinois), 36, 86–88
Omnivore, 115, 185
Ooze, 114
Open space, 147
Open water zones, 21–22
Orchids, 139, 144
Oregon, 46, 69, 179, 180
Organic matter, 95
Orland Park (Illinois), 31
Osprey, 67
Ostracods, 104, 118
Otters, 116, 139

Overcup oak, 128
Overflow areas, 135
Overstory layer, 129
Oviedo (Florida), 25
Owls, 128
Oxbow wetlands, 79
Oxygen:
  in bogs, 139
  in lakes/ponds, 88, 94, 96, 97, 99, 100, 111–112
  seasonal levels of, 94
  soil, 16
  in streams, 77
Oysters, 66
Ozark region:
  bog plants for, 141
  flowing-water plants for, 80–81
  forested-wetland plants for, 130–131
  lake and pond plants for, 106–107
  marsh/wet meadow plants for, 121–122
  shrub-wetland plants for, 136

Pacific coast, 7, 69–70. *See also* West Coast region
Pacific cord grass, 66, 68
Painted turtles, 117
Palm Beach Gardens (Florida), 4
Palmetto, 128
Palm warbler, 139
Palustrine Aquatic Beds, 23
Pamphlets, 41
Panfish, 117
Pans, 64–65
Parula, 140
Peat, 11, 16, 96, 138, 185
Peat bogs, 96
Peatland, 11
Peat moss, 144
Pelicans, 117
Pelican Preserve (Fort Myers, Florida), 150
Penalties, 26
Pennsylvania, 19, 73
Perches, 43
Perdido Key (Florida), 33, 52
Periphyton, 72, 77, 100–101, 185
Permits, 15, 20, 24–26, 42, 176, 177
Persistent emergent plants, 30
Pesticides, 4, 31, 112
Phantom midges, 100
Phosphorus, 5, 89, 95, 96, 138
Photosynthesis, 30, 72, 97, 99
Phragmites, 23, 53, 71, 109
Physiognomy, 72, 74, 185

Phytoplankton, 30, 72, 96, 97, 99, 186
Phytozones, 49–51
Pickerel, 101
Pickerel frogs, 140
Pickerelweed, 19, 57, 110, 113
Piers, 113
Pike, 78, 117
Pileated woodpeckers, 128–129
Pill clams, 77
Pines, 57, 67, 128, 129
Pine flatwoods, 48, 54, 128, 129
Pine grosbeak, 79
Pine siskin, 79
Pintails, 116
Pitcher plants, 139
Plankton, 65, 78, 98, 99, 104, 117, 186
Plants, 160–162
    bog, 139–144
    classification system for, 159
    estuarial, 63–64, 66, 69–71
    forested-wetland, 128–134
    height of, 105
    in lakes/ponds, 98–99, 105–109
    lotic, 79–85
    in marshes/wet meadows, 113–114,
        118, 120–126
    removal of exotic, 55–57
    selection of, 44–53
    shrub-wetland, 135–138
    and wetlands delineation, 175–176
    wild, 144
Plantain, 110
Planting depths, 109, 110
Plateaus:
    bog plants for, 142
    flowing-water plants for, 82–83
    forested-wetland plants for, 132
    lake and pond plants for, 108
    marsh/wet meadow plants for, 123
    shrub-wetland plants for, 137
Playability, 19
Plunge pools, 112
Pollution, 120
Ponds, *see* Lakes and ponds
Pond cypress, 129
Pond holes, 64–65
Pond pine, 129
Pondweed, 30, 104
Pools, 186
    spring, 77
    stream, 72, 74, 78
Posters, 93
Potassium, 138
Pot holes, 68, 114

Prairie plugs, 86, 87
Precipitation, 8
Preservative, wood, 105
Primary production (photosynthesis), 72
Privet, 85
Problematic wildlife, 17, 59, 135
Pro shops, 7, 151
Protection of Natural Resources Act
    (Maine), 178, 180
Protozoans, 78, 99–101, 159, 164, 186
Pulmonate snail, 67
Pumpkin ash, 20
Pumpkin Ridge (Cornelias, Oregon), 46
Purple finches, 79
Purple gallinules, 101
Purple loosestrife, 85, 109, 125
Pussy willow, 135
Pytozones, 48–51

Quackgrass, 109
Quality, water, *see* Water quality

Raccoons, 67, 104, 115–117
Rails, 67, 115, 116
Rainfall, 120, 134
Rainwater, 72
Raised cart paths, 17, 46
Rakes (tools), 112
Range End Golf Course (Dillsburg,
    Pennsylvania), 73
Rapids, 72
Raptor Bay Golf Club (Estero, Florida),
    48–51
Rare species, 20, 51
Razor clam, 67
Red alder, 133
Red efts, 101
Red maple, 30, 57, 79, 128, 139
Red osier dogwood, 135
Red-spotted newts, 101
Redtop grass, 43, 91
Red-winged blackbirds, 67, 101, 115–117
Reeds, 9, 40, 66, 71, 85, 109, 110
Reed canary grass, 109
Reefs, 66
Regulations, 25, 26
Regulatory issues, 175–181
Repellents, 59
Reproduction, 32
Reptiles, 117, 148, 160, 165
Reservoirs, 9
Resources, wetland, 169–174
Respiration, 97
Restoring wetlands, *see* Wetland restoration

Reynoldsburg (Ohio), 8
Rheotropism, 186
Rhizopods, 100
Rhode Island, 179, 180
Ribbed mussel, 67
Ribbon grass, 73
Rice cut-grass, 30
Richardson, Nancy, 38
Richmond (Virginia), 3
Richness, 100, 186
Riffles, 72, 74, 77, 78, 186
Rill erosion, 186
Ring-necked ducks, 101, 139
Riparian forests, 40, 72, 84–85
Riparian zones, 74
Riprap, 80
Rivers, 7–9. *See also* Flowing-water systems
River bulrush, 30
River-scouring rush, 110
Riverweed, 30, 99
Robert Trent Jones Golf Club
    (Gainesville, Virginia), 24
Robins, 79, 116
Rock outcroppings, 93
Rocky Mountains region:
    bog plants for, 142–143
    flowing-water plants for, 83
    forested-wetland plants for, 132–133
    lake and pond plants for, 108
    marsh/wet meadow plants for, 123–124
    shrub-wetland plants for, 137
Roosting boxes, 43
Roots, 5, 30, 98–99, 126, 128
Roped boundaries, 27, 148
Rose mallow, 66
Rosemary, 139
Rotifers, 101, 159, 164
Rotten-spot pans, 65
Routing plans, 32
Royal fern, 135
Rubble, 77, 78
Ruddy ducks, 101
Runoff, 3, 4, 28
    and buffer areas, 18
    and forested wetlands, 134
    from irrigation, 9
    lotic system, 5
    from pesticides, 73
    and stream levels, 8
    and water quality, 49, 51
Rushes, 2, 9, 45, 57, 66, 68, 89, 110, 113
Rye, 43

Saddle Rock Golf Course (Aurora,
    Colorado), 119

"Safety shelves," 93
Safeway (store), 5, 7
Sago pondweed, 30
Salamanders:
    in flowing-water systems, 78
    introduction of, 111
    in lakes/ponds, 95, 102–104
    in marshes/wet meadows, 117
    movement of, 32
Salinity:
    estuarial, 62–71
    gradient of, 65
    seasonal, 63
    vertical, 63
Salmon, 96
Saltmarsh mosquito, 67
Salt-meadow cord grass, 68
Salt water, 7
Saltwater cord grass, 66, 68
Salt wedge, 64
Saltwort, 68
Sanctuary Golf Course (Sanibel Island,
    Florida), 89
Sandhill cranes, 4
Sandpipers, 78, 101
Sand Ridge Golf Club (SRGC) (Chardon,
    Ohio), 20–23, 126
Sanibel Island (Florida), 89
San Joaquin Valley, 95
Saturation, 2, 15, 41
Scientific names of organisms, 159–167
Scout troops, 152
Screech owls, 128
Scuds, 104, 118
Sea blite, 66
Sea ducks, 115
Sea lavender, 65, 66
Seaside sparrow, 67
Seasons, 148
    and estuaries, 63, 66
    and forested wetlands, 127, 128
    and lakes/ponds, 88–89, 94–95, 104
    and marshes/wet meadows, 9, 116
    and runoff, 8
    and stream temperature, 74, 77
Second-order streams, 74, 76
Section 401 (Clean Water Act), 176
Section 404 (Clean Water Act), 175, 176
Sedges, 2, 9, 11, 15, 19, 30
    in bogs, 139
    in lakes/ponds, 104
    in marshes/wet meadows, 113, 114
    obtaining, 45
Sedge wrens, 116
Sedimentation, 53, 62

Sediments, 5, 17, 18, 40, 53
Seeds, 42, 43, 58, 85, 105, 134
Seed shrimp, 118
Seepage, 72, 77, 186
Selective cutting and thinning, 85
Self-assessment checklist, 153–157
Self-guided tours, 41
Sensitive fern, 135
Sessile, 65, 186
Shallow water, 98–100
Shallow-water swamp forests, 10, 128
Sharp-tailed sparrow, 67
Sheep laurel, 139
Shoreline Management Act (Washington),
    179
Shoreline Management Program
    (Wisconsin), 180
Short-tailed shrews, 116
Short-tailed weasels, 116
Shovelers, 116
Shrews, 116, 139
Shrimp, 104
Shrubs, 11, 66, 128
Shrub bogs, 144
Shrubby willows, 128
Shrub-scrub thickets, 126
Shrub wetlands, 10–11, 66, 134–138
    physical characteristics of, 134
    plants/animals of, 135
    plants by region for, 135–138
    restoration/management of, 135
Side swimmers, 118
Sierra Club, 170
Signage, 17, 27, 29, 48, 148, 151, 152
Silky dogwoods, 135
Silt, 72, 78, 95–96
Silt fences, 40, 56
Silver Lake Country Club (Orland Park,
    Illinois), 31
Silver maple, 128
Silversides, 67
Site preparation, 43–44
Skunk, 115
Skunk cabbage, 110
Slash pine, 57, 129
Slopes, 42
Snags, 88
Snails, 59, 99, 112, 114, 115, 118
Snakes, 101, 109, 117, 128
Snapping turtles, 101, 117
Snipe, 116
Snow geese, 115
Snowy egrets, 40, 101
Society for Ecological Restoration, 170

Society of Wetland Scientists, 170
Softstem bulrush, 30, 110
Soils, 175
    and flowing-water systems, 72, 73
    and restoration, 42
    and wetlands delineation, 16
    and wet meadows, 114
Soil Conservation Service, see Natural
    Resources Conservation Service
Soil probe, 16
Soil survey, 15
Song sparrows, 116, 139
South Carolina, 147, 179
Southeastern region:
    bog plants for, 140–141
    flowing-water plants for, 80–81
    forested-wetland plants for, 129–130
    lake and pond plants for, 105–106
    marsh/wet meadow plants for, 120–121
    shrub-wetland plants for, 135–136
Southern bog lemming, 139
Spanish moss, 129
Sparrows, 67, 115, 116, 139
Spawning beds, 93
Spearscale, 66
Sphagnum mosses, 11, 139, 140
Spicebush, 135
Spike grass, 66
Spike-rush, 57, 66
Sponges, 99, 101, 117, 159, 164
Spotsylvania (Virginia), 152
Spotted turtles, 101
Spot treatment, 73
Springs, 77
Spring (season), 186
Spring overturn, 89, 94
Springtails, 99
Spruce, 139
Squirrel, 115, 128, 129
SRGC, see Sand Ridge Golf Club
    (Chardon, Ohio)
Staff guages, 118
Stakes, 80, 86
Standing water wetlands, 4
Star-duckweed, 30
States, 176
    with comprehensive wetland laws for
        inland waters, 180
    natural heritage programs of, 45
    with wetland protection programs,
        178–179
Steamboat Springs (Colorado), 44
Sterile triploid grass carp, 112, 125
Stevinson (California), 38

Stevinson Ranch Golf Club (Stevinson, California), 38
Sticklebacks, 67, 117
Stinkpot turtles, 101
Stomata, 30, 99, 186
Stone flies, 78
Straw blankets, 86
Streams, 7–9. *See also* Flowing-water systems
   classification of, 74, 76
   as corridors, 34
Stream buffers, 15
Striped skunk, 115
Structures:
   for erosion control, 68
   man-made, 118
   nesting, 67
   for water control, 40, 42, 105, 120, 129, 135
   for wildlife, 27, 71, 88, 109–111, 126
Submerged plants, 30, 99
Subsidies, 175
Substrate, 30, 186
Successional process, 9–10, 96, 134, 140
Suckers, 78
Sulfur, 95
Sundews, 139
Sunfish, 101, 111
Sunlight, 74, 77, 97, 111
Suspended plants, 30
Swallows, 115
Swamps, *see* Forested wetlands
Swamp azalea, 135
Swampbuster Provision (Food Security Act), 175
Swamp rose, 135
Swamp sparrow, 115, 116, 139
Swamp tupelo, 30
Swans, 101, 114–115
Sweet bay, 129
Sweetgale, 139
Sweet pepperbush, 135
Switch grass, 43
Synthetic fertilizers, 111–112

Tadpoles, 112
Tahoe Regional Planning Agency, 6
Tall reed grass, 23
Tall saltwater cord grass, 66
Tamarisk, 85
Tardigrades, *see* Water bears
Teal, 101, 115
Telescopes, 41
Temperature:
   and bat houses, 111

in lakes/ponds, 88–89, 99
   stream, 74, 77
Terns, 67, 115
Terrace pools, 95
Terrene Institute, 170
Thermocline, 89, 186
Thinning, 85
Third-order streams, 74, 76
Three-square bulrush, 66
Thrushes, 79, 128
Tides, 7, 62, 66, 67, 185
Tidal flats, 62
Tidal flushing, 68
Tidal marshes, 63–64, 66
Tidal Wetlands Act (Maryland), 178
Tidal Wetlands Act (New York), 179
Toads, 115, 117
Topsoil, 42, 118
Tortoises, 48
Tours, 151
TPC of Michigan, 53
Trails, 27, 40, 48
Trail guides, 150, 151
Transpiration, 99, 186
Trees, 42
Trout, 78
Trout Unlimited, 170
True flies, 78
Trust for Public Land, 170
Tube-dwelling annelids, 78
Tube worms, 100
Tufted titmouse, 79
Tules, 40
Tupelo, 30, 128, 129
Turbidity, 30, 88, 96, 97, 101
Turk's cap lily, 79, 118
Turtles:
   in flowing-water systems, 78
   forested-wetland, 128
   in lakes/ponds, 101
   in marshes/wet meadows, 117
   sources for obtaining, 59
Tussocks, 113, 186
Twin Rivers Golf Course (Oviedo, Florida), 25

Undecomposed plant matter, 138
Undercutting, 64
U.S. Army Corps of Engineers (ACE), 179
   addresses for, 171–172
   and Clean Water Act, 25, 175
   and delineation of wetlands, 37
   permit review process of, 176, 177
   permitting process by, 15, 26
   regional offices of, 176

U.S. Department of Agriculture, 170
U.S. Department of Commerce, 171
U.S. Department of Interior, 172–173
U.S. Environmental Protection Agency, 173–175
U.S. Fish and Wildlife Service, 39–41, 172, 175, 179
U.S. Forest Service, 170–171
U.S. Geological Survey (USGS), 102, 172
United States Golf Association, 146
Upland swamps, 129
Upland-wetland connections, 32–33
USGS, *see* U.S. Geological Survey
Utility lines, 22

Valley oak, 40
Valley pools, 95
Vegetated buffers, 18–19
Vegetated filter strip, 18
Vegetation, 15. *See also* Plants
   and bank stabilization, 80
   and restoration, 42–43
   and wetlands delineation, 16
Vegetation zones, 29–31
Velocity, stream, 74
Vermont, 180
Vernal pools, 94–95, 104, 148, 187
Vertebrates, 160, 164–167
Viewing stations, 150
Vines, 128
Vireos, 128
Virginia, 3, 24, 152, 179
Virginia rails, 101
Visibility, 96
Volcanic areas, 95

Wading birds, 51, 101, 116
Walkways, 27
Warblers, 128, 139–140
Ward, David, 86
Washington (state), 69, 179
Wastewater, 21, 23, 96, 97
Water arum, 110
Water bears, 100, 159, 164
Water boatmen, 78, 101, 117
Water control structures, 40, 42, 105, 120, 129, 135
Water crowfoot, 30
Water cycles, 95
Waterdogs, 78
Water fleas, 30, 104, 117
Water flow, 27
Waterfowl, 22, 23, 28, 38–41, 59, 65, 114
Water hickory, 128

Water hyacinth, 30, 125
Water level, 31, 119–120, 127, 140
Water lilies, 30, 104, 110, 112, 113
Water lotus, 105
Watermeal, 30, 113
Water milfoils, 30, 109
Water moccasins, 117
Water moss, 72, 101
Water naiad, 30, 105
Water ouzel, 78
Water pepper, 110
Water quality, 3–5
   and buffer areas, 18
   at Raptor Bay Golf Course, 48–51
   at Sand Ridge Golf Course, 21
   and waterthrushes, 78
Water quality protection, 153–155
Water quality standards, 176
Water Resources Development Act (Wisconsin), 180
Water Resources Management Act (Vermont), 180
Water scorpions, 101
Watershed, 3, 41
Water shield, 23, 30
Water shrews, 139
Water smartweed, 110
Water snakes, 117
Water striders, 78, 117
Water table, 74, 127
Waterthrushes, 78, 139
Water tupelo, 129
Waterweed, 30, 99
Water willow, 139
Wave action, 5, 71
Wax myrtle, 57
WCI Communities, Inc., 48
Weasels, 116
Wells, 118
West Coast region:
   bog plants for, 143
   estuarial plants for, 69–70
   flowing-water plants for, 84–85
   forested-wetland plants for, 133–134
   lake and pond plants for, 109
   marsh/wet meadow plants for, 124–125
   shrub-wetland plants for, 138
Western arborvitae, 133
Western grebes, 115
West Indian marsh grass, 55
Wetlands, 1–11
   bogs as, 11
   definition of, 2–3
   delineation of, 16

Wetlands *(cont'd)*
  estuaries as, 7
  Fish and Wildlife definition of, 179–181
  forested, 9–10
  importance of, 4–5
  lakes/ponds as, 9
  legal definition of, 175
  marshes/wet meadows as, 9
  Old Brockway Golf Course case study of, 5–7
  overall loss of, 36
  protection of, 15, 17
  resources concerning, 169–174
  rivers/streams/creeks as, 7–9
  shrub, 10–11
  size of, 148
The Wetlands Act (Delaware), 180
The Wetland Conservation Act of 1991 (Minnesota), 180
Wetland consultants, 16
Wetland creation, 14, 15, 23
Wetland delineation, 16, 153
Wetland preservation, 14
Wetland Protection Act (Massachusetts), 180
Wetland restoration, 14, 15, 35–59
  of bogs, 140
  definition of, 36
  of estuaries, 67–68
  exotic-species control in, 53–58
  of flowing-water systems, 79–80
  of forested wetlands, 129
  hydrology involved in, 41–42
  of marshes and wet meadows, 118–120
  for migratory waterfowl, 38–41
  plant selection for, 44–53
  of shrub wetlands, 135
  site preparation for, 43–44
  and soils, 42
  and vegetation, 42–43
  wildlife considerations for, 59
Wetlands International, 170
Wetlands Regulation Center, 170
Wetland topsoil, *see* Muck
Wet meadows, *see* Marshes and wet meadows
Whirligig beetles, 117
White amur, 125

White cedar, 128, 139
White pelicans, 117
White pine, 128
White-tailed deer, 59, 109, 139
White-throated sparrow, 139
Whitetop grass, 30
White water lily, 30, 110, 113
Widgeons, 114–115
Widgeon grass, 30, 65, 68
Wild celery, 99
Wildflowers, 73, 118
Wildflower preservation societies, 45
Wildlife:
  considerations for, 59
  introduction of, 71
  movement of, 32
  problematic, 17, 59, 135
Wildlife Habitat Council, 170
Wildlife Links, 146
Wild raisin, 23
Willets, 67
Willows, 40
  in bogs, 139
  in forested wetlands, 128
  in lakes/ponds, 104, 109
  in marshes/wet meadows, 119
  in shrub wetlands, 134
Winterberry, 135
Wisconsin, 180
Woodcock, 116
Wood ducks, 40, 43, 78, 101, 127
Wood frogs, 140
Woodpeckers, 128–129
Wood preservative, 105
Woolbright, Larry, 32, 33
Worms, 159, 164
Wrens, 101, 116

Yardage books, 151
Yarrow, 44
Yellow birch, 79
Yellow-headed blackbirds, 115
Yellow iris, 73, 109
Yellowlegs, 101
Yellow pond lily, 30, 105, 110, 113
Yellow-rumped warbler, 139–140
Yellowthroats, 115, 139

Zooplankton, 96, 99, 187